CELLULOID SAINTS

Celluloid

Sai

Images of Sanctity in Film

Theresa Sanders

Mercer University Press, 2002

ISBN 0-86554-750-5 (hardback)
MUP/H560
0-86554-775-0 (paperback)
MUP/P217

© 2002 Mercer University Press
6316 Peake Road
Macon, Georgia 31210-3960
All rights reserved

First Edition.

Library of Congress Cataloging-in-Publication Data

Sanders, Theresa, 1963–
Celluloid saints : images of sanctity in film / Theresa Sanders.
p. cm.
Includes bibliographical references and index.
1. Religion in motion pictures.
2. Motion pictures--Religious aspects--Christianity. I. Title.
PN1995.9.R4 S345 2002
794.43'682--dc21
2002004822

Contents

For George Garrelts, and for my parents,
Ervin and Mary Catherine Sanders

Acknowledgments

Numerous people assisted in the completion of this work. The following read early portions of the manuscript and offered valuable advice: Alan Berger, Ariel Glucklich, William McFadden, Joseph Murphy, Frederick Ruf, and James Walsh. Vincent Lapomarda generously shared information for the chapter on saints of the Holocaust. Helen Scimeca and the staff at the Media Resource Center of the Baltimore Archdiocese offered kind assistance in locating in locating copies of some movies. Fred Boehrer and the members of Emmaus House in Albany offered insights into the life of Dorothy Day. Finally, I am indebted to Elizabeth McKeown for the title of the book.

Preface

This book grows out of my twin loves of theology and film.

Theology, of course, is usually defined as the science or study of God. The word comes from two Greek roots: *theos*, meaning God, and *logos*, which we usually understand to mean science. However, this is not the only meaning that *logos* can have. The word also means "story." Theology, as I understand it, is stories of God. It is stories about the deepest meanings of our lives. It is stories about, as theologian Paul Tillich puts it, "ultimate concern."

If we think of theology as rooted in story, it should come as no surprise that some of the most profoundly theological works of the past century have been movies. Movies do more than entertain, though they surely do that. They also shape our hopes and our desires. They tell us who we are and who we ought to be. They give us a language to express our loves and our fears and the full scope of our messy, complicated humanity. That humanity is contemptible and noble, craven and courageous, pitiable and dignified. As members of it, we share one thing in common: a desire that something matter. We long for something to devote our lives to with all our heart and with all our mind and with all our strength.

Finding that "something" and having the courage to commit themselves to it without reservation is what sets the saints apart from the rest of us. Saints are not necessarily "good" people. They are not always temperate or polite or affectionate or even kind. There are many whom we would not want as friends, much less as roommates or family members. Yet the saints intrigue us because they have an extraordinary passion: a passion for God.

This passion is, I believe, the most consistent marker of what we call holiness. Unfortunately, films about lives of the saints vary in their ability to portray this unique characteristic. Many are dreary affairs with plodding scripts and wooden acting. In this book I have tried to give as little attention as possible to movies that are, in the end, simply not very interesting. Instead I have focused on works that convey something of the complexity of saints' lives and of their reputations for holiness. I have also kept to a minimum discussion of the innumerable documentaries about saints. A number of these are quite well done and are invaluable for communicating the biographies of holy men and women. However, because the "story" element in many of them is muted, they do not fit well with the project of this book. There are exceptions, of course; some documentaries have a quite clear narrative line. Others have such exaggerated ideological perspectives that failing to examine and critique them would be irresponsible. Still others are included in this book simply because they are the only cinematic portrayals available of a particular saint.

The book is written with two goals in mind. The first is to give film viewers some background and context for evaluating what they see on screen. By and large, Hollywood is not very conversant with theological issues. Occasionally, movies base their plots on a fundamental misunderstanding of religious practice. Consider, for example, the popular movie *Dogma*. The premise of the film is that two angels have been cast out of heaven forever for disobeying God. Longing to return home, the angels are searching for ways back to heaven. When a Catholic cardinal declares that anyone passing through the arches of a particular church will receive a plenary indulgence, the two angels think that they have found a loophole that will enable them to gain entrance to paradise once again. According to the film, a plenary indulgence is "a little-known Catholic belief which offers all that pass through [the church's] arches a morally clean slate." One angel tells another, "By walking through the archway, all your sins are forgiven."

In fact, however, in Catholic theology a plenary indulgence does not at all offer forgiveness for sins. What a plenary indulgence offers is simply the remission of any temporal punishment that a person's sins might have incurred. It cannot change the decision of whether or not someone goes to heaven; it merely removes any penance that a heaven-bound person must perform before entering paradise. In other words, all it can do is "speed up" (to put it in highly imagistic and indeed over-simplistic terms) a person's journey towards the salvation that God has already granted him or her.

Such an error in representing Catholic belief does not, of course, make the film less pleasurable or indeed provocative to watch. The movie strikes a chord with its audience precisely because it is willing to ask questions about faith and religion that are too often ignored. As critic Roger Ebert observes, *Dogma* occasioned so much controversy upon its release precisely because it takes religion absolutely seriously: "And if a movie dares to deal with what people actually believe, all hell, so to speak, breaks loose."[1] Nonetheless, the movie is an example of how Hollywood can mislead viewers with inaccurate presentations of religion. Purporting to represent authentic Catholic teaching, it instead offers erroneous information and then bases its entire plot on the error.

Such lapses occur frequently in movies, but an equally significant if not more serious problem is that too many films are simply flat-footed in their approach to faith: overly simplistic or cynically dismissive of religious traditions. Members of faith communities are often portrayed as unthinking rubes who refuse to wake up to all that contemporary culture has to offer. Think, for example, of the anti-dancing preacher in *Footloose*. Or, conversely, religious people are idealized into holier-than-thou cardboard figures who float through life untouched by the struggles that plague the rest of us (e.g. the title character in *The Song of Bernadette*).

Giving readers the tools they need to interpret and critique cinematic portrayals of religion and the religious dimension of culture is one goal of this book. The second goal, however, is to show students of theology how the ideas that they encounter in often highly technical language might play themselves out on the big screen. One of my most fundamental convictions about theology, one I repeat to my students so many times that it has become something of a mantra, is that theology always begins with an experience. Any theology worth its salt begins in human experience. If a theology cannot be translated into the language of events and emotions, dreams and love, despair and fulfillment, then it has lost its way. Revelation is always revelation *to someone*. To be meaningful, it has to be able to render itself in a language that people understand.

That language, I am suggesting, can be film. Looking back on my own days in college and graduate school, I can remember very few of the words that my professors said. By contrast, I remember frame after frame of the movies that I saw, many of them in the classroom. Film is an extraordinary medium. It can literally change lives. Used wisely and intelligently, it can be a powerful tool for expressing theological insights.

Celluloid Saints is arranged in sections that correspond roughly to the development of sainthood itself. That is, following two short chapters dealing with the meaning of sainthood, on the one hand, and the relationship between religion and film, on the other, Chapter 3 focuses on examples of cinematic martyrdom. Martyrs were the first to be recognized as specially holy by the developing Christian community, and they have been given pride of place in the collective memory of the faithful.

As early persecutions of Christians died out and opportunities for martyrdom grew scarce, however, holy men and women turned to asceticism to express their devotion to God. Chapter 4 examines the relationship between asceticism and mysticism as it has appeared in film.

Nearly from its conception, Christianity has been a missionary religion. When in the fourth century the Emperor Constantine legitimized worship of Jesus, Christian efforts to evangelize increased geometrically. Chapter 5 looks at missionary saints and explores both the glory and the shame associated with evangelization.

From this, the next section flows naturally. Entitled "The Miracle Worker," Chapter 6 offers a short examination of the role that wonder-working plays in saintly lives. Some saints are credited with accomplishing miracles during their time on earth; missionaries especially are remembered as performing astonishing feats to convert tribal kings and warriors to Christianity. Nearly all of the saints, however, are believed to have interceded with God after their deaths to perform wonders for the living. Just what exactly a miracle is, and how miracles are portrayed on film, is the subject of Chapter 6.

Chapter 7 is entitled "Blessed are the Poor" and looks at saints who have devoted their lives to serving the people many of us would like to forget. These saints teach, heal, preach to, and sometimes live among the destitute of the world. The chapter explores why so many Catholic saints have committed themselves not only to serving the poor, but also to being poor themselves.

Chapter 8 takes us to one of the darkest events in human history: the Holocaust. Over fifty years later, the world is still just beginning to grapple with the horrors that were perpetrated by Nazi Germany in the twentieth century. At this writing, two people who died in Nazi concentration camps have been canonized (that is, officially declared to be saints worthy of veneration by the entire Catholic Church). More than 100 others whose lives were intimately affected by the Holocaust have undergone beatification, the last step before canonization, and hundreds of others are being considered for nomination to the process. Their stories as told in film, and the debates surrounding those stories, form one of the most controversial chapters of cinematic sainthood.

Chapter 9, "Hail Mary, Full of Grace" departs from the loosely historical framework around which the other chapters are arranged. It examines a sampling of the extraordinary number of films featuring the Virgin Mary, the mother of Jesus. Historical information about this saint is minimal. By contrast, cinematic portrayals of her are legion and continue to grow in number. Mary's image appears in movies ranging from the pious to the pornographic, and she is used to symbolize everything from repressive sexual mores to feminist power. How this saint went from obscure mother of an executed criminal to star of the silver screen is the subject of this chapter.

Chapter 10 is entitled "Saint or Psychotic?" and explores the often very thin line that separates holiness from mental illness. It is no secret that many of those who have been canonized have not been what one would call psychologically healthy. This section of the book looks at how movies have dealt with saintly figures who are suspected of being mentally ill by those who surround them. The chapter pays particular attention to Saint Joan of Arc, who was burned at the stake in the fifteenth century. During Joan's own day, the term "mental illness" did not exist. The warrior-saint was thought instead to be possessed by a demon or of having willingly married herself to Satan. However, modern scholars have speculated at length about the "voices" that Joan confessed to hearing, and at least some of them have concluded that the saint suffered psychotic episodes.

The movies included in this book fall into several categories. Some of them attempt to represent, whether in documentary or dramatic form, the life of a historical person who has been canonized as a saint by the Catholic Church. For example, *The Reluctant Saint* tells the story of Saint Joseph of Cupertino, also known as "The Flying Saint." Many others depict men and women whose causes have been introduced for sainthood but who have not yet been canonized. For example, *Entertaining Angels* is about Catholic Worker founder Dorothy Day, whose cause for canonization has only recently been put forth. Still others feature fictional characters whose lives are based on the lives of particular holy people. The priest in *Au Revoir, Les Enfants*, for example, was modeled on Père Jacques, a Carmelite priest who died shortly after the liberation of the Nazi concentration camp Mauthausen. Finally, several movies feature characters not based on historical people at all. Instead, these figures lead lives that mimic or are touched by saintly lives. Sister Agnes in *Agnes of God*, for example, is largely a fictional creation. However, because she is described by others in the film as a saint, and because her life mirrors that of countless saintly visionaries, her story is included here.

Perhaps an additional word is in order regarding which films have been included and which have not. In each chapter I analyze works that represent a variety of theological perspectives so that readers can become familiar with the issues and controversies that have marked thinking about the saints. Beyond that, I confess that my choices have been, of necessity, somewhat idiosyncratic. Some movies were chosen because of their status as classics. Others represent a world-view so intriguing or so problematic that it cries out for analysis. Still others appear in these pages simply because I enjoy watching them and thinking about them, and I want to share them with others. Making such choices means, of course, that numerous movies have been left out. I have included a selected list of other movies featuring saints at the end of the book.

Virtually all of the movies under discussion are available to the general public either at video stores or via the Internet. My hope is that by the time you finish reading *Celluloid Saints*, you will want to watch or re-watch all of them. One caution: readers should be aware that though I have made every effort not to reveal more than necessary about the plots of the movies under consideration, in some cases it is simply not possible to refrain from giving away a film's surprises. In certain instances, a fruitful interpretation of characters and events can only be done if the plot's twists and turns are taken into account. If you believe that your pleasure in watching the films will be muted because of what you will read here, I urge you to view the relevant movies beforehand.

CELLULOID SAINTS

1

What Is a Saint?

Introduction

In 1975, *Time* magazine featured a picture of Mother Teresa of Calcutta on its cover. Mother Teresa, who spent most of her adult life caring for the sick and dying on India's streets, was universally regarded as an example of true holiness. *Time*'s cover proclaimed in bold letters that she was among the world's "Living Saints."[2]

What is a saint? What distinguishes saints from the rest of humanity? It's difficult to generalize, of course, since saints, like all people, lead unique lives conditioned by the times and places and circumstances in which they live. Yet there are some characteristics that seem to arise again and again in descriptions of holy people. A century ago, the famous psychologist and philosopher William James attempted to summarize these characteristics in what he called "a certain composite photograph of universal saintliness, the same in all religions."[3] It may be overstating the case to claim that sanctity is thought of in the same way by every faith tradition. Still, all of the world's great religions recognize some people as special—as exemplifying the tradition's highest values or attaining its ideal of spiritual perfection.

For example, Islam looks to the *awilyā* or "friends of God," people who are believed to have been caught up into the divine. Some forms of Judaism have held the *tsaddiqim* to be living embodiments of the Law of God and have counted on them to intercede with God on behalf of the faithful. In Hinduism, *gurus* serve as models to be imitated along the path to spiritual liberation, and in Mahayana Buddhism, the *bodhisattva* is thought to extend compassion to all living beings. To be sure, the practices and beliefs of these various men and women differ widely. Still, all are recognized by their own communities as being spiritually extraordinary, and in that sense they are comparable to Catholicism's saints.

Thus James's work is a good starting place for our journey into saintly lives. After getting a sense of holiness "in general," we can then narrow our focus to sanctity within the Catholic tradition, and to how Catholic saints have been represented in film.

The Features of Sainthood

The first feature that James identifies as characteristic of saintliness is what he calls "a feeling of being in a wider life than that of this world's selfish little interests." Saints, says James, have the conviction that there exists an ideal power against which our everyday projects, hopes and fears must be measured. In Christianity this power is personified as God; other traditions conceive of it differently. What is important is simply that saints see the toils and cares of human existence against a larger, more perfect horizon.

Consider, for example, the way Saint Augustine (d. 430) described himself prior to his conversion to Christianity. In his *Confessions*, he recalls, "I was held back by mere trifles, the most paltry inanities, all my old attachments. They plucked at my garment of flesh and whispered, 'Are you going to dismiss us?'"[4] Augustine struggled for years with his fondness for good food and good wine and the attentions of women, praying famously, "Give me chastity and continence, but not yet." It was only after a revelatory experience during which he randomly opened a collection of Saint Paul's writings and read, "...arm yourselves with the Lord Jesus Christ; spend no more thought on nature and nature's appetites" (Romans 13:14) that he was able to let go of his desires. Later, he could say to God, "You are merciful. You saw how deep I was sunk in death, and it was your power that drained dry the well of corruption in the depths of my heart."[5]

We need not go back as far as the fifth century to find an example of someone discovering a wider life than that of this world's selfish little interests, however. Innumerable movie plots revolve around precisely this theme: a character whose eyes are suddenly opened to the beauty and mystery at the heart of life. Think, for example, of *A Christmas Carol*'s

Ebenezer Scrooge who in a single night is transformed from a miserable miser into a man filled with joy and generosity. Or think of George Bailey in Frank Capra's classic *It's a Wonderful Life*. George has never been what the world would call a success, though he is a kind and decent man. When his business begins to fail, he becomes distraught and asks for help from a local banker. The evil banker inspects George's life insurance policy and tells him mockingly that he is worth more dead than alive; George believes him and so tries to commit suicide. Only the intervention of a kindly angel saves him from the icy river into which he's jumped, and it is this angel who must point out to him how skewed his priorities have become. Caught up in the little interests of this world, and feeling himself worthless because he is not a business success, George has forgotten the "wider life" of love. By the end of the movie he realizes that in the light of this larger horizon, he is truly a rich man.

This brings us to the second characteristic of saintliness that James identifies: namely, a sense that the ideal power of which we are aware stands in friendly continuity with our lives. This power is not something alien or frightening that violates our sense of self. Instead, we (or at least the saints) feel that surrendering to it is good and right. When George in *It's a Wonderful Life* continues to see his life as worthless even after he is rescued from his suicide attempt, his angel companion arranges to show him what the world would have been like had he never been born. We discover that George's younger brother would have died in a sledding accident because George wasn't there to save him. A pharmacist's life would have been ruined because George wasn't there to catch a fatal mistake the man had made while filling a prescription. George's entire hometown, his beloved Bedford Falls, would have been turned into something tawdry and ugly because George's decent and gentle presence wasn't there to stop the evil banker who was bent solely on making money. Seeing all of this, George comes to realize that what had seemed to be a disappointing life haphazardly thrown together and amounting to nothing had actually been guided all along by a power wiser than he.

Cardinal John Henry Newman, who was declared "Venerable" by the pope in 1991, spoke of the guidance of God in this way:

> God has created me to do Him some definite service; He has committed some work to me which He has not committed to another. I have my mission—I may never know it in this life, but I shall be told it in the next.... Therefore I will trust Him. Whatever, wherever I am, I can never

be thrown away. If I am in sickness, my sickness may serve Him; in perplexity, my perplexity may serve Him…. He does nothing in vain… He knows what He is about. He may take away my friends, He may throw me among strangers, He may make me feel desolate, make my spirits sink, hide my future from me—still He knows what He is about.[6]

This sense that the ideal power "knows what it is about" offers to the saints a tremendous sense of elation and freedom, according to James. They no longer feel compelled to protect their own selves and egos at all cost. Instead, the borders that separate them from others melt away, and the saints feel themselves united with all that lives.

James notes that when the self is no longer obsessed with securing itself against all other beings, it undergoes a kind of shift: "towards 'yes, yes,' and away from 'no,' where the claims of the non-ego are concerned."[7] Saints, in other words, place themselves entirely at the disposal of others. They are less concerned with preserving themselves than with offering aid and care and joy to everyone they meet. Father Damien de Veuster, for example, whose biography is told in the Peabody Award-winning one-man film *Damien* (1978), spent twelve years working with victims of Hansen's disease (what used to be called leprosy) on the island of Molokai in Hawaii. Reflecting in the film on the probability of his dying of the fearful illness, the priest says with a shrug, "Well, if it's God's will, I'm prepared. By remembering that those worm-infested ulcers are the wounds of Christ, that's how I manage to go from day to day." Rather than abandon people who desperately need his help, Damien chooses to minister to them: "They must have one priest who belongs to them, if only to prove to them that God has not forgotten them." Father Damien did eventually contract Hanson's disease and died in 1889.

The Fruits of Sainthood

The characteristics of sainthood, James observes, play themselves out in very practical ways. For one thing, they lead many of the holy to practice asceticism, or to sacrifice and self-denial. Not all saints have been ascetics, but many have gone through at least one period in their lives when they denied themselves food or sleep or other creature comforts. In the documentary *Mother Teresa* (1986), we see the famous nun walk through a building that has been donated as a convent for the Missionaries of Charity (the religious order that she founded). She marches with the authority of a field marshal as she briskly declares that her nuns have no need for so many luxuries. Carpets and mattresses are rolled up and thrown out the window, tossed aside as unnecessary extravagances. When asked why she and her sisters don't use washing machines or fans, and why they don't attend movies or parties, Mother Teresa replies, "These are natural things, and there is nothing wrong in having them. But for us, we have chosen not to have them." The reason, she explains, is so that she and the sisters can better identify themselves with the poor.

In *Mother Teresa* we also see another of what James calls the practical consequences of sainthood: strength of soul. Strength of soul involves relinquishing all the fears and anxieties that normally prevent us from being who we ought to be. All of our inhibitions, our shyness or laziness, our need for guarantees and successes, our smallness and stinginess— these disappear, and a deep serenity takes their place. Mother Teresa speaks of this as a kind of total surrender to God. In her halting English, she says, "To be where He wants you to be. If he puts you in the street...to accept to be in the street at that moment. Not for you to put yourself on the street but to *accept* to be put there. This is quite different. To accept if God wants you to be in a palace, well then to accept to be in the palace, as long as you are not choosing to be in the palace."

Her words might sound as if they are encouraging a deliberate help- lessness or the type of passivity that led Karl Marx to speak of religion as an opiate that keeps poor people poor. This interpretation doesn't fit with the determined nun on the screen, however. It is quite clear from the film that during her life, Mother Teresa could be doggedly persistent in pursuing her goals, whether they were obtaining land for her charitable organizations in Guatemala or persuading government officials to let her into Beirut during the height of the war in Lebanon. In the film she is unabashed in asking for what she wants, asking several times if she has to; however, she also displays equanimity in the face of failure. This equa- nimity is what James means when he speaks of strength of soul. It is a sense that, as he says, "Come heaven, come hell, it makes no difference now!"[8]

Another consequence of sainthood, according to James, is purity, or the drive to eliminate from one's life any elements not in tune with one's deepest commitments. For example, in the sixteenth century, Saint John of the Cross advised that "...every pleasure that presents itself to the senses, if it be not purely for the honour and glory of God, must be renounced and completely rejected for the love of Jesus Christ.... I take this example. If there present itself to a man the pleasure of listening to things that tend not to the service and honour of God, let him not desire that pleasure, nor desire to listen to them."[9] In other words, if you are committed to treating people as if they are made in the image of God, then you should strive not to listen to malicious gossip, to music whose lyrics express contempt for human beings, to jokes that diminish a particular gender or race, or to speeches filled with hate. Purity doesn't want to hide from the world, but it does want to make people's interactions with the world consistent with what they believe to be good and true.

For some, the drive towards purity takes an unusual form. The film biography entitled *The Life of Charles de Foucauld* (1996),[10] for example, tells the story of the playboy-turned-missionary who lived in the desert in Algeria and who was killed in an anti-French uprising in 1916. The Venerable Charles de Foucauld reflects in the film, "The older I get, the more I realize that the simple life, a life in loving communion with God, through prayer and penance, is the only means that can help us humans really find our way out of our forlorn condition." As an explanation for why his search for the simple life led him to the sands of North Africa, he offers the following bit of wisdom: "You have to go into the desert and live in it to receive God's grace because that is where you eliminate everything that is not of God." Eliminating everything that is not of God is what James means when he speaks of the saint's search for purity.

The last consequence of sainthood that James discusses is charity, or a shifting of the saint's emotional center outwards in tenderness and care for one's fellow creatures. Saints, James says, love their enemies and treat the most loathsome beings as their brothers and sisters. Such charity finds extreme expression in *The Spiritual Dialogue* of Saint Catherine of Genoa. Catherine, who lived in fifteenth-century Italy, discovered in her dealings with the poor that the sight of lice made her want to vomit. According to the *Dialogue*, God helped her to overcome this aversion to the insects by commanding her, "Take a handful of them, put them in your mouth and swallow them. That way you will free yourself of your nausea."[11]

Likewise, in *Molokai* (1999), another film about Father Damien, the saint is strictly enjoined by his bishop not to touch any of the infected people on the island. Damien promises to obey his superior's order, but he breaks his promise almost immediately by shaking hands with a young boy who has volunteered to serve as his altar-boy and who is afflicted by the disease. Damien also kisses the forehead of a man hideously maimed by ulcerous sores, and he buries the dead with his own hands. Confronted with the fact that he will almost certainly contract Hanson's disease through such intimate contact, the priest explains matter-of-factly that God and the Virgin Mary will keep him alive as long as he is needed.

Examples such as this show the joyful and even reckless abandonment of self that charity makes possible.

Making Saints[12]

If we now have some sense of what holiness means, we can narrow our focus to saints within the Catholic Church. How exactly are saints made?

In Catholicism, the process of saint-making, called "canonization," begins when a bishop sets up a committee to gather evidence about a person reputed to be holy. Normally, the person in question must have been dead for at least five years, though exceptions have been made, most notably in the case of Mother Teresa. In any case, no living person can be officially designated a saint. Once the cause has been introduced, interviews are then conducted about the deceased, now called "Servant of God." His or her writings are carefully examined for doctrinal orthodoxy, and objections to the person's cause are raised and answered. The resulting file is sent to the Vatican to be examined, and if all goes well, the case is sent on to the office of the pope. If that office determines that the Servant of God has practiced to a heroic degree the virtues of faith, hope, and charity, or died as a martyr, the holy person may officially be called "Venerable."

Another investigation must take place, however, before the candidate can move on to the next step in the process. Even if it can be demonstrated beyond a shadow of a doubt that a person lived a life of heroic virtue, one further criterion must be met before the cause can advance: the working of miracles.

In determining what counts as a miracle, the Vatican has two questions to consider. The first question is, is a particular unusual event truly an intervention of God? After all, strange things happen all the time in this world, and what we don't understand about biology and physics and astronomy vastly exceeds what we do know. The Vatican employs teams of investigators to exhaust all possible explanations for an unusual occurrence. Only when something happens that has no scientific explanation, and that acts to increase people's faith in God, can the word "miracle" be used. For example, a water stain on a wall that resembles the face of Jesus can simply be chalked up to coincidence; it has a perfectly natural explanation and would not be called a miracle. Likewise, if the population of an entire city suddenly died for no apparent reason, we might be tempted to use words like "supernatural" or "demonic," but we would not call the event miraculous.

The second question investigators must ask is whether or not the unusual occurrence in question can be attributed to the intercession of the person in question. Suppose, for example, that a woman is on her death bed, ill with terminal cancer. Her friends place a picture of a saint-to-be on her pillow and ask him or her to intercede with God on the sick woman's behalf. If the woman at that moment were to spontaneously and completely recover, it would be reasonable to credit the holy person with the cure.

On the other hand, suppose that the same woman is dying and that five of her friends are praying for her. One lights a candle to Saint Jude, the patron saint of hopeless causes. Another prays the rosary, asking that the mother of Jesus intercede on the woman's behalf. Another simply prays, "Please, God, save my friend." Another places a picture of Saint Joseph (the father of Jesus) on the woman's bed, and still another prays to a holy person who has not yet been canonized. If the woman recovers, the cure cannot count as a miracle worked through the intercession of the not-yet-canonized person. The circumstances surrounding the cure are simply too ambiguous.

If after rigorous scrutiny a miracle is believed to have occurred due to the prayers of a particular holy person, that person may be beatified, or declared "Blessed." If a person undergoes beatification, he or she may then be venerated at the local level. A "Blessed" person from the United States, for example, might be honored in American churches but not elsewhere, or the founder of a religious order who is beatified might be venerated by the worldwide members of that order but not by others. Not all people with a miracle to their credit undergo beatification, however. The pope may decide for various political, social, or religious reasons that it would not be appropriate to beatify a particular person at a particular time. Causes can wait for years before they come to fruition, if they do so at all.

We should note that in the case of martyrs, the process of beatification is somewhat different. For one thing, a martyr can be beatified without having produced a miracle. For another, what must be demonstrated in the case of martyrs is not that they showed virtue to a heroic degree but that they died in defense of Christian faith. This is not quite as simple as it might seem. For example, suppose a priest is teaching peasants to read so that they can free themselves from poverty. The government of the country may see an educated lower class as a threat to its power, and so it may murder the priest. If this happens, can we say that the man died for his faith? After all, Jesus instructed his disciples to feed the hungry and clothe the naked, and this is in a sense what the priest was doing. On the other hand, numerous people teach others to read with no religious motive whatsoever.

Or consider the case of Maximilian Kolbe, who took the place of a condemned man during the Holocaust. In the concentration camp known as Auschwitz, the Nazis had chosen at random ten men to die of starvation. When one of the men began to cry, pleading that his wife and children would suffer if he died, Kolbe offered himself in the man's place. For this act of extreme charity and because his life as a whole was thought to exhibit heroic virtue, Kolbe was beatified; afterwards, however, there was pressure from the Polish Church to have him declared a martyr. This presented a problem. After all, there was no indication that the man originally chosen to die had been singled out because he was a Christian, and the Nazis performing the execution would have killed Kolbe regardless of his faith. Nonetheless, at Kolbe's canonization, the pope declared that Kolbe would henceforth be known as a "martyr for charity."[13]

For a person to be canonized, or placed on the list of those worthy of universal veneration, at least one miracle beyond beatification is required, even for martyrs. Not everyone who is beatified goes on to be canonized. Some cases simply fall to the wayside due to lack of interest or, quite frequently, lack of funding. One scholar puts the cost of canonization in the neighborhood of a few hundred thousand dollars and notes that some religious congregations have spent as much as several million dollars to see a canonization through to the end.[14]

It is also the case that historically, some types of people are far more likely to be canonized than others. For one thing, saints come more often from wealthy families than from poor ones. This is due not only to the high cost of canonization, but also to the fact that the wealthy tend to be more visible and powerful than the poor, and they have more access to education and thus to writing. If you live and die as an illiterate peasant, it is not likely that your case will come to the attention of the pope, no matter how holy you are.

Second, a large proportion of saints come from three countries: Italy, France, and Spain. Indeed, as historian Catherine C. Mooney observes, "Even factoring in the larger Catholic populations in these areas, there is little significant correlation between the numbers of Catholics in each territory and the percentage of persons canonized."[15] Mooney explains this fact by pointing to the historically friendly relations that these countries have had with the pope. A country that enjoys such "social proximity" is more likely to have its candidates accepted for sainthood.

Third, between the years 1000 and 1987, only about one in five saints formally approved by the pope for sainthood were women, and over half of those were canonized in the twentieth century.[16] Men historically have had more economic power and more access to education than women, and so it makes sense that they would have a more visible presence among the holy just as the wealthy are more visible than the poor. Moreover, men have frequently been of the opinion that women are less suited to sanctity than men are. Saint Thomas Aquinas, for example, speculated in the thirteenth century that women were actually deformed males. He believed that the male seed would naturally produce male children, and that the only explanation for girls being born was that something had gone wrong in the reproductive process. What might cause such a terrible malformation? Aquinas offered several explanations, including the effect of an external influence such as a moist south wind.[17] Likewise, Saint Augustine in the fifth century held that women by themselves were not truly made in the image of God, though when completed by their husbands they could be considered to be so. A man, on the other hand, was "the image of God as fully and completely as when the woman is joined to him in one whole."[18]

It's difficult to be a saint if you are defective and misbegotten and not truly made in the image of God!

One other group of people is frequently left out of the saint-making process as well, though it's a group that contains most of the adults on the planet: married people. Catherine Mooney reports that of the 393 saints recognized by the papacy between the years 1000 and 1987, fewer than twenty percent were laypeople, (that is, people who were not nuns, monks, or priests). Of these, over half had never married. Moreover, many of the married saints who were canonized were recognized not because they had lived lives of heroic virtue but because they had been martyred.[19] Apparently the saint-makers feel that it is difficult to live a saintly life if you are somebody's husband or wife.

This issue arises in one of the best films about the process of canonization, Agnieszka Holland's *The Third Miracle* (1999). The plot of this movie follows one woman's journey towards canonization from the day of her death to her beatification and beyond. Along the way, various questions about the meaning of sanctity are raised, and the politics of saint-making play a key role in the story's development. At a meeting to decide if the woman's case should be sent on to Rome, an archbishop challenges the notion that a married woman caught up in the everyday concerns of her husband and daughter could really be holy: "True sainthood is of another world," he declares. In the archbishop's eyes, sexual intercourse, even within the bounds of marriage, degrades a person. It is, he contends, "a contamination of the spirit by the flesh." Fortunately, his voice does not prevail.

Called to Be Saints

When we consider all the questions that can be raised during an inquiry into a person's life, and when we consider the tremendous obstacles (financial, bureaucratic, and so on) that the process of canonization presents, it is a miracle that anyone actually obtains official sainthood. Only an infinitesimal percentage of the Catholics who have ever lived have been canonized. This does not mean, though, that these are the only real saints. In Catholic tradition, anyone who is with God in heaven is a saint, whether or not that person has been officially declared to be so. The Church remembers all of the uncanonized but nonetheless holy people each year on November 1, the Feast of All Saints. This day, which follows All Hallow's Eve (Halloween), commemorates all those who now enjoy life in heaven. It is a celebration of what Catholic tradition calls the communion of saints, or the bond that the holy dead maintain with the living and with God.

In fact, the history of the word "saint" shows that originally it did not refer merely to a few extraordinary people singled out for special recognition. Originally, it meant all of the followers of Jesus: all those struggling to live as he had. For example, when Saint Paul was writing his letter to the Christian community at Corinth, he addressed it "to those who are sanctified in Christ Jesus, called to be saints, together with all those who in every place call on the name of our Lord Jesus Christ" (1 Cor 1:2). In Paul's eyes, all Christians were saints in that all had been called to holiness. It was only as Christianity grew and developed that a few of the holy dead were held up as specially worthy of veneration.

Moreover, from the perspective of Catholic theology, anyone who has been blessed with heavenly life is a saint, regardless of what religion he or she may have practiced in life. In earlier times, Catholics used the term "baptism of desire" to acknowledge that all people are part of God's salvific plan. The old *Baltimore Catechism*, which generations of Catholics memorized in grammar school, explained, "An unbaptized person receives the baptism of desire when he loves God above all things and desires to do all that is necessary for his salvation."[20] In other words, people who tried to live a life dedicated to God's will could be saved regardless of whether or not they belonged to the Catholic Church.

More recently, the Catholic theologian Karl Rahner has expressed much the same idea by pointing to the all-encompassing grace of God. He observes, "However little we can say with certitude about the final lot of an individual inside or outside the officially constituted Christian religion, we have every reason to think optimistically—i.e. truly hopefully and confidently in a Christian sense—of God who has certainly the last word and who has revealed to us that he has spoken his powerful word of reconciliation and forgiveness into the world."[21] In short, there is no reason from a contemporary Catholic perspective to believe that only those who have undergone baptism can share eternal life with God.

In sum, then, Catholicism believes that all people are called to be saints, and there is hope that all of the dead in fact *are* saints—that they enjoy a life of peaceful bliss in a world beyond this one. A book written about that kind of sainthood, though, would be entirely unmanageable. If all of us are destined for heaven, then virtually any movie containing a human character could find a place in *Celluloid Saints*. Given the overwhelming nature of such a task, we must, alas, limit ourselves here to films about the "official" saints of Catholicism.

For the purposes of this book, then "saint" will be used most often in its narrowest sense, referring only to those who have been canonized by the Catholic Church. The word will also be used to refer to someone whose cause for sainthood is in process, as well as to fictional characters whose lives mimic or are based on the lives of saints. The hope, however, is that by looking at these few, the rest of us might learn something useful—not only about what we believe it means to be holy, but also about how we might come to deserve the title ourselves.

2 Celluloid Saints

Introduction

Imagine that you are a filmmaker and that you want one of the characters in your film to undergo a religious experience. The first difficulty you will have is defining what exactly a "religious" experience is. Which of the following, if any, would fit your definition?

1. After fasting and standing motionless in the hot sun for days, a young Native American man has a vision in which his guiding spirit teaches him to chant.
2. After taking a hallucinogen, a graduate student has a vision of Jesus.
3. A young woman is convinced she is hearing the voice of God. Concerned relatives take her to the hospital, where she is diagnosed as schizophrenic.
4. A woman watches as a statue of the Virgin Mary exudes drops of oil that look like tears.
5. A boy reads from the Bible during his bar mitzvah ceremony. As he does so, he is thinking about a conversation he had with a friend earlier in the day.
6. A college senior eats a bowl of his favorite cereal. He later tells his roommates that this was, for him, a religious experience.
7. While viewing the Grand Canyon, a high-school sophomore has a feeling of peace and harmony.

Do any of the above reflect your idea of a religious experience? If your definition includes the notion that such an event must have no rational
explanation, you will probably discount scenarios 1, 2, and 3. After all,
anyone standing in the sun for a long time or taking drugs might have
hallucinations—there is nothing very unusual about that. If a woman is
suffering from mental illness, you might simply attribute the voices she
hears to an imbalance of brain chemicals. However, before dismissing
these examples, you should be aware that many cultures have honored as
visionaries or shamans the people whom our society would call mentally
ill. Likewise many cultures have used hallucinogens or ascetic practices as
time-honored ways of opening up communication with the spirit world.
The famous psychologist William James observed that "our normal waking
consciousness, rational consciousness as we call it, is but one special type
of consciousness, whilst all about it, parted from it by the filmiest of
screens, there lie potential forms of consciousness entirely different."[22]
James, writing in 1902, was willing to admit that people under the effects
of nitrous oxide or ether, for example, could have genuinely mystical experiences.

Let's move on to the example in which a statue of Mary seems to cry
tears of oil. This seems to be an event of supernatural origin, assuming
that it is not merely a clever trick. Is it "religious" though? Imagine that
the woman who is watching the statue is a chemist trying to prove that the
tears are a fraud. Or imagine that what is exuding oil is not a statue of
Mary but rather a statue of Mickey Mouse. Would the experience still
count as religious?

The truth is that it's difficult to pin down just what is "religious"
about religious experiences. The boy reading during the bar mitzvah ceremony is performing an overtly religious act, but his mind is on other
things. The college senior eating cereal claims that the act is religious, but
from the outside it may be difficult to see why. The girl who feels peace
and harmony while viewing the Grand Canyon might simply be
responding on an aesthetic level; there need be nothing "religious" about
her experience.

Religious Experience

One thinker who tried to isolate the religious element of experience was a
German scholar named Rudolf Otto. Otto's *The Idea of the Holy* has
become a classic in the study of religion, and his definition of the Holy is

frequently cited by scholars in the field. According to this definition, an experience of the Holy is an experience of an awesome, overwhelming mystery: what Otto calls the *mysterium tremendum*.[23] The Holy, says Otto, is a mystery not only because it is beyond our comprehension but also and primarily because we experience it as "wholly other"—as something utterly different from ourselves. The word *tremendum* conveys the sense of awe that Otto believes the Holy inspires in us. We perceive the Holy to be absolutely unapproachable and forbidding in its majesty and energy, and yet, says Otto, we are at the same time fascinated by it; we are drawn to it and we long for it. While it may appear to be, he says, "so overwhelmingly great that it seems to penetrate to the very marrow, making the man's hair bristle and his limbs quake," it may also at times "steal upon him almost unobserved as the gentlest of agitations, a mere fleeting shadow passing across his mood."[24]

As an example of what he means by an experience of the *mysterium tremendum*, Otto points to the last few chapters of the Book of Job in the Bible. According to this ancient story, the man Job was upright and God-fearing. However, precisely because of his outstanding piety, he became the focus of a wager between God and ha-satan (whose name means "the accuser"), an angel in God's court. For his part, ha-satan claims that Job praises God only because God has been good to the man: "But just reach out and strike everything he has, and I bet he'll curse you to your face" (1:11).[25] God accepts the wager and allows ha-satan to do anything he wishes to the unlucky Job: anything, that is, short of killing him.

What follows is a litany of disasters for Job and his family. First the man's donkeys, sheep and camels are all killed. Then a messenger arrives to report that while Job's children were feasting together, a great wind knocked down their house and killed them all. On top of this, Job is afflicted with boils from head to toe, and his friends make fun of him, accusing him of having sinned and thus of being justly punished by God.

Job, however, knows that he is innocent. In summing up his case against God, he cries out, "But what good has virtue done me? How has God rewarded me? Isn't disgrace for sinners and misery for the wicked? Can't he tell right from wrong or keep his accounts in order?" (31:2–4).[26] At this point God answers Job in the form of a voice coming from within a whirlwind. The voice thunders, "Who is this whose ignorant words smear my design with darkness? Stand up now like a man; I will question you: please, instruct me" (38:1–3).[27] God then asks a series of questions. Where, God wants to know, was Job when God planned the earth? Who gives the horse its strength, and who teaches the hawk to fly? Who guides dawn to its place each morning, and who makes the wilderness blossom? In other words, who is Job, insignificant miserable little Job, to question the ways of God?

In referring to this story, Otto points out that it is not God's argument *per se* that puts an end to Job's questioning. After all, Job is already well aware that he is not himself the master of the universe. In an earlier verse he acknowledge, "Any plant will instruct you; go learn from the fish in the sea. Which of them does not know that God created all things?" (12:8–9).[28] What quiets Job's complaints, Otto says, is not an explanation; rather, God's rebuttal "relies on something quite different from anything that can be exhaustively rendered in rational concepts, namely, on the sheer absolute wondrousness that transcends thought, on the *mysterium*, presented in its pure, non-rational form."[29] It is the power of God made manifest in the whirlwind that humbles Job. Not ideas, but rather an awareness of the Wholly Other causes Job to conclude, "I will be quiet, comforted that I am dust"(42:6).[30] This sheer absolute wondrousness is what makes God *God*. An encounter with it, according to Otto, is what makes an experience "religious."

Now return to our original question. How would you, as a filmmaker, present this kind of an encounter on screen? How would you portray an experience of the Wholly Other? More specifically, if you chose to make a movie about the Book of Job, how would you depict the meeting between Job and the Almighty? If you chose to film a whirlwind and then to make that whirlwind speak, how would you convey to your audience that the one who speaks is God, the Holy, the *mysterium tremendum*, rather than simply a tornado with personality? How, in other words, can the world we see on film speak of the world of the divine?

In one sense, of course, film can't capture the Holy. What is Wholly Other by definition cannot be represented in any literal way. Yet, as professor of religion and film interpreter Michael Bird explains, "If art cannot give a direct representation of the dimension of the holy, it can nonetheless perform an alternative religious function: art can disclose those spaces and those moments in culture where the experience of finitude and the encounter with the transcendent dimension are felt and expressed within culture itself."[31] In other words, if we cannot capture the Holy, we can nonetheless capture those times when people feel themselves to have been touched by it. We can convey something of religious experience even if we cannot convey what, exactly, is being experienced.

Film and Religious Experience

How best to do this? Before we can answer that question, we have to consider how film functions in the first place—that is, what the relation is between what we see on screen and the universe that we inhabit every day. There are several schools of thought when it comes to this question, but two from the history of film interpretation stand out as particularly important.

The first, called the Formative school, takes the position that the role of film is not to record reality so much as to transform it in the way that a painting or that literature might. One of the principal advocates of this position is Rudolf Arnheim, whose book *Film as Art* has been one of the most influential works on film theory. Arnheim seeks to refute those who would say that film is not an art: that it merely records reality and is thus only a mechanical process. He explains that in truth there is no such thing as a simple or "objective" recording of the world. Even something as basic as photographing a cube presents challenges. Photographs, after all, are two-dimensional, and so a photographer or film-maker interested in the cube must decide how a two-dimensional medium can best convey the object's three-dimensional nature. Thus Arnheim explains that "people who contemptuously refer to the camera as an automatic recording machine must be made to realize that even in the simplest photographic reproduction of a perfectly simple object, a feeling for its nature is required which is quite beyond any mechanical operation."[32]

Arnheim spells out several of the features of photography and film that should make us hesitate before dismissing these media as merely technical reproductions of reality. For example, lighting and color can be used to alter what the unaided eye would see. Choosing to film something from a great distance or from very close up can affect how that thing is understood, and placing some people or objects in the foreground while others remain in the background can tell us something about their relative importance. Film can take liberties with time and space, presenting events in an order other than that in which they occur, or showing what is going on at the same time in two different parts of the world. Through the use of montage, a movie can create imaginative and original associations between things that would not normally be thought of as in any way alike; just as poetry uses similes and metaphors to suggest relations, presenting scenes in quick succession, or placing diverse photographs side-by-side can shape how we interpret them. All of these processes are important to the art of film, says Arnheim: "Art begins where mechanical reproduction leaves off, where the conditions of representation serve in some way to mold the object."[33]

In contrast to the Formative school of film, representatives of the Realist school see the virtue of photography as being precisely its ability to represent the world without distortion. German theorist Siegfried Kracauer, for example, notes that creative efforts are important in film, but only "as long at they benefit, in some way or other, the medium's substantive concern with our visible world." Kracauer's concern is that in contemporary culture we are too easily swayed by images that may or may not have any relation to reality. As a corrective to the reels of propaganda produced by the Nazi party during its rise to power, for instance, we need to see footage taken when the Allies liberated places like Auschwitz and Dachau. When we view the tortured bodies of Hitler's victims, "we redeem horror from its invisibility behind the veils of panic and imagination. And this experience is liberating in as much as it removes a most powerful taboo."[34] For realist filmmakers, the point of film is not to improve upon reality but rather to reveal it.

So which approach to film can best convey religious experience: Formative or Realist? If we think of the Holy as something that breaks into our world only sporadically and as something essentially foreign to it, we are more likely to opt for a Formative strategy of film making. We will attempt to transform reality through montage, special lighting, unusual camera angles and so on in order to convey the idea that something other-than-natural is going on. Think, for example, of Steven Spielberg's *Raiders of the Lost Ark* (1981), in which archeologist Indiana Jones attempts to find the chest containing the original Ten Commandments before his Nazi enemies do. In the film, Jones explains, "An army which carries the ark before it is invincible," and thus Hitler wants to find the ark and use its powers for his own evil designs. Of course, when the Nazis actually do open the chest, they get more than they bargained for: a pyrotechnic explosion that melts their faces. In this movie, the presence of the divine is conveyed using spectacular special effects and cinematic sleight of hand.

In contrast to this approach, if we believe that the Holy has some intrinsic relationship to this world, that it underlies or is connected to reality in something other than an accidental way, then we may be more likely to choose a Realist methodology. Rather than manipulating the world through cinematic means, we will try to show the mystery that lies at the heart of life. Not special effects, but rather the depth found in ordinary reality will be our concern.

For Protestant theologian Paul Tillich, the choice between these two conceptions of the divine is clear. We must understand God not as a being or as one thing among other things in the universe, says Tillich; God is not the kind of thing that can be stored in a box, as *Raiders of the Lost Ark* might lead us to think. Instead, he says, we must think of God as the ground of being or as being-itself. Tillich writes, "Being-itself infinitely transcends every finite being." He continues, "On the other hand, everything finite participates in being-itself and in its infinity."[35] As the ground of being, God is not limited by space and time in the way that beings are. God has no limitations at all. At the same time, though, God is what underlies all finite beings. Without such a ground, no finite beings could even exist.

In other words, experiences of God are not like meetings with a stranger, with someone whom we might or might not happen to run into as we make our way through life. Quite the contrary. Religious experience for Tillich occurs when the ordinary world reveals to us the power of being that lies underneath it: when "a segment of finite reality become[s] the basis for an assertion about that which is infinite."[36] Any segment of reality can disclose the power of being that grounds it; literally anything in the world can become a site of access to the Holy. Indeed, looking at the history of religions, one can see the enormous diversity of objects, people and events that have taken on this revelatory character. Sacred trees, mountains, rivers, books, shrines, colors, words, melodies, jewelry, leaders, statues, buildings, births, deaths—the number and variation of such items are limitless. Nothing is holy in itself, but everything can become holy if we experience it in light of the Holy that underlies it.

Such points of encounter with the divine Tillich calls "symbols." A symbol, he says, differs from a sign in an important way. Both signs and symbols point to something beyond themselves. For example, a red light, which is a sign, means that cars should stop. However, there is no intrinsic relation between the color red and the act of stopping. We stop our cars simply because we have learned to associate the color with the act, and not because there is anything inherent in "redness" that demands that we draw to a halt. For Tillich, this is what differentiates a sign from a symbol. A sign has merely an extrinsic and accidental relation to what it points to.

A symbol, on the other hand, is not arbitrary. A symbol participates in what it symbolizes. Think, for example, of the use of water in the

Christian ritual of baptism. In the ritual, water symbolizes death to one's old life and entrance into a new relationship with God. It symbolizes the washing away of sin as well as the growth of the human spirit towards love and freedom. All of these things (death, life, washing, growth) have an intrinsic relationship to water. Submersion in water can cause drowning, but at the same time we cannot live more than a few days without slaking our thirst. Water washes away dust and grime, and at the same time it causes plants to grow. It is not merely an arbitrary sign of renewal, but rather it bears in itself the reality which it symbolizes.

For Tillich, symbols are not merely the medium by which we become aware of the mysterious depth of the world; in them we also experience the ground of our *own* being. In a realization of this ground, he says, "Man is driven toward faith by his awareness of the infinite to which he belongs, but which he does not own like a possession. This is in abstract terms what concretely appears as the 'restlessness of heart' within the flux of life."[37] Faith, in Tillich's lexicon, is defined as "ultimate concern." It is a longing for the depth at the heart of life, for meaning and for truth. It is not to be confused with belief, or with the declaration that there exists a divine being somewhere in the universe. For Tillich, such a declaration would reduce God to a being among other beings and would make God too small. Rather, faith is an awareness of our ground and the ground of all reality.

Faith expresses itself, Tillich says, in symbols and myths. Here "myth" does not mean a belief that isn't true, as in, for example, "Five Myths About Weight Loss." Rather, it refers to stories that express the deep truths about our lives: stories that tell us who we are and who we ought to be. Myths are symbolic tales of divine-human encounters that convey something about the purpose and meaning of life. For example, says Tillich, the story about Eve and Adam in the Garden of Eden is not a historical account of something that happened long ago. Rather, it is a poetic description of the tragic character of human freedom. In order to be truly human we must be separated from God, the ground of our being, and this separation brings with it both freedom and suffering.

It is important to point out that for Tillich, myths are not merely a primitive form of religious expression. They cannot be mined for their meaning and then discarded as old-fashioned or primitive. On the contrary, myths are indispensable to faith; they are the language of faith. Like poetry, art, and music, they can never be reduced to a moral or a thesis. We could, for example, summarize Michelangelo's *Pieta*, by saying that it is a depiction of the Virgin Mary's sorrow over Jesus's death; the "meaning" of the sculpture is fairly simple. However, such a summing up of the masterpiece could never adequately express the multiple emotions and thoughts that the work evokes. A sculpture cannot be replaced by something other than itself. Its meaning is dependent on its form and cannot be separated from it. Likewise, says Tillich, a myth cannot be reduced to a set of statements or propositions. Myths grow and live precisely because of their ability to capture our imaginations and to express things that literal language never could.

Tillich's theology of symbols and myths can help us to see how film, particularly narrative film, relates to religion. The Bible's myths were first of all stories passed on from generation to generation, tales shaped by the oral tradition in which they grew and lived. They sustained peoples who did not or could not write, tying the wisdom of the past to the needs of the present. We, however, do not live in such a story-telling culture. Most of us do not gather around campfires at night remembering the ways of our ancestors and telling the wondrous tales that they told. Our myths come to us rather on the big screen. They come in the form of movies about people larger than life who nonetheless tell us about ourselves and the world we live in. We compare ourselves to characters in the movies; we relate our experiences to theirs. We judge ourselves by the lives that we see on screen, making sense of reality by looking at its celluloid counterpart. The truths of our lives are not related by oral storytellers but by movie-makers.

It is important to add that in Tillich's theology, symbols and myths are able to articulate our experience of the divine precisely because they do not pretend to encapsulate the divine. Symbols and myths by definition point beyond themselves. They urge us to look beyond them, and they remind us that they are about something more than what they themselves are. Explains Tillich, "That symbol is most adequate which expresses not only the ultimate but also its own lack of ultimacy."[38] Religious experience must be articulated symbolically because otherwise we might be tempted to equate the Wholly Other with a particular representation of it. We might, in other words, create idols for ourselves, mistaking an idea about God or an image of God for what is beyond all ideas and images.

This point is especially important when we turn to film, a medium that, as we have noted, has an intimate relation with the real. What we see on film seems true to us, even if we know in our heads that what we are watching is a simulation. We tend to believe that, as the saying goes, the camera doesn't lie. One woman, after having watched Spielberg's film about the Holocaust entitled *Schindler's List* (1993), emerged from the theater commenting, "Now I know it really happened."[39] Seeing a fictionalized version of genocide somehow had the power to convince the woman that what she had merely read about or heard about had really occurred. Visual evidence is powerful: seeing is believing. If it is possible to mistake a depiction of a historical event for the event itself, it is no less possible to mistake an on-screen version of God for the real thing. Movie makers must find some way to remind their viewers that their films are about something outside of or beyond any image.

Using the insights of Tillich's theology, we can conclude that the best way to do this is not to try to depict God-in-godself, but rather to show the divine dimension of all reality. But how can this be done? How can a film convince us that it is about more than simply what appears on screen? How can it clue us in to the fact that it is seeking the depth of reality rather than merely its surfaces? Rudolf Otto, whose *Idea of the Holy* we discussed above, considered three techniques by which artists (primarily painters and musicians) can point towards the Holy, if only indirectly. The first of these is the use of darkness, a "semi-darkness that glimmers in vaulted halls, or beneath the branches of a lofty forest glade, strangely quickened and stirred by the mysterious play of half-lights...." The second is the incorporation of silence, which he notes is the reaction of anyone overcome by the feeling of being in the presence of the divine. The third is the portrayal of emptiness, "a negation that does away with every 'this' and 'here,' in order that the 'wholly other' may become actual."[40] All of these techniques, Otto notes, are essentially negative: they utilize an absence to express a presence beyond all expression.

One can see these techniques at work in numerous films. The somber, brooding tones of Maurice Pialat's *Under the Sun of Satan*, the play of light in Robert Bresson's *Diary of a Country Priest*, the long periods of quiet in Ingmar Bergman's *Winter Light*, the spare scenery in Alain Cavalier's *Thérèse*—these tell us that what we are watching is as much an interior drama as an external one. We know that the camera is attempting to convey not only people and objects, but the significance of those people and the meaning of the objects.

Filmmakers also use other methods to indicate to us that they are dealing with the sacred rather than simply the secular. Perhaps the most common of these is to take explicitly religious symbols and incorporate them into the storyline. For example, when we see the protagonist in Luis Buñuel's *Viridiana* gather the homeless, poor, blind and lame around her and then join them for a meal, we know that the scene is meant to evoke Jesus's Last Supper. Likewise, when Bess in *Breaking the Waves* walks along a tortuous path, tormented by children who jeer and throw stones at her, we call to mind Jesus's agonizing road to Calvary. Neo's resurrection from the dead in the science fiction thriller *The Matrix* is a traditional religious symbol given new cinematic contextualization. The use of such common religious imagery in what otherwise might appear to be a non-religious movie tells readers that something more than the ordinary is going on.

Celluloid Saints

What role does cinema play in the contemporary process of saint-making? In the earliest days of Christianity, people were recognized as saints simply through popular acclamation. When martyrs were slain, people spontaneously gathered at their graves and built shrines, venerating the deceased as God's fortunate ones and petitioning them for favors. The popularity of martyrs was directly proportional to the excitement generated by their *passios*, or the stories of their deaths. As Saint Gregory of Tours explained in the sixth century, Saint Patroclus of Troyes had been all but forgotten because his *passio* had been lost: "It is the custom of the man in the street to give more attentive veneration to those saints of God whose combats are read aloud."[41] Only when a military expedition returning from Italy brought back a document claiming to be "The Passion of Saint Patroclus" did the saint's popularity take off.[42]

The purpose of martyrdom tales was to make the saint present to the living once again. As historian Peter Brown observes, "When the *passio* was read, the saint was 'really' there.... Without a *passio* the *praesentia* of the saint lacked weight."[43] In the ancient culture of early Christianity, the human voice could conjure up realities that were otherwise absent. Storytelling not only called to mind but brought into being the deeds of ancestors and heroes, inviting listeners to relive the past in the present. In our day, movies perform this function. We participate vicariously in the exploits of people real and imagined, far away or far in the future, by watching them on screen.

Thus movies are our modern *passios*. Paulist priest Ellwood Kieser recalls that when the movie *Romero* (which he had produced) was released, the slain archbishop's friends were stunned by its power: "For a while I thought Oscar was alive again," one commented. Some who viewed it characterized the film as being the most powerful cinematic experience of their lives; others said that it brought about an experience of God. Concludes Kieser, "What more could a priest-producer want?"[44]

The ability of a film to affect those who view it is not necessarily a blessing, however. When the made-for-television movie *The Courage to Love* (2000) was released, those promoting the cause of Henriette Delille were apprehensive. Mother Delille was the first person of African-American descent to have had her cause officially opened by the Catholic Church. A free woman of color who lived in New Orleans in the nineteenth century, Delille founded the Sisters of the Holy Family, an order of religious, mostly African-American women. The *Courage to Love* tells the story of how the Servant of God gave up a life of relative luxury to work among the poor and sick of New Orleans.

In the movie, the role of Delille is played by Vanessa Williams, a former Miss America whose nude photographs were published (notably, without her consent) in *Penthouse* magazine. The postulator for the saint's cause for canonization commented that Williams "was not the most appropriate actress to have played the role of Henriette Delille," and, pointing out several historical inaccuracies in the film, alleged that its producers "fictionalized many things to excite the audience and for viewer appeal." Though he doubted that the movie would "desanctify" the Servant of God, he clearly wished that it had never been made at all.[45]

Movies are powerful. They shape our world and our perception of the people in that world. That is why it is so important to view cinematic portrayals of saints with an appreciative and yet always-critical eye. Viewers should ask themselves about the relation between what they see at the theater and the historical record, paying as much attention to what the film leaves out as to what it chooses to include. They should be aware of the theological assumptions underlying a work and take note of any discrepancies between those assumptions and their own. In a world saturated by images, we cannot afford to accept passively whatever appears to us on the big screen.

3 # Holy Blood

Introduction

There is a scene in Alejandro Jodorowsky's strange film *Santa Sangre* ("Holy Blood") that captures the complexity of Christians' relations to their bodies and to death. The scene takes place at a shrine dedicated to "the saint with no arms," a local girl who was mutilated and killed during a rapist attack. In the shrine is a pool filled with red liquid: apparently the blood of the child-martyr. Viewers watch as a young woman dressed in flowing white garments slowly immerses herself into the pool, reveling in her bloody baptism.

How are Christians to think about death? If the body is merely a temporary and ill-fitting covering for the soul, then death is not a tragedy but rather a form of liberation. At death the soul can fly free from the mortal bonds that have held it captive. The young woman swimming through the martyr's blood would be ritually anticipating the glorious day when her own fleshly imprisonment would come to an end.

On the other hand, the fact that the young woman is merely *swimming* through the blood (which, the movie will reveal, is not really blood at all but merely water dyed red with paint) and not adding her own to it complicates the picture. If death were an unmitigated good, then all of the worshipers at the saint's shrine should simply slit their wrists and fall into the pool in an exultant gesture of deliverance. That they do not indicates that they are reluctant to surrender their flesh too quickly. Perhaps then the body is more essential to us than we might like to admit. Perhaps death signals the loss of something precious and irreplaceable.

Conceptions of death and of the body are inextricably bound up with one another. Is the body something to be despised and gotten rid of as quickly as possible, or is it something to be cherished and loved, a temple and a gift from God? Is the body insignificant to our identity, merely clothing for an invisible, immaterial, immortal soul, or is it an indispensable part of who we are? Remarkably, Christianity has managed to embrace all of the varying answers to these questions about the flesh (and, consequently, about death) not only enthusiastically but often even simultaneously. Throughout its history, Christianity has both denigrated the body as a prison and looked forward to its resurrection. It has both posited an immortal soul as the center of human beings and asserted that on the Last Day, bodies will be indispensable to people's heavenly existence. It has both held the body to be of little consequence and looked to the body of Jesus as the source of the world's salvation.

Nowhere is Christianity's ambivalence about the body more apparent than in the martyr tales that it has told and retold for nearly 2000 years. On the one hand, the death of a martyr is presented as a tragedy: the slaughter of an innocent victim by a cruel despot. On the other hand, however, Christianity and in particular Catholicism has gloried in its martyr tales. There are even accounts of Christians seeking out martyrdom, throwing themselves into harm's way so as to be able to sacrifice their lives for Christ. According to one early Christian text, Saint Andrew the Apostle refused to be taken down from his cross even after his friends had persuaded the Roman proconsul to halt his execution: "What kind of friendship and love and habituation to the flesh is this?" protested Andrew as his friends tried to rescue him. "How long will you be taken up with earthly and temporal things? ...Leave me now to be put to death in the manner you see, and let no one release me in any way from these bonds."[46]

The question of Christians' relation to the body is made more complex by the fact that even when martyrs themselves seem to hold their bodies in little regard, their loved ones do not share this estimation. In tale after tale, the remains of a martyr are gathered up by the faithful and venerated as sacred objects. They are enshrined in reliquaries or entombed in the altars used for the celebration of the Eucharist. In the fourth century, the Roman Emperor Julian complained about the way that followers of Christ would process through the streets carrying the bones and skulls of their departed saints. They seemed to him to have an unhealthy fascination with mortal remains. Exasperated by their bizarre behavior, the emperor charged, "You keep adding many corpses newly dead to the corpse of long ago. You have filled the whole world with tombs and sepulchres."[47]

If Christian theology has been marked by ambivalence regarding the meaning of death, films about martyrdom have been just as divided over the issue. In the epic *Quo Vadis?* (1951), Christian prisoners sing triumphant hymns as they march off to meet the beasts in the arena. Holding the body to be irrelevant to their true selves, they willingly sacrifice the flesh in order to enjoy a life in heaven. Saint Thomas More in *A Man for All Seasons* (1966), on the other hand, is in no hurry to lose his head; he looks for ways to avoid his decapitation and accepts it only when it is clear that he has no viable alternative.

Most interesting, however, are films that not only portray the complexities of Christians' acceptance or horror of martyrdom but also explore the potent mix of death, religion, and sexuality in the martyr tales. *Santa Sangre*'s fictional saint enshrined in blood brings to mind the real life of Saint Maria Goretti, a young girl who was killed because she fought off her attacker's attempts to rape her. Goretti was canonized in 1950 as a "martyr of chastity"; her canonization was controversial in that it seemed to suggest that death was preferable to surrendering one's virginity. In numerous stories of virgin martyrs, innocent Christian maids are subjected to sexual humiliations such as being stripped naked or being forced to enter a brothel or enduring attempts at rape before they are killed. Such sexualizing of the martyrs can be found in numerous movies ranging from Cecil B. De Mille's *Sign of the Cross* to Derek Jarman's homoerotic *Sebastiane*.

This chapter will attempt to make sense out of what seems to be a contradictory and confusing jumble of ideas about the human body, its sexuality, and its mortality as presented in film. First we will look at the history of Christians' conceptions of the flesh, tracing those conceptions' roots back to both Greek and Jewish sources. Second, we will examine how Christians' ideas about the body have affected their views of death—both the death of Jesus and the deaths of the martyrs. At that point we will have some of the tools necessary to interpret the deaths of Christians on the big screen: cinematic portrayals of martyrdom.

"Who Will Rescue Me From This Body of Death?"

In the year 399 BCE,[48] the Greek philosopher Socrates was sentenced to death by an Athenian jury on the charges of corrupting the city's youth and refusing to worship the city's gods. After hearing his sentence, Socrates bade farewell to the men who had condemned him with these words: "Now the hour to part has come. I go to die, you go to live. Which of us goes to the better lot is known to no one, except the god."[49]

However, if at the time of his sentencing Socrates professed not to know whether life or death was preferable, at the moment of his execution he seemed to have had utter confidence that his was the better part of the bargain. We read of the death of Socrates in an account called the *Phaedo* left by his student Plato. According to Plato, Socrates looked forward to his demise not only with peace and equanimity but with genuine optimism. On the day he was to drink the poisonous hemlock, Socrates gathered his friends and disciples around him and quizzed them about the meaning of death. He asked, "Is it anything else than the separation of the soul from the body?" No, they replied. Socrates continued, "The lovers of learning know that when philosophy gets hold of their soul, it is imprisoned in and clinging to the body, and that it is forced to examine other things through it as through a cage and not by itself, and that it wallows in every kind of ignorance."[50] Gradually, he says, philosophy is able to loosen the soul from its corporeal bonds by ignoring the passions and desires of the flesh.

Death, then, is simply the final escape of the soul from the body. At death, the soul of the philosopher, which is gradually trained to disdain the claims of the body, makes its way to "beautiful dwelling places which it is hard to describe clearly."[51] Only in death is the philosopher able to get hold of the truth. Only in death can the soul find real peace and liberation.

For Socrates, as indeed for much Greek thinking, the soul is "like the divine, deathless, intelligible, uniform, indissoluble, always the same as itself," while the body is "like that which is human, mortal, multiform, unintelligible, soluble and never consistently the same."[52] Who we are is determined by our soul rather than by our body. Our bodies are merely packaging, and disposable packaging at that. They house our essence but are quite separate from it.

This Greek way of thinking about the body rings true for many of us in contemporary Western society. We tend to think of ourselves as having a constant identity as we go through our lives despite the tremendous changes that take place in our physical being. Every day we lose millions of our body's cells, and yet we do not think that we are different people before we wash our hands or brush our hair than we are afterwards. If I were to cut off the tip of my finger while slicing carrots, or if my skin darkened from exposure to the sun, I would not find myself in a crisis of identity. Even major changes to our bodies do not always alter our ways of thinking about ourselves. Actor Christopher Reeve once played the part of Superman in the movies. After he was paralyzed from the neck down in a riding accident, he wrote an autobiography detailing his life both before and after the injury. The title of his memoir was *Still Me*.[53]

The Greek conception of the body finds its way into contemporary movies as well. The plot of the blockbuster hit *Ghost* (1990) revolves around the ability of a woman's dead husband (played by Patrick Swayze) to visit his wife (Demi Moore) via the body of a storefront medium (Whoopi Goldberg). The unquestioned assumption in the movie is that the dead man is still himself regardless of whether he is "in" his own body before his death, in someone else's body (as when he speaks through the medium), or in no body at all. The same plot device can be found in numerous other Hollywood productions, including *All of Me*, *Switch*, *Freaky Friday*, *Heart and Souls*, *Goodbye Charlie*, and comic Chris Rock's *Down to Earth*.

However, we need to ask ourselves how well the Greek conception of the body really fits our everyday experience. Would it really make no difference if Patrick Swayze, a white male, were suddenly to become Whoopi Goldberg, an African-American female? Are our gender, stature, facial features, genetic coding, health, diet, sexual histories, wrinkles, voices, physical talents and scars really that irrelevant to who we are? Would we be the same person if we had the body of Michael Jordan or Marilyn Monroe? Would we be the same if we had the body of a tiger or a cricket? In other words, is our identity entirely determined by an invisible, immaterial soul, or does the body play some role in what makes me "me"?

Ancient Judaism opted for the second answer: that we are to a significant degree contiguous with our bodies. In fact, for much of its history, Judaism assumed that death was the end of the individual. Those who died simply went to Sheol, a shadowy underworld with little relation to the life that had been left behind. As the character Job remarks in the book of the Bible that bears his name, "As the cloud fades and vanishes, so those who go down to Sheol do not come up; they return no more to their houses, nor do their places know them any more" (7:9–10). Neither do those in Sheol look forward to an individual resurrection. Job continues, "As waters fail from a lake, and a river wastes away and dries up, so mortals lie down and do not rise again; until the heavens are no more, they will not awake or be roused out of their sleep" (14:11–12).

This is not to say that the ancient Jews thought that humans were merely material beings. They used the word *nephesh* (which is often translated as "soul") to talk about what differentiates a living person from a mere corpse.[54] They did not, however, believe that this *nephesh* would survive the body except in a vague and shadowy way. It animates the flesh, but apart from the living flesh it is nothing. Human beings, in this way of thinking, are naturally mortal. When they die, they are entirely dead. Nothing about them continues.

Even when later on many Jews came to adopt a belief in resurrection (this began just a few centuries before the birth of Jesus), they did not think of it as the continued existence of an immortal soul. Rather, resurrection would be the raising up of the entire person. After all, if in this life my identity depends on my being embodied (this way of putting it seems more appropriate than saying that my identity depends on my "having" a body), then if my body were absent in the afterlife, how could I still be me? For the ancient Jews as well as Jews at the time of Jesus, a person was a unified whole, in life, in death, and in the resurrection.

Thus we are presented with two very different versions of what it means to be a person, what it means to die, and what it means to live on after death. In a Greek way of thinking, I am an immortal soul imprisoned in a disposable body, and at death my soul will finally fly free of its bonds. In an ancient Jewish way of thinking, I am an animate body that is naturally mortal. When I die, I shall be entirely dead. If I am to be raised up (Jews at the time of Jesus disagreed about whether or not resurrection was really a possibility), it will not be because there is anything naturally immortal about me, but only because God has intervened on my behalf. Moreover, such a resurrection will involve my whole person, including, in some way or other, my very human body.

What is surprising about Christianity is that as it developed it managed to adopt both of these quite different conceptions of life and death. For example, some of the earliest Christian scriptures were written by a Jew named Saul, whose name was changed to Paul after he came to profess faith in Jesus as the Messiah. In the letters of Paul, we see very clearly a Jewish mind at work. Paul's writings show that he does believe in a resurrection after death; however, the resurrection that he looks forward to is of the whole person and not merely of a soul. To be sure, he thinks that our bodies will be different in the next life. They will no longer be fleshly but will be what he calls "spiritual bodies." Still, they will be our bodies, continuous with the bodies that are so central to who we are here and now.

In fact, Paul, who was writing in the first century, thought that the dead had to wait until the Second Coming of Jesus before they would be resurrected. The dead would be dead in every sense of the word until some point in the future. They would not be souls hanging around waiting for their bodies to join them. Rather, wrote Paul, only at the sound of the trumpet, when Jesus came to earth for the second time, would those who had died be raised up to be with the Lord forever (1 Thess 4:16–17).

Moreover, Paul, unlike Socrates and Plato, did not think of the body as something undesirable or as something to be despised as an obstacle to people's spiritual journeys. Rather, he said, the body is a temple; it is a sanctuary of the Holy Spirit. "Therefore," he urged his friends, "glorify God in your body" (1 Cor 6:19–20). The body is a gift from God and a means of giving thanks to God. Far from being an impediment to our true nature, it is central to who we are as part of the divine creation.

Of course, in Paul's eyes, the body is liable to sin. It is not sinful in itself, but because we are physical people, the body participates in our sins. Often when Paul is talking about the sins we commit as embodied beings, he uses the Greek word *sarx* or "flesh." He says, for example, "Now the works of the flesh are obvious: fornication, impurity, licentiousness, idolatry, sorcery, enmities, strife, jealousy, anger, quarrels, dissensions, factions, envy, drunkenness, carousing, and things like these" (Gal 5:19–21). However, again, it is not that the body itself is evil; the body is a holy gift from God. Rather, Paul's contrast is between living as embodied people for God, on the one hand, and living as embodied people as if God were not important, on the other.[55] When we do the latter, we are living according to the *sarx*, he says: living according to the flesh. We are using our bodies not to praise God but to cause hatred and sorrow. Paul, then, stands firmly in the Jewish tradition regarding bodies and their worth. When he asks, "Who will rescue me from this body of death?" (Rom 7:24) it is not his physical being that he longs to escape, but rather his sinfulness.

It didn't take long, however, before Greek ways of thinking began to seep into Christian life and beliefs, and the body came to be seen as wretched and loathsome. In the fourth century a theologian named Athanasius wrote a biography of a famous monk named Saint Anthony. Anthony, according to Athanasius, spent his days as a hermit in the

Egyptian desert groaning and longing for the mansions of heaven. "He used to say," Athanasius wrote, "that we should give all our time to the soul, rather than to the body." Indeed, Anthony was apparently so humiliated by the fact that he had a physical body that he was embarrassed to be seen eating: "For when going to food and sleep and the other needs of the body, shame came on him, thinking of the spirituality of the soul."[56]

For Anthony, the body was distressing and disgusting, something we should flee from rather than cherish. This view was so widespread in the first few centuries of the common era that many Christians came to deny that Jesus of Nazareth could ever really have had a human body. Bodies were wicked, they thought. Bodies were evil. How could God have had a body? Christians who thought this way were called Docetists, a term that comes from a Greek word that means "to appear." They believed that Jesus had only appeared to be physical. In reality, they said, he wore a human body in the way that one might wear clothes. His flesh was not really a part of him but was merely an outer covering used to make him visible to us.

Indeed, the Docetists not only denied that Jesus had had a body, but they also denied that Jesus had really died on the cross. An early Docetic document called the *Second Treatise of the Great Seth* depicts Jesus mocking those who thought they were tormenting him in the crucifixion. Jesus says, "I *visited* a bodily dwelling. I cast out the one who was in it first, and I went in.... And I am the one who was in it, not resembling him who was in it first. For he was an earthly man, but I, I am from above the heavens.... it was another, Simon, who bore the cross on his shoulder. It was another upon whom they placed the crown of thorns.... And I was laughing at their ignorance."[57] In this scenario, Jesus could not really have suffered because he had no flesh with which to feel pain. He was merely visiting another's body, himself immune to the tortures of the cross.

Docetism was eventually declared a heresy. In the fifth century, bishops from all over the Christian world met at a meeting called the Council of Chalcedon and formally declared that Jesus was "truly God and truly man, consisting also of a reasonable soul and body," and that he was "like us in all respects, apart from sin." This should have put an end to the matter. The Definition of Chalcedon proclaimed without hesitation that Jesus had truly had a human body just like ours. However, for one reason or another, docetic ideas have continued to live on in Christian tradition.

For example, several years ago the movie *The Last Temptation of Christ* opened to waves of protest from angry Christians who felt that the film portrayed Jesus in an unfavorable light. One of the main criticisms of the movie was that in one scene, Jesus dreams about marrying Mary Magdalene, having sex with her, and fathering several children by her. An open letter to Universal Pictures from the American Society for the Defense of Tradition, Family, and Property denounced the film, declaring that "[Jesus's] sublime perfection assures us that He practiced the virtue of chastity in the most absolute way and always maintained that state of perfect chastity which is intrinsically superior to the matrimonial state."[58]

And yet, if Jesus was truly "like us in all respects" and was really an embodied person, it is inconceivable that he would not have had sexual thoughts and longings. As Catholic novelist Andrew Greeley remarks, "Those who would exclude the poignancy and joy of erotic desire from the life of Jesus wish to deny Him full humanity to protect Him from what they take to be evil. They are possessed by the curious notion that God made an artistic and ethical mistake in ordering the dynamics of procreation and nurturing of human young."[59] The furor over the film shows that many Christians continue to have a docetic vision of Jesus, one in which Jesus is fully God but not really very human. They are uncomfortable with a physical Jesus and prefer to think of him as somehow "above" the shame of having a body with all of its urges and needs.

This is so despite the fact that both Christian scriptures and orthodox Christian theology have steadfastly maintained that the earthly body of Jesus played a crucial role in the drama of salvation. That body wasn't merely a covering for the real Jesus but was indispensable for the atonement that Jesus enacted. More than this, both Scriptures and theology have affirmed that Jesus's body was not left behind when the sacrifice on the cross had been completed. Rather, it was raised up into glory and remains an integral part of the post-Easter Christ. And, says Christianity, what happened to Jesus will happen to all the faithful.

Contemporary Christians are often surprised to discover that their tradition professes a belief in the resurrection of the body. Many of them feel, on the contrary, that their bodies will simply waste away in the ground, and that what will live on is their soul or spirit. They think, in other words, much like the ancient Greeks. But this was not how the earliest followers of Jesus saw the matter. Again, we can see this in a letter that Saint Paul wrote to a group of Christians in Corinth. In Paul's epistle, he told the Corinthian community not to grieve too much for friends who had died. The dead sleep in Christ now, he said, but when Jesus comes again the bodies of the faithful will be rescued from the grave: "For as all die in Adam, so all will be made alive in Christ. But each in his own order: Christ the first fruits, then at his coming those who belong to Christ" (1 Cor 15:22–23). In other words, just as the body of Jesus had arisen from the tomb, so too would the bodies of all Christians be raised up, albeit in a transformed way.

"A Sacrifice Rich and Acceptable"

One of the most interesting developments in the history of Christianity is the insistence of the early disciples that the death of Jesus was somehow salvific. Christians did not simply look to Jesus as a fallen hero. Nor were they content to describe him simply as a god who had died and come back to life, like the Greek god Dionysus. Rather, they claimed that there was something in his death that affected not just him but the very cosmos as well. When he died, all creation groaned, and when he was raised up, all creation was transformed. How exactly this happened has been a matter of disagreement among theologians. However, *that* it happened is one of the central proclamations of Christianity.

We should first be clear about the historical details of the death that Jesus endured. Scholars are unable to date with any precision the year of Jesus's birth, nor can they say exactly when he died, though most would situate his life as having occurred sometime between the years 4 BCE and 33 CE. During his ministry as a prophet, teacher, healer and exorcist, Jesus managed to come to the attention of both the authorities in the Jewish Temple and the Roman government that had been occupying Palestine for some time. It was the latter, the Roman regime (possibly influenced by some Temple administrators) that ordered and enacted Jesus's crucifixion. Jesus was executed as thousands of other Jews had been executed before him: as a threat to the Roman establishment.[60]

However, unlike the executions of those unnamed thousands, this death came to be seen as salvific. One of the earliest ways of understanding the death of Jesus was that it was a sacrifice offered to God on behalf of all people. This model relied on the idea of sacrifice as it was practiced in the Jewish Temple. In Judaism, the faithful gave offerings of animals (for example, doves or sheep) to God as tokens of their own repentant hearts. The sacrifice was a way of offering not only the animal but also one's own self to God's service. It was a way of rededicating oneself to God and of vowing to live with renewed generosity and compassion.

Thus, to call Jesus a sacrifice was to say that his death was a way for all people to reconcile themselves to God. In a letter to a group of Christians in Corinth, Paul wrote, "Now you are the body of Christ and individually members of it" (1 Cor 12:27). Thus, not just one man had been offered on the cross, but all people who were willing to identify themselves with Jesus were offered as well. To be a member of the body of Christ was to be part of his sacrifice and to be made new in relation to God.

There have been many other ways that Christians have understood the atoning death of Jesus, but the sacrifice model remains the most prevalent. What is fascinating is that Christians have seen the deaths of the martyrs as re-presenting over and over again that one perfect offering. An ancient document called "The Martyrdom of Polycarp" depicts Polycarp, a Christian who was eighty-six years old at the time of his execution, turning his eyes heavenward as he was bound to the stake: "O Lord God Almighty," he prays, "I bless thee for granting me this day and hour, that I may be numbered amonsgst the martyrs, to share the cup of thine Anointed...a sacrifice rich and acceptable...."[61]

It was common in the early centuries of Christianity to depict the sufferings of the martyrs as patterned on the Passion of Jesus. Polycarp, according to the story, was arrested after having been betrayed by one of his houseboys, a figure who is explicitly compared to Judas. When soldiers arrive at Polycarp's house, the old man holds a meal for them and then asks for an hour during which he might pray undisturbed. He refuses to try to escape, saying merely, "God's will be done." When his hour is up, he is mounted on an ass and taken to the nearby city, where he is mocked and reviled by soldiers. As he is being burned at the stake, his body looks "like a loaf baking in the oven" (a Eucharistic allusion), and at his death a soldier pierces him with a lance. At this point blood gushes from his side, "such a copious rush of blood that the flames were extinguished," and a dove appears.[62] All of these details in the story mimic events from the suffering and death of Jesus.

The early Christian device of portraying martyrs as dying *in imitatio Christi* is continued in many Hollywood versions of martyrdom. For example, the last fifteen minutes of John Duigan's *Romero* show the Salvadoran Archbishop Oscar Romero praying in agony as he foresees his death: "I can't," the priest prays desperately to God. "You must. I'm Yours. Show me the way." His words echo the lament of Jesus in the Garden of Gethsemane: "Father, if you are willing, remove this cup from me; yet, not my will but yours be done" (Luke 22:42). Romero then enters a town where he is taunted by soldiers who remove his clothes in a search for weapons. A woman steps forward from the crowd around him to offer him a cloth with which to cover himself (reminiscent of the legendary Veronica wiping the face of Jesus), and Romero then begins a celebration of the Mass: a remembrance of the last supper Jesus had with his followers. A few scenes later, Romero is killed as he offers wine to God during a Mass held in a hospital chapel. At the moment of his death, as the assassin's bullet enters his body, the archbishop throws his arms back in a cruciform position, and his blood spills into the communion cup he has been holding. As the movie comes to a close, Romero's voice is heard, saying, "I have often been threatened with death. If they kill me, I shall arise in the Salvadoran people." From arrest to execution to resurrection, Romero's life as portrayed in his cinematic biography follows the pattern familiar to Christians from their reading of the gospels.

Celluloid Martyrs and Sexuality

The Sign of the Cross

One of the earliest full-length portrayals of sainthood in the movies is the classic *Sign of the Cross* directed by Cecil B. DeMille (1932). The film is set during the reign of Nero and opens with a scene of the besotted emperor playing his fiddle while all Rome burns around him. The conflagration that nearly destroys the city is blamed on a new and subversive religious movement called Christianity, and immediately an order goes out that all Christians are to be arrested and executed. Meanwhile, a budding romance is developing between a beautiful Christian girl named Mercia and a handsome Roman soldier named Marcus who is sworn to serve the emperor.

As the persecution of the Christians intensifies, Mercia's younger brother Stephan, an idealistic adolescent, is arrested and tortured. In his pain, he reveals the secret place where the Christians meet to worship their God, and a legion of soldiers is dispatched to massacre them. The slaughter of the Christians by Roman soldiers is interrupted by Marcus, who had hoped to warn the Christians of the impending attack. However, Marcus arrives too late; Mercia's father and several others have already been slain. The Christians left alive are all taken to prison, with the exception of Mercia. She is brought instead to the house of Marcus where an orgy is in progress. Marcus hopes to convince Mercia to renounce her faith, indulge herself in hedonistic pleasures, and ultimately become his bride.

At this point a remarkable scene takes place in which Marcus persuades a friend named Ancaria, "the most wicked and, uh, talented woman in Rome!" to dance around Mercia singing a hymn called "To the Naked Moon." Ancaria caresses the virgin Mercia's body, thrusting her hips towards her and kissing her lasciviously. Mercia, for her part, swears that she will never abandon her faith no matter how much Marcus wishes her to. Ancaria continues her steamy dance until she is interrupted by the sound of the condemned Christians being marched to the arena, singing their hymns of faith in the Son of God. A Roman soldier bursts into the house and, despite Marcus's protests, carries Mercia off to be thrown to the lions along with the others.

Cecil B. DeMille is not known for his use of understatement, but the segment of the movie that follows Mercia's arrest is truly over the top. We see Nero presiding at games in the Colosseum, flanked on one side by his wife and on the other by a naked youth who holds a tray of grapes for the emperor's enjoyment. Nero looks supremely bored as pairs of gladiators battle each other in the arena, and he does not hesitate to turn thumbs-down at the end of the contest, thus compelling each victor to butcher his opponent. After the gladiatorial games are over, various prisoners are tortured for the amusement of the crowd. One man has his head trampled by an elephant, another unfortunate is tossed about by a bull, and a scantily-clad young woman, bound hand and foot and screaming for mercy, is menaced by crocodiles. These events are followed by a fearsome battle between what a sign outside the arena advertises as "Pygmies from Africa" and "Barbarian Women from the North." Amazons decapitate exotically dressed pygmy warriors while at the same time exhibiting themselves in erotic poses. Violence and sexuality mingle in an extraordinary carnival of animalistic desire.

All of this is, of course, merely appetizer for the main event in which the Christians will be eaten by lions. Mercia and her companions can hear the roar of the crowd as they wait in their dungeon below, and together they pray the "Our Father" to keep their courage up. When one prisoner asks in despair, "Where is God now?" Mercia replies, "He is closer to us now than he has ever been." As they hear the sound of the trumpet announcing that the time of their execution has arrived, they weep and wail and stumble and fall, but they nonetheless manage to sing bravely as they march up the stairs and into the teeth of the ravenous beasts.

The *Sign of the Cross* is significant not simply because it is an early cinematic portrayal of martyrdom; in fact, versions of the same story had been made by other directors in 1909, 1910, and 1914. What makes the film so fascinating is rather the mixed messages it sends regarding the role of the human body in life and death. On the one hand, the Christians profess a kind of Platonic sensibility in which the body is essentially irrelevant to identity. When the young Stephan is overcome with remorse for having betrayed the site of the Christians' prayer meeting under torture, his sister tells him, "It was only your body that was weak, not you!" To this Stephan responds, "Yes, it was my body, wasn't it! I tried, but I couldn't." The true Stephan, in other words, would never disclose the secret meeting-place of the Christians. It was only his body, and not his real self, that failed.

Moreover, the martyrs in the *Sign of the Cross* believe themselves to be immortal. Of course, they know that they will be ground to bits by the lions' teeth, but they are convinced that when this happens they will not truly die. In the scene in which the Christians have gathered secretly to pray and worship, their leader Titus praises Jesus because, he says, "He proved there is no death, only a crossing over to the Father's life everlasting." Later in the dungeon Mercia invokes Titus's words in order to give her fellow prisoners strength and hope.

To say that there is no death is, in point of fact, to contradict orthodox Christian belief. Indeed, early Christian creeds fought against such a claim by affirming that even Jesus had really and truly died. Regarding Jesus, the Apostles' Creed declares, "He descended into Hell"; in other words, Jesus descended into Sheol, the realm of the dead, the place that Job feared so much because he thought that no one could return from it. To say that Jesus had not really died would be to fall into the heresy of the Docetists. It would be to deny that Jesus had been truly human.

Nonetheless, the martyrs in the *Sign of the Cross* go off to their fate believing that their souls will simply pass over into heaven without having been touched by death. This is the gospel preached by Mercia to Marcus when he comes to visit her in her dungeon. Marcus, still enraptured by the Christian maiden and regretting the humiliations he subjected her to at the hands of the dancer Ancaria, decides to accompany Mercia into the next world. As he wraps his cloak around her and the two of them head towards the waiting lions, Marcus observes, "I'm happy. I'm full of strange hope."

The world-and-body-denying message preached by the Christians is, however, at the same time consistently and quite effectively undercut by the persuasive case the film itself makes for licentiousness. At one point Nero speaks with glee about, "the food, the wine, the delicious debauchery!" As Nero's wife Poppaea (Claudette Colbert) pampers herself by frolicking nude in a milk bath, the camera ogles not only her bare breasts but also the luxuriant body of her friend Dacia who is standing nearby. Lest anyone in the audience miss the homoeroticism of this scene, Poppaea orders Dacia, who has come to relate the latest gossip to her, "Take off your clothes and get in here!"

In interviews, DeMille claimed that he included such scenes of the depraved Roman empire only in order to highlight the Christians' purity and moral superiority. When the movie was released, however, Christians responded to his work with outrage, and their anger was one of the factors that led to the founding of the Legion of Decency in 1934.[63] The Legion recruited millions of Catholics to its ranks, asking them to pledge, in part, "I condemn absolutely those salacious motion pictures which, with other degrading agencies, are corrupting public morals and promoting a sex mania in our land. I shall do all that I can to arouse public opinion against the portrayal of vice as a normal condition of affairs and against depicting criminals of any class as heroes and heroines, presenting their filthy philosophy of life as something acceptable to decent men and women."[64]

The fact is, though, that the *Sign of the Cross* merely offers a cinematic version of the salacious details that have been part of martyr-tales throughout Christianity's history. According to the medieval *Golden Legend*, Saint Agnes (who is supposed to have lived in the fourth century) was a girl of thirteen when she caught the eye of a local nobleman. When she spurned his advances, her would-be-suitor charged her with the crime of being a Christian and had her stripped naked and taken to a brothel. There he invited his friends to rape her and attempted to do so himself, but a miraculous light engulfed her, and all of the men's efforts were thwarted. Agnes was finally killed when a soldier thrust a dagger into her throat.[65]

Likewise, Saint Agatha is believed to have been a highborn woman of great beauty who came to the attention of a consular official some time during the third century. This man had Agatha brought before him so that he might claim her as his own, but when she refused his offers, he "turned her over to a procuress whose name was Aphrodisia and her nine daughters who were as lascivious as their mother." These women tried to convert Agatha to their ways, but she resisted them and so was imprisoned instead. Her admirer, frustrated in his efforts to seduce her, ordered his executioners "to twist her breast for a long time and then cut it off." When that torture failed to persuade the young virgin, Agatha was rolled naked over potsherds and live coals, and eventually she perished.[66]

It is impossible to ignore the sexual element in these martyr-tales. Before being murdered, Agnes and Agatha are stripped for the enjoyment of their tormentors, and they are threatened with rape, perhaps the most traumatic violation any woman can undergo. It is disturbing, however, that these women's failure to respond erotically to the abuse that they received is often interpreted as a heroic act of chastity. Butler's *Lives of the Saints*, for example, notes that after she had been abducted and imprisoned in Aphrodisia's brothel, "Agatha suffered assaults and stratagems upon her honour more terrible to her than torture or death, *but she stood firm.*"[67] The implication seems to be that being sexually assaulted was a temptation for Agatha but that by force of will she overcame her desire to be raped and so was able to maintain her virginity.

Love's Bravest Choice

A similar attitude can be found in a most troubling short documentary aimed at teenagers entitled *Love's Bravest Choice: The Life and Legacy of St. Maria Goretti*. The film is narrated by Molly Kelly, founding president of the Pennsylvania Pro-Life Educational Foundation and author of two books entitled *Let's Talk To Teens About Chastity* and *Saved Sex: Chastity Because You're Worth It!* (Kelly informs viewers, "I'm known as the Chastity Lady!") The purpose of *Love's Bravest Choice* is to inspire girls to the same respect for chastity that the documentary says Saint Maria Goretti exhibited.

Maria Goretti was an Italian peasant girl born in 1890. When she was not quite twelve years old, a young man from her village attempted to rape her. Maria fought off the attack, protesting, "No, no, God does not want this!" but in her struggle she was stabbed thirteen times. Before she died, she was asked by a priest if she could find it in herself to forgive her attacker; she responded that she did forgive him and that she hoped to see him in heaven.

As the poet and spiritual writer Kathleen Norris has pointed out, there is surely something remarkable in Maria's resistance to her would-be-rapist, as well as in her ability to forgive him. In a culture where girls are taught from an early age to submit to the power of men, any girl who refuses to do so will strike us as significant. Norris writes, "We take it as a matter of course that girls will be stalked, raped, murdered—if not on the streets, in our popular entertainment. If one dares say to her attacker, 'Some things are worth dying for,' there is nothing joyful about it, except possibly deep within, some inner defiance, purity, and strength that defies the sadist and the power of his weapons."[68]

In Norris's view, Goretti can rightly be called a saint because, as she says, "The mystery of hope, of holiness, infuses such defiance."[69] Norris does not suggest that Goretti would have been any less holy if she had submitted to the rape as a way of preserving her life. If she had submitted, that too might have been a form of defiance against the most unthinkable of violations and an expression of hope for life despite and beyond that violation. Nor does Norris contend that Maria's resistance was the determinant factor in whether or not the young man's attempted rape was successful; surely many women have fought against their attackers but have been raped anyway. Instead, what Norris suggests is that in the moment of the assault, Goretti had to make the most personal of choices, and that the very fact that she did choose, that she refused to surrender her freedom and her personhood to the invader who sought to strip both from her, is what makes her a model. It is not the particular choice that she made, but rather her summoning up the courage to make it, that most distinguishes her—that, and her ability to forgive.

For if legend is to be believed, Maria's pardon of her attacker was not only unusual in the realm of human affairs but had a supernatural dimension to it as well. The young man who killed Goretti was sentenced by an Italian court to thirty years in prison for his crime. According to testimony, he at first refused to take responsibility for the girl's death and blamed her for leading him on. At some point during his incarceration, however, it seems that he had a dream in which Goretti appeared to him and forgave him, and from that time on his life was changed. Whether or not such a dream occurred, it is indisputable that after his release from prison, the killer sought forgiveness from the young saint's mother, affiliated himself with a Franciscan religious order, and penned a letter of repentance in which he warned others to stay away from "immoral books and bad companions."

It is this story, the story of a girl's death and her murderer's conversion, that the little movie *Love's Bravest Choice* seeks to tell. It does so, however, lacking the nuances of Norris's writing, and proceeding from a point of view that begs for close and critical examination. Self-described as a docu-drama, the movie mixes photographs and interviews with re-enact-ments of events in Maria's life. It also, however, includes discussions with contemporary girls about their views concerning sexuality, and it is here that its disturbing implications become apparent.

Reflecting on Maria Goretti's life, narrator and "Chastity Lady" Molly Kelly notes that in the contemporary world, teenagers can be confused about how to integrate their sexuality into their lives as Christians: "Young people need to answer the questions: how far do you go, and how do you say No?" Several girls appear on camera resolving to maintain their chastity despite pressure from peers, and the film ends with the admoni-tion, "Let Maria Goretti be your model, and chastity your choice!" The implication is that Maria had a choice about being sexually violated—that if the rapist had succeeded in penetrating her, it would have been her own fault. She would have been guilty of not choosing the chastity that Kelly is enjoining on the girls in the documentary. "Like Maria," she tells these impressionable young women, "we are all given the right of free choice." Presumably then Maria "chose" not to be raped. She, the eleven-year-old peasant girl—not the man eight years older, much larger and heavier and several times stronger—was the one on whom the burden of morality lay.

Related to this is the unspoken but unavoidable conclusion that girls who are in fact raped are somehow "lesser" than their virgin sisters. The movie several times equates virginity with purity, implying that Maria would have been impure if her attacker had penetrated her body. Pope John Paul II is quoted urging that Christians "be capable of defending your purity of heart and body," and again, the implication is that if one cannot defend oneself, one falls from purity into defilement.

The most pernicious aspect of the documentary is its unarticulated but unavoidable judgment that it is morally preferable to be "pure" and dead than to undergo a sexual assault and to survive. The movie is not simply suggesting that some women will find rape such a traumatic occurrence that they might, tragically, wish for their own deaths. Rather, by presenting the fact that Maria's attacker did not succeed in raping her as the girl's free choice in favor of chastity, the film encourages all girls toward the choice of death over rape. It explicitly enjoins girls to make Maria's murder "a living [sic] example of something they can follow and practice." Tragically, it is not simply *Love's Bravest Choice* that implies that it is better to be dead than raped. When Pope Pius XII beatified the young girl in 1947, he did so with the justification that she had died as a martyr in defense of the Christian virtue of chastity—as if being overpowered by an attacker and "allowing" oneself to be raped would be an unchaste act.

Sebastiane

In contrast to *Love's Bravest Choice*, Derek Jarman's *Sebastiane* (1976) is not at all concerned with the morality of sexual involvement. Though the title character is executed because he refuses another man's libidinous advances, it is not chastity *per se* that is at stake for him. Sebastiane rebuffs his captain's attempts to seduce him simply because he is enraptured by the love of another: the love of Christ.

Sebastiane is one of the most remarkable films about a Catholic saint ever made. Inspired by the eroticism evident in numerous paintings of Saint Sebastian, a third-century martyr, the work features nude Roman soldiers frolicking on the beach and engaging in homosexual love-play while trading insults and obscenities in Latin. Indeed, the film's entire script is spoken in Latin, though English subtitles translate the dialogue for those unacquainted with the ancient tongue. Based loosely on the legend of the saint, who was executed during the reign of the Roman Emperor Diocletian, *Sebastiane* is both an unabashed celebration of homo-eroticism and an exploration of saintly sensuality.

Set in the year 303 CE, *Sebastiane* opens with an orgiastic dance performed in the court of the emperor. Nearly-naked men holding enormous phalluses gambol in a circle until their dance culminates in an orgasmic finale. Next, a man in a leopard-skin loincloth bares his teeth and rips into the throat of an accused Christian while the court looks on approvingly. At this point Sebastiane, favored soldier in the emperor's army, utters a protest against the horrific display of savagery and as punishment is exiled to a desert outpost.

The remainder of the film takes place entirely in this desolate wasteland. As the relentless sun beats down on their unprotected bodies, Sebastiane and his fellow soldiers practice at swordplay and wrestling, preparing themselves for an enemy attack that both they and their commander know will never occur. In the long hours of the afternoon, they stage mock battles among the black beetles that populate the desert sands, tell each other stories, and engage in feverish attempts at seduction and fornication.

It does not take long before it becomes clear that Sebastiane is different from the other soldiers at the camp. He is a Christian, and this fact leads him eventually to throw down his sword, refusing to duel with his comrades. For this offense his captain, Severus, whips him brutally, but Sebastiane refuses to surrender his convictions. Taking more extreme measures, Severus orders that Sebastiane be stripped and left spread-eagled against the hot desert sands, his arms and legs secured with wooden stakes.

When Sebastiane's friend Justin comes to offer him comfort during his agonizing hours in the sun, the martyr tries to explain why he cannot give up his new-found love. He explains, "His eyes are so beautiful. He has sky-blue eyes. His hair is like the sun's rays. His body is golden like molten gold. This hand of his will smooth away these wounds. His is Phoebus Apollo.[70] The sky is his burning kiss."

This extravagant love for Christ is precisely what prevents Sebastiane from acceding to the sexual desires of Severus later in the movie. Severus is in love with the saint, and he is angry not only because Sebastiane has abandoned his duties as a soldier but also because he has given his heart to another. In an intoxicated rage he attempts to rape Sebastiane, who responds contemptuously, "Poor Severus. You think your drunken lust compares to the love of God?" Frustrated in his desires to make Sebastiane his own, the captain orders that the Christian be executed. Sebastiane is tied naked to a pole and shot full of arrows.

It is important to note here that *Sebastiane* does not depict the saint's struggle as a battle between the flesh and the spirit. On the contrary, Sebastiane's love for Christ is unabashedly sensual, if not sexual. He is not denigrating or renouncing the body and its desires; instead, he finds the fulfillment of those desires in the tortures that the captain inflicts on him. His execution is not so much a death as the ecstatic consummation of his deepest longing. Director Jarman, commenting on the numerous depictions of the martyrdom of Saint Sebastian that have an undeniably erotic flair, contends that the saint "sports his wounds on a thousand altars like a debutante."[71] Martyrdom in *Sebastiane* is not at all an attempt to flee from the body. It is instead a way of glorying in the body's capacity to suffer and thus share in the pains of Christ. Sebastiane's wounds bring him closer to his beloved. In his adoration of Christ, the martyr professes, "He takes me in his arms and caresses my bleeding body. I want to be with him. I love him."

Celluloid Martyrs and Politics

Having looked at portrayals of martyrdom in the ancient world, we are now prepared to turn in a more focused way to their cinematic counterparts. Immediately, though, we are faced with a question: what exactly is a martyr? In the eighteenth century, Pope Benedict XIV established strict criteria for determining who could be considered a Christian martyr. According to these criteria, anyone promoting a saint-to-be's cause must demonstrate that the martyr was killed as a direct result of his or her profession of Christian faith.[72] The word "martyr," after all, comes from a Greek word that means "witness": martyrs are believed to have witnessed to Christ through their suffering and death.

Deciding who does and does not die "for the faith" can be difficult, however. Maria Goretti died after she was brutally attacked by a neighbor; she was canonized not because she had defended Christianity *per se* but because in the eyes of the pope she had defended the Christian virtue of chastity—a development that journalist Kenneth Woodward calls "a significant though by now routine expansion of the grounds on which a candidate can be declared a martyr."[73] In 1981, Pope John Paul II declared Maximilian Kolbe a martyr not because he had died explicitly for the Christian faith but rather because he had freely offered himself in the place of a condemned man in a concentration camp. Kolbe is remembered as a "martyr of charity."

The question of who is and is not a martyr becomes more complicated when the holy victim is killed at least in part for his or her opposition to a political regime. In such cases it must be asked whether the person's death was a martyrdom for the faith or for a more secular cause. To illustrate this point, let us look at two cinematic martyr tales. The first, entitled *To Kill a Priest*, is a fictionalized version of the life and death of Father Jerzy Popiełuszko, a Polish Catholic priest who was murdered in 1984 because of his protests against Poland's then-Communist government. The second tells the story of Archbishop Oscar Romero, who was shot to death in 1980 because of his opposition to a corrupt government in Catholic El Salvador. Both Popiełuszko and Romero have been put forth as candidates for canonization.

The title of Agnieszka Holland's *To Kill a Priest* (1988) tells viewers exactly how the film will end. There are no secrets here; the story of the capture and murder of Father Alek (Jerzy Popiełuszko's cinematic counterpart) by Communist Poland's secret police unfolds very much as we might expect, with few surprises or twists. Given that the plot and its outcome are known from the start, the movie must engage viewers by drawing them into the drama of the story: its pain, pathos, courage, and tragedy. This it does with only limited success.

Perhaps the reason that the film does not fully convince viewers of the import of its cause is simply that it focuses too much on the killer instead of on the victim. *To Kill a Priest* opens on the evening of 12 December 1981, when martial law is imposed on Poland; it ends in 1984 with the death of Father Alek and with the aftermath of his murder. Though the priest appears in several of the movie's scenes, the real protagonist of the film is rather the character named Stefan, an agent of the secret police who is determined to put a stop to Father Alek's work with the newfound Solidarity movement that is opposing Poland's Communist government.

We learn quite a bit about Stefan (played by Ed Harris). He is unhappily married and has a son who questions Communism's fierce opposition to religion. His father is a dedicated Communist who encouraged his son to follow in his footsteps. He has doubts about his job and at least from time to time admires the strength and beauty of Catholicism. He is ambitious and hopes to move ahead in the party through his relentless persecution of the Church.

By contrast, we learn next to nothing about Father Alek. As film critic Roger Ebert observes, "The priest, a handsome young man played by Christopher Lambert, stands in the pulpit and recites Solidarity sermons of crushing banality. In his private life, he is so solemn and stolid we find it difficult to care about him...."[74] We do see him in some cliché-filled scenes with a female friend who is clearly in love with him. At one point the two characters playfully chase each other about until they (accidentally, of course) tumble to the floor, the priest's body on top of his admirer's. Later, when the woman begs for "just one kiss," Alek answers stoically, "I'm not that strong." (Lest anyone in the audience suspect Alek of simply not being attracted to women, the movie includes a scene in which the priest laughs out loud at a joke his driver tells about "faggots.")

Aside from these few details, we know very little about Father Alek. We have no clue how he became involved in the Solidarity movement, why he did so, or even when. His motives, thoughts, and feelings remain for the most part obscure. When his bishop (an unnamed version of the real-life Cardinal Józef Glemp) accuses him of using the Church to advance his own "petty, personal ambitions," we don't have sufficient reason to disbelieve the charge. In fact, a scene in which Alek is carried through the streets on the shoulders of a cheering throng might lead us to believe that the allegation is true. Though clearly the film intends us to feel the same outrage that Alek does when his motives are questioned, we simply haven't been given enough reason to do so.

Moreover, the priest's spiritual life is portrayed in a way that lacks authenticity. After some relatively mild harassment from the secret police (including a short and uneventful stay in prison), Father Alek declares to one of his friends, "I don't hate them anymore. They can beat me, kill me, and I sincerely can pray for them. Do you understand? I'm free. I'm really free." Given that he has yet to be harmed in the least by the Communist government, his statement comes across as callow rather than as courageous.

To Kill a Priest uses several devices to link the suffering of Father Alek with the suffering of Jesus. When the unnamed bishop berates Alek for antagonizing the Polish government and thus risking his life, asking, "Who do you think you are? A new Jesus Christ with dreams of martyrdom?" the priest responds by paraphrasing words of Jesus as recorded in the Gospel of Matthew: "He who gives himself saves himself. He who protects himself loses himself." At one point during this argument, Alek stands up from his chair and clasps his hands tightly in front of him. The intended meaning of this peculiar gesture becomes clear a few seconds later. As Alex strides angrily from the room, the bishop catches sight of a painting on the wall; the painting depicts Jesus being tormented by soldiers, his hands bound together in front of him. After gazing at the picture for a moment, the bishop slowly lowers his eyes in embarrassment and shame.

The connection between Alek and Jesus is strengthened near the end of the movie when Stefan overhears a sermon preached by the Solidarity priest. At this point it is clear that Stefan's plans to kill Alek are about to come to fruition, and so Alek's homily takes on heightened significance. Speaking before a group of seminarians, the priest offers this prayer: "The trial of Christ is still in progress. Its actors are still among us. Only the names have changed. All those who hate, all those who use violence, all those who cause the suffering of their brothers and sisters, all those who take away their freedom, participate in the trial of Christ. We ask you, O Lord, to have pity on those who use force against our brothers and sisters." As Jesus prayed for the forgiveness of those who tortured him (Luke 23:34), so Alek prays within the hearing of his assassin that God might take pity on the one who will murder him.

Despite the clear comparison that it draws between Alek and Jesus, the film makes no attempt to pattern the torture and death of the priest on the Passion of Jesus. This fact is curious. As we have seen, Christianity has modeled its martyr-tales on the story of Jesus' trial and execution practically from its inception. *To Kill a Priest* deviates from this tradition by presenting Alek's murder as a haphazard affair planned and carried out by incompetent bunglers. The three secret police agents in the film responsible for killing Alek (Stefan and two companions) are not so much diabolical as comical. They bumble about with the efficiency of Keystone Cops, and it is a wonder that they manage to pull the job off at all. Their car fails to start just as they are about to begin tailing the priest on what will turn out to be his final journey. After push-starting the vehicle, they putter along, the car's engine hiccuping the whole time, until they finally capture Alek, beat him, and stick him in the car's trunk. At one point they pull off to the side of the road to check the sputtering engine, and one of the agents attempts to open the car's hood. Instead, he pulls the wrong lever and releases the lid of the trunk, thus allowing Alek a brief escape. After the trio finally capture and kill the priest and dump his body into a river, one of the agents stands on the bridge panicking, screaming that the body won't sink. All in all, they are not the most impressive of villains.

This is, I would suggest, precisely what the film intends. The murder of Father Alek is patterned not on the Passion of Christ but rather on the very mundane (and at times pathetically absurd) details of the actual death of Father Jerzy Popiełuszko.[75] The effect is to remind us that what we are witnessing is a crime. Murder is an ugly business, and if we glorify it we do a disservice to its victims.

There is a tendency in both visual and literary depictions of martyr-doms to give victims' deaths a kind of cosmic significance. In the New Testament's Acts of the Apostles, for example, when the deacon Stephen is about to be stoned, he is first allowed to make a long speech to his accusers recounting the entire course of God's salvific action in history. When he gazes at the heavens, Stephen sees Jesus standing at the right hand of God, and as his killers fling rocks at his broken and bruised body, the martyr kneels and prays, "Lord Jesus, receive my spirit" (7:59). One can almost see the halo encircling his head and hear the choirs of angels sing.

Such dramatizations of death serve a purpose. They grow, as Susan Bergman observes, "from a perception that all history is caught up in meaning greater than a single event can reveal, meaning that has been showing itself through the ages...."[76] Yet the risk is that if we understand a death as having universal significance, we will forget that death's very dirty, bloody, slow, messy, and haphazard particularities. Martyrs are not killed by villains but by men and women. Romanticizing a victim's murder can have a detrimental effect, as it encourages us to judge negatively any death that does not live up to the kind we read about in idealized hagiographic[77] literature.

This consequence can be seen in the process that led to the beatification of Blessed Isidore Bakanja. Bakanja, who was murdered in 1909 in what is now the Democratic Republic of Congo, acted as servant to a Belgian master named Van Cauter. Van Cauter opposed the Catholic Church's work in Congo at the time because he felt that the missionaries stirred up too much trouble; they taught the Congolese that in the eyes of God, Africans were equal to Europeans. In his anger at Catholics, Van Cauter had his servant Bakanja (who had been baptized some years earlier and who always wore a scapular of Our Lady of Mount Carmel around his neck) beaten severely. The servant's wounds became gangrenous ulcers, and the young man died of his injuries six months later. He was beatified in 1994.

Isidore Bakanja's beatification was controversial for several reasons. The most significant of these for our purposes is the fact that, as one of the members of the committee investigating his case observed, "there would seem to be missing in the servant of God, in the act of torture, the note of heroic strength that is usually found in the victims of vexation for the faith. Under the blows, in fact, poor Isidore 'whimpered and screamed' and his cries were so loud that they awoke Van Cauter's concubines who were sleeping in a den some distance from the site where the whipping took place...."[78] In other words, the fact that Bakanja cried out in agony led some to believe that he was not a true martyr for the faith. As this case shows, human memory has a nearly irresistible desire to cleanse martyr tales of their pain and blood and gore. We prefer martyrs who have haloes around their heads and who spare us the discomfort of having to imagine their tortures. *To Kill a Priest* does not let us off the hook so easily. We hear the screams. We see the blood.

As Bakanja's case also demonstrates, martyrdoms are seldom clear-cut instances of purely religious persecution. Issues of race, ethnicity, nationality, political affiliation and social status frequently factor into a martyr's death, and it is difficult to separate the victim's faith out from his or her other commitments. Clearly, Bakanja was killed because he was a Catholic. Just as clearly, he was killed because he was an African servant in a colonized country, and he was perceived to be a threat to European sovereignty in that land.

The reasons behind Father Jerzy Popiełuszko's murder are equally diverse and equally complex. It would be simplistic to say that the priest was killed solely for being a Christian. He was killed also because he was chaplain to the Solidarity movement that was challenging Communist rule in Poland. In *To Kill a Priest*, Father Alek preaches that "a government by brute force is not a government," and he does not hesitate to raise his fingers in Solidarity's V-for-Victory gesture during one of his Masses. He calls on Mary, the mother of Jesus, to watch over "suffering, independent, ever-faithful Poland," and when Christmas comes he builds a manger scene featuring the red and white flag of the Solidarity movement. The government would have had reason to kill him regardless of his Christian faith.

The same is true of the Catholic archbishop of El Salvador as he is portrayed in John Duigan's movie *Romero* (1989). Oscar Romero, who was assassinated in 1980, directly challenged the government of his country, even going so far as to write a letter to then-President of the United States Jimmy Carter to request that no more arms be sent to the Salvadoran government. He preached openly against wealthy aristocrats who exploited the land and labor of the poor, and he supported efforts to teach poor *campesinos* to read, write, and vote. As in the case of Popiełuszko, the government would have found it necessary to kill Romero even if he had not been a Catholic archbishop.

Unlike *To Kill a Priest*, however, the film *Romero* is explicitly and thoroughly hagiographical in both its aims and its execution, modeling Romero's life and death on the ministry and Passion of Jesus. The movie also has specific theological points to make; it attempts to represent in dialogue and visual imagery a trend in contemporary Christian thought known as liberation theology.

Put simply, liberation theology reflects critically on political, social, and economic realities in light of Jesus's message of good news for the poor. As Peruvian liberationist Gustavo Gutiérrez puts it, the role of the theologian should be to "be engaged where nations, social classes, people struggle to free themselves from domination and oppression by other nations, classes, and people."[79] From this perspective, theology demands personal involvement of its practitioners. A liberation theologian cannot stand on the sidelines of history but must plunge into its confusions guided by the light of the Gospel and by the conviction that God wills freedom and happiness for all people.

This kind of commitment to the needs and struggles of the poor and exploited is illustrated in the very first scene of *Romero*, in which peasant farmers are led by a priest in a consciousness-raising group, also known as a *comunidad de base* or a base community. One of the farmers describes how he loved his land deeply until soldiers came and burned it. Reflecting on the misfortune of the farmer, one of the other *campesinos* murmurs, "It's God's will." Challenges another, "Who says it's God's will? I think that God looks at these things and vomits!" Reacting against an ideology that has told them to accept suffering in silence and obedience, these peasant farmers are beginning to challenge the notion that God wishes the poor to be poor. Instead, they are taking to heart the mission of Jesus as articulated in the Gospel of Luke: to proclaim release to captives and recovery of sight to the blind, and to bring freedom to all who are oppressed (4:18).

Romero himself, as portrayed in the film by Puerto Rican actor Raul Julia, is at first skeptical of what he perceives to be a radical and dangerous liberationist message. He warns his friend Rutilio Grande (a fire-brand preacher on the order of John the Baptist) that his work with the *campesinos* is subversive. Referring to Jesus, Grande replies, "Remember who else they called such names." After Grande is murdered by government operatives, Romero's eyes are opened to the oppression that the peasants face and that is tearing his country apart, and he assumes the mantle of his prophet-friend. He begins to preach to the poor of the countryside, and before long he is surrounded by eager crowds of listeners and by adoring children whom he clasps to his side.

One scene in *Romero* sums up in a few short minutes the message of both the film and the liberation theology that inspires it. The scene is actually a turning point: the moment that transforms Romero from timid cleric to courageous champion of the poor. It takes place in the town of Aguilares, which has recently been occupied by the Salvadoran army. Soldiers have taken over the local church and turned it into a barracks, and when Romero enters the building in order to remove the Eucharist from the tabernacle, he finds the place filled with cigarette smoke and the blare of radios. He approaches the altar but is stopped by an American GI (perhaps meant to highlight the United States's involvement in El Salvador's civil war) who tells him that he has no business in what is now army property. Before Romero's astonished eyes, the soldier takes a machine gun and sprays the church's altar with bullets, destroying it, the crucifix that hangs behind it, and the tabernacle housing what Catholics believe to be the body of Christ.

At this point Romero turns and leaves the building, deciding that discretion is the better part of valor. Outside, however, he is confronted by the weary and hopeless faces of the local *campesinos* who have all but reconciled themselves to their desperate situation and to the violence that ravages their homeland. After looking into their eyes for one long moment, Romero turns abruptly and re-enters the church, striding purposefully towards the bullet-ridden altar. He kneels and begins to gather up the broken pieces of the Eucharist, not stopping even when bursts of machine gunfire rip into the wall next to him and above his head.

Leaving the church once again, and cradling the broken pieces of bread in his hands, Romero gets into his car and signals the driver to take him back to his home in San Salvador. Silence follows as the archbishop's car drives off into the dust; the townspeople and their priests glance at each other as if to say, "Well, what did we expect? Why would he be any different? Why did we think that he could free us from our hopelessness when no one else has?"

As it turns out, however, Romero is not like everyone else. Within minutes his car re-appears on the screen and pulls up outside of the church/barracks. The archbishop emerges from the back seat and begins donning his priestly vestments. Armed with nothing more than his faith, he walks resolutely towards the church, facing down the soldiers and their guns. Astonished, but aware of a new hope taking root in their midst, the peasants and priests fall into step behind the archbishop. Together, they march past the loaded rifles of the soldiers and the raised pistol of the army sergeant.

Inside the church, Romero gazes out at the assembly and begins to speak:

> We are here today to retake possession of this church building and to strengthen all those whom the enemies of the Church have trampled down. You should know that you have not suffered alone. For you are the Church. You are the People of God. You are Jesus in the here and now. He is crucified in you just as surely as he was crucified two thousand years ago on that hill outside of Jerusalem. And you should know that your pain and your suffering, like his, will contribute to El Salvador's liberation and redemption.

The scene has some basis in fact, though its details have been altered to dramatize the incident. In actuality, one month after the Salvadoran army occupied the city of Aguilares in 1977, several thousand peasants and hundreds of priests and nuns descended on the town to hear Oscar Romero preach in its church. Following the service, a procession followed the archbishop through the town and towards the city hall. Suddenly, eleven soldiers stepped forward and blocked Romero's path. "Go forward," the archbishop urged the crowd, and together they moved into the path of the soldiers' guns. "As the people passed in front of the guards," recalls one witness, "they sang: 'But where, where, where is our Lord? He is with the humble and the persecuted.'"[80] By including this incident (albeit in altered form), the film is not simply presenting history for its own sake. Rather, it offers a particular interpretation of history in which imitating Jesus is acting on behalf of the poor, and in which the holy are those willing to sacrifice themselves, like Jesus, to make the Kingdom of God a reality.

Moreover, the scene offers a complex though unspoken theology of the Eucharist. When Romero first enters the church to remove the blessed bread from the tabernacle, his focus is on the bread itself. That is, his reason for approaching the altar is to rescue the body of Christ, an object of adoration, from the disrespect that the soldiers are showing it. When the army sergeant grabs a machine gun and sprays the altar with bullets, Romero is willing to leave the bread behind in order to spare his own life.

It is only upon seeing the faces of the peasants outside the church that the archbishop changes his mind and heads back towards the altar, ignoring the shouts of the sergeant and the blasts of gunfire over his head. The camera at this point moves in closely as Romero, sweating profusely, his glasses slipping down his nose, gathers up the fragments of the sacramental bread. A connection becomes clear: the broken lives of the peasants outside are the broken bread/body of Christ inside the church. Theologian Gustavo Gutiérrez, reflecting on the relationship between justice on the one hand and the Christian ritual of Communion on the other, explains the connection in this way: "The bond which unites God and man is celebrated—that is, effectively recalled and proclaimed—in the Eucharist. Without a real commitment against exploitation and alienation and for a society of solidarity and justice, the Eucharistic celebration is an empty action, lacking any genuine endorsement by those who participate in it."[81] When Romero re-enters the church after having been chased out the first time, he does so not to rescue an object but rather to make real Christ's commitment to and presence with the poor.

This theme is reinforced later in the film when portions of the real-life archbishop's sermons are pronounced in voice-overs by the cinematic Romero. The homilies are preached as a variety of images appear on the screen: peasants cutting cane in the fields, for example, and a young woman lying dead in the street as schoolchildren stare at her naked body. As we watch these scenes of poverty and violence, Romero proclaims, "The mission of the Church is to identify itself with the poor and to join with them in their struggle for justice. By so doing, the Church finds its *own* salvation!"

Romero's willingness to involve himself in politics is demonstrated several times throughout the movie, not least when he calls the newly-elected president of El Salvador a liar. However, it is the following declaration that sets the stage in the film for his eventual assassination: "I believe economic injustice is the root cause of our problems. From it stems all the violence. The Church has to be incarnated in those who fight for freedom, and defend them, and share in their persecution!" Soon after, Romero is murdered as he celebrates Mass.

Unlike *To Kill a Priest*, the movie *Romero* does not hesitate to alter the details of history in order to make a theological point. While it is true that the archbishop was assassinated during the ritual of the Mass, in the film he is struck down during the consecration of the wine/blood of Christ, whereas in reality he was shot before that part of the liturgy had begun. The effect of the film's version is that the connection forged earlier between the Eucharist and the poor is made complete. As he stumbles backwards from the force of the assassin's bullet, and as the cup of consecrated wine spills from his hands, Romero embodies the suffering Christ, the Christ whose blood was spilled on the cross and whose blood Catholics drink in ritual form each Sunday. He also embodies the people of El Salvador, victims of brutality and oppression. As Jesus was murdered, as his friend Rutilio Grande was murdered, as the peasants are murdered, Romero too is cut down by violence. His blood mixes with Jesus's as he falls to the floor, one more martyr in the struggle for the justice that Jesus preached. If in theory it is difficult to assess who, precisely, is a martyr, in the memories of the faithful matters are much simpler. Those who die out of commitment to and love for Christ deserve the title "martyr" as well as the title "saint."

Conclusion: Holy Blood

How shall we respond to these various cinematic presentations of saintly martyrdom? Are they appropriate reminders of men and women who have made the ultimate sacrifice for their faith? Are they voyeuristic indulgences of Hollywood's insatiable appetite for sex and violence? Are they horrible exercises in a misguided piety that glories in death?

The answer, of course, is all of the above. When watching movies about men and women murdered for their religious beliefs, we must be extremely careful to analyze what, precisely, the movie is telling us. What interpretation of the body does it present, and what interpretation of sexuality? How does it understand death? If it patterns the martyr's death on the death of Jesus, what does that tell us about the victim, and what does it tell us about the filmmaker's view of Jesus?

Asking these questions will help us form intelligent and informed responses to cinematic martyrdoms. We will need to ask similar questions as we approach the next chapter, which looks at movies' depictions of ascetics and mystics.

4   Ascetics and Mystics

Introduction

Towards the end of Alain Cavalier's cinematic biography *Thérèse* (1986), there is a scene in which Saint Thérèse of Lisieux lies dying from tuberculosis. Her body is wracked by coughing, and she is attended both night and day by the other sisters in her convent. Convinced that Thérèse is truly holy, one of her nurses performs a gesture both horrifying and fascinating. She stares at the bowl of the young woman's clotted and bloody sputum for what seems like an eternity. Then slowly, deliberately, she does what the audience both knows that she will do and dreads that she will do: she drinks from the bowl.

    Making sense of that scene, and of others like it, is the aim of this chapter. It is not an easy task. Why, after all, would anyone purposely put herself in harm's way by ingesting contagious fluids? Why have many Christians throughout history insisted on injuring, causing pain to and even endangering their own bodies? Blessed Clare of Rimini, who lived in the fourteenth century, wore a hair shirt next to her body and fasted severely. She kept bands of iron next to her skin, and on Good Fridays, in commemoration of the scourging of Jesus, she had herself bound to a pillar and whipped. Saint Catherine of Genoa ate the lice that infested the sick whom she cared for, and Saint Catherine of Siena drank pus from the sores of a woman with cancer. Charles of Blois bound his chest with knotted cords until sores formed, and he whipped himself until the blood ran.[82]

No doubt, the trials undergone by saintly Christian ascetics have inspired many along their spiritual journeys, encouraging them to new heights of religious devotion. Just as surely, however, the self-imposed rigors of asceticism have had the opposite effect, causing alarm and even revulsion rather than admiration. The Romanian philosopher Emile Cioran once remarked, "You are lost if saints don't disgust you."[83]

Not all saints, of course, are ascetics. The word "ascetic" comes from a Greek word that means "to exercise." Unlike athletes, who exercise their bodies in the interest of greater physical strength and endurance, ascetics perform bodily exercises in order to enhance their *spiritual* well-being. Asceticism has been practiced in virtually all of the world's religions. One need only think of the fasting that Muslims perform during the month of Ramadan, or of Hindu seekers who sacrifice the comforts of civilization to live as hermits, or of Native American vision-quests in which a young man might live for days without food or water. Asceticism has been particularly influential in Christian tradition, and though not all saints engage in ascetic practices, holiness and asceticism frequently go hand in hand. As the age of martyrdom came to a close in the fourth century, Christians began to look for new ways to show their devotion to God. They developed practices ranging from fasting to self-flagellation to sitting atop pillars in the desert. They pierced their own bodies with nails, put pebbles in their shoes until their feet were bloody and raw, and conducted all-night vigils in which they refused to gratify their bodies' need for sleep.

There are a number of explanations for such behavior, and no one of them by itself is adequate. Christian asceticism, as we will see, at times seems to be the result of psychological deviance. At other times it stems from a disgust with the body similar to that which we identified in the last chapter. However, to reduce asceticism simply to mental illness or to hatred of the flesh would be to miss its genuinely creative and, perhaps, redemptive possibilities. Ascetics often see their sufferings as a form of discipline: not as a good in itself, but simply as a way to tame their passions so that they can be more free to do God's work. At other times, ascetic practices are understood as a form of penance. Pain becomes payment both for the saint's own sins and for the sins of others. Sometimes, ascetics offer their torments as a sacrifice, a gift given to God either in hope of securing some divine favor or simply as a gesture of love. In other cases, ascetics use physical mortification as a way of gaining spiritual or healing power. In still others, they see their agonies as participation in the salvation brought about by Christ. By suffering as Jesus suffered, they seek to join their bodies with the body that Christians say redeemed the world. Finally, many ascetics seem to turn to pain when they feel that they are overwhelmed by an experience of the divine. When God seems unbearably near and yet, in the end, so far away, pain can both express the mystic's spiritual suffering and soothe it at the same time. All of these explanations for ascetic behavior have some element of truth to them, and nearly all of them have found expression in film.[84]

Asceticism and Psychological Deviance

In the fourteenth century, Blessed Henry Suso devised a series of torments for himself. These included wearing an undergarment studded with sharpened nails and wearing gloves fitted with tacks so that if during his sleep he tried to remove the garment, he would end up gashing his own flesh. In addition, he fashioned a cross for himself with thirty nails protruding from it which he wore against his bare back both day and night. He scourged himself and slept on a wooden door rather than on a mattress. In the winter he avoided warm rooms, and for years he never bathed because he felt that to do so would be surrendering too much to his comfort-seeking body.[85]

How should we interpret Suso's behavior? He himself says that he inflicted these tortures so that he might make his flesh subject to his spirit and thus overcome his "lively" nature.[86] Can we accept his explanation for what, by any measure, is extremely bizarre behavior? Or might something else be going on?

Psychiatrist Armando Favazza has little patience with people who claim that there are valid religious reasons for self-harm. He calls such explanations "mystical mumbo-jumbo," and he writes, "Although therapists should try to utilize powerful religious and shamanic symbols in selected cases, the fact remains that self-mutilators are neither gods nor saints but rather frightened prophets manqué."[87] To Favazza, people who hurt themselves are in need of immediate medical intervention. Their example is neither to be admired nor imitated.

It is easy to see why Favazza feels as he does. Confronted with patients who slash their skin with blades, repeatedly bang their heads against walls, or rip out their own eyes, one might certainly be moved to feel dismay or compassion rather than reverence. Given the prevalence of self-destructive behaviors in our society, the last thing that a responsible psychiatrist would want to do is to encourage people to hurt themselves in the name of religion. Favazza notes that in one study of female undergraduate students enrolled in a basic psychology course, roughly one in seven (14.5 percent) had an eating disorder, and about one in twenty had a history of deliberate self-harm.[88]

Favazza's explanation for the self-mutilation that he sees among his patients is that it functions as a desperate attempt at self-therapy when the symptoms of a mental disturbance become intolerable. For example, self-inflicted pain can offer a kind of stimulation for children raised in sterile institutional environments. It can also be used as a temporary cure for the depersonalization or the loss of a sense of selfhood that some mental patients experience. One person under Favazza's care remarked, "It's all right to hurt yourself because it proves you are real."[89] In addition, self-harm is sometimes used by people who feel that they have no control over their environment. Though they cannot take charge of the world around them, they can control their own bodily sensations. Pain provides a focal point that can help calm erratic thoughts and emotions. Thus in Favazza's understanding, the self-harm of the mystics might be read as dysfunctional attempts to soothe mental anguish. Though Favazza does acknowledge that there are culturally and religiously sanctioned uses for mutilation, he is loathe to accept those uses as anything other than misguided.

Along similar lines, historian Rudolph Bell attributes much of the fasting of medieval saints to a form of illness that he calls "holy anorexia." The term is ironic since in his opinion there is nothing at all "holy" about starving oneself to death. In his writing, Bell examines the lives of a number of Christian women mystics, including Saint Catherine of Siena. Catherine, one of only a few female saints to have been named a "Doctor of the Church" by the pope, died in the year 1380 at the age of thirty-three. Her death was caused by a long period of self-imposed fasting during which she neither ate food nor drank water.

Bell's thesis is that anorexia (an eating disorder characterized by loss of appetite or aversion to food), both in its modern-day forms and in the Middle Ages, stems from a need for control in an insecure world. He notes that the disease most often afflicts girls: girls who feel, in his words, "hopelessly inadequate and ineffective." Regulating what they eat and drink is one way for these young women to take command of their lives.

The need for control manifests itself, Bell argues, in accordance with the priorities of the society in which each girl lives. Thus the disorder might look different in our contemporary culture than it did in the Middle Ages. Bell writes, "In both instances anorexia begins as the girl fastens onto a highly valued societal goal (bodily health, thinness, self-control in the twentieth century/spiritual health, fasting, and self-denial in medieval Christendom)."[90] While the goals of physical health (in our day) and holiness (in the Middle Ages) may seem laudatory, in victims of anorexia these objectives mask what is essentially a psycho-physiological illness. Regarding the death of Catherine of Siena, Bell remarks, "In the end she had committed the sin of vainglory and had starved herself to death. It had been her will, not [God's], that had triumphed all these years and that now lay vanquished."[91]

Despite the differences between medieval society and our own, anorexia that expresses itself in religious terms still finds resonances in contemporary culture. In the movie *Agnes of God* (1985), for example, Meg Tilly plays a young woman sent to a convent in Montreal after the death of her parents. Utterly naive and perhaps feeble-minded, Agnes as a girl lived a sheltered life, watching no television and being schooled at home by her abusive, alcoholic mother. She now harbors a self-hatred that borders on the vitriolic, parroting to herself the insults that she heard from her mother during her childhood. One day the superior of the convent comes across Agnes lying face-down in the chapel with her arms spread out beside her. The superior asks Agnes why she has stopped eating. Agnes replies that she has been commanded by God to fast. When asked why, she responds, "There's too much flesh on me. I'm a blimp. I have to be attractive to God. He hates fat people. It's a sin to be fat."

The superior attempts to reason with Agnes, but the young nun is resolute. She gestures towards statues of saints in the chapel to make her point, noting that all of them are thin: "That's because they're suffering." Agnes believes that people have to be thin in order to squeeze into heaven. Moreover, she continues, "Suffering is beautiful. I want to be beautiful." When asked, she admits that it was her mother who told her all these things. "Your mother is dead," cries the exasperated superior, but Agnes is unfazed: "She watches. She listens," she replies solemnly. Agnes declares that she can live on the Host alone—that the bread of the daily Eucharist is enough to sustain her. At this point her palm begins to bleed as if it had been pierced. As the superior looks on in disbelief, Agnes sobs, "I'm being punished!" Clearly Agnes is suffering the effects of a childhood marked by cruelty and neglect. Her ascetic practice has roots in a distorted self-image and in harsh parental judgments that have left her with nothing but despair about her life in the body.

Illness such as that suffered by Agnes has surely been the cause of some saints' ascetic practice. No one of us can claim that we are not, at least at times, vulnerable to mental and/or emotional impulses that are destructive, and the saints are no exception. We should not assume that because they possess a dedication to holiness, the saints are therefore immune to the complexities and pitfalls of the human psyche. If we confine ourselves to the insights of Favazza and Bell and others like them, saintly asceticism will always be judged as merely sickness masquerading as sanctity. Yet, as we will see in chapter 10 (and in fact in *Agnes of God* itself), the line between mental illness and holiness can be extremely difficult to draw. Moreover, examination of the lives of Christian ascetics will reveal other motivations for saints' actions besides psychological dysfunction.

Heavenly Medicine

One of these motivations is a desire to discipline the will by disciplining the body. In his sixteenth-century spiritual masterpiece *The Ascent of Mount Carmel*, Saint John of the Cross urged his readers to renounce any pleasures that were not purely for the greater glory of God. In order that they might more easily habituate themselves to an austere way of life, he advised, "Strive always to prefer, not that which is easiest, but that which is most difficult; Not that which is most delectable, but that which is most unpleasing.... Not that which is restful, but that which is wearisome.... Strive to go about seeking not the best of temporal things, but the worst."[92]

Indeed, many Catholic religious orders have instructed their members to engage in forms of self-mortification such as lightly whipping themselves on Fridays or wearing slightly uncomfortable bands around their thighs. The purpose of these practices was (and still is, in some cases, though the ritual has all but disappeared in recent decades) not to cause bodily harm but simply to fortify a person's commitment to avoiding sin and living a life dedicated to God. The practice has been referred to as a kind of "heavenly medicine."

Such discipline seems to be the motivation of the ascetic holy man in Luis Buñuel's short film *Simon of the Desert*. The movie is a fanciful depiction of Saint Simon the Stylite, a fifth-century hermit who spent thirty-seven years of his life living atop a pillar in the desert. In Buñuel's portrayal, Simon is a genuinely holy man who preaches wisdom to the monks who come to visit him and who is able to restore miraculously the amputated hands of a repentant thief. In his saintly simplicity, Simon has no sense of personal property. When a visiting monk observes that much of the world's trouble stems from the words "yours" and "mine," the saint is unable to comprehend what the monk is saying. He does not understand what "mine" means.

For sustenance, Simon takes only a little water, a bit of bread, and some lettuce, and the latter he shares with a hungry rabbit. He does not hate his body, but neither does he indiscriminately indulge its desires. Instead of eating food immediately when it is passed up to him in a basket, he waits until sundown so as to discipline his wants. He urges his listeners to use asceticism as a way to build a bridge from earth to eternity.

Viewers accustomed to Buñuel's usual biting satire regarding religion will be surprised to find in this film a genuine fondness for and admiration of Simon's single-minded devotion. Of course, this devotion is not without its costs. When Simon's mother comes to him and begs him to embrace her, he ignores her plea, granting only that she might live in the shadow of his pillar-home if she wishes. She spends the rest of the film gazing longingly at the son who steadfastly ignores her. Later, a monk observes that Simon's asceticism is, in the end, of very little use to humanity.

Nonetheless, the hermit's way of life is for the most part vindicated by the end of Buñuel's film. During the course of the movie, Satan comes three times to tempt Simon away from his perch. The first time, the devil comes in the likeness of a voluptuous woman dressed as a little girl— though wearing stockings and garter belts as well. The second time, Satan arrives in the form of a woman dressed as Jesus (complete with fake beard and mustache) and carrying a lamb. This Jesus tells Simon, "I weep for you, my beloved. Your penance saddens me. The excess of your sacrifice! Indulge yourself in pleasure. Then you will be near me." The third time that Satan approaches, it is as a woman in a coffin. The woman rises from the coffin and magically appears on top of the pillar where the hermit lives. She then tells him that he has no choice but to accompany her to a devilish destination. "They are coming for us now!" she exclaims, and, literally out of the blue, an airplane arrives on the scene.

Satan takes Simon not, as we might expect, to the fiery pits of Hell, but rather to a twentieth-century disco. We watch for several minutes as electric guitars screech out music and young people twitch on the dance floor as if having seizures. Simon, now with sideburns and a Beatles haircut, smokes a pipe and pours drinks for Satan and himself as he gazes impassively at the dance floor. When he asks the devil what the dance is called, she replies, "Radioactive Flesh! It's the latest—and the last!" Released in 1965 at the height of the Cold War, *Simon of the Desert* recognizes that humanity has brought itself to the brink of nuclear disaster. Though Buñuel steadfastly resists attempts to reduce his film to a "message," the implication seems to be that if Simon's way of life is useless, the alternatives that we have found for ourselves since his time are not much better.

Oh My God, I Am Heartily Sorry

Another motivation for ascetic behavior is the desire to do penance. In its very earliest days, Christianity held to the conviction that once a person was baptized, he or she would sin no more. Baptism was seen as entrance into a new life with Christ. In this new life the old unconverted self would be set aside, and a Christian self would emerge cleansed by the blood of the Savior. It did not take long, however, before Christians realized that even the Spirit of Christ did not always prevent people from sinning. By the third century CE, a system was developed by which those who had committed very serious sins could be reconciled to both God and the Christian community. The system involved public confession of one's offenses, a prolonged period of prayer and fasting, a ritual of re-entrance into the Church, and the making of a lifelong commitment to penitential practices. Because of the rigors involved and because the ritual could only be undergone once, many Christians put off seeking reconciliation until their deathbeds. That way they could atone for the greatest number of sins with the least amount of effort and with the least risk of backsliding.

By the fifth century, it had become clear that allowing Christians only one chance at reconciliation simply wasn't working. In light of this, Irish monks developed the practice of repeatable, private confession and penance: what has come to be known in the Catholic Church as the ritual of Confession or Reconciliation. By confessing one's sins with sincere repentance and by performing a prescribed penance, one could gain forgiveness from God through the agency of God's representative on earth, the priest.

This development led to the writing of carefully detailed penitential manuals which established penances for everything from gluttony to adultery. For example, in the early Middle Ages, manuals instructed that someone who committed homicide should spend seven years eating nothing but bread and water; even little boys who struck one another were sentenced to one week on that meager fare. No aspect of life was left untouched. One manual commanded, "He who gives to anyone a liquor in which a mouse or a weasel is found dead shall do penance with three special fasts."[93]

The word "penance" comes from the Latin *poena* (from which our word "punishment" is also derived). Behind the notion of penance is the idea that pain can be used as a kind of currency. My pain can act as payment in satisfaction for any wrongs I have committed against another person or against God. Not merely deterrence ("I am punishing you so that you won't do this again") but the desire for reparation ("You must pay your debt to society") is at work in rituals of penance.

This is the case when, in the movie *Thérèse*, the mother superior in the Carmelite convent has herself whipped by one of the younger sisters. The mother superior has just been told by the convent's doctor that young Thérèse Martin (later known as Saint Thérèse of Lisieux) is dying of tuberculosis. The doctor recommends frequent massages for his patient, and he prescribes high doses of morphine in anticipation of the pain that will wrack Thérèse's body in the days to come. The mother superior rebuffs his advice, explaining, "We're on earth to suffer as our husband [Jesus] did. He's in agony till the world ends." The doctor, barely able to contain himself, blurts out, "Suffering is hideous!" To this the nun replies, "Not here."

The truth is, however, that the mother superior is not withholding medication from Thérèse out of a holy desire for her to share in the sufferings of Jesus. Quite simply, she wants Thérèse to suffer because she is jealous of her. She is jealous of the girl's simplicity and goodness and of the spontaneous love and affection showered on her by the other nuns in the convent. Knowing the darkness of her own heart, she prostrates herself before the altar in the convent chapel, hands another sister a small branch cut from a tree, and bares her back for punishment. The other sister, aware of the superior's jealousy, strikes her once but then throws the branch away in a gesture of disgust. Patiently, the penitent mother retrieves the instrument and hands it back, reminding the nun that as superior, she expects her orders to be obeyed. She wishes to offer her own bloody back in reparation for her sins.

Sacrificial Asceticism

Willingly undergoing pain is not always an exercise in penance, however. At times, physical suffering is understood instead by those who seek it as a kind of sacrifice offered to God. In the first scenes of *Thérèse*, for example, the young saint reads in the newspaper that an unrepentant murderer is about to be beheaded by the government. Thérèse prays for the convict and abstains from drinking water; her thirst is an offering to God on the criminal's behalf. When she reads the next day that the prisoner kissed a crucifix before his execution, thus indicating sorrow for his sins, she exclaims, "He's saved! I saved him! I won!" Later in the same movie, a dying Thérèse rises from her bed and limps around her sickroom with as much energy as she can muster. When her nurse scolds her for exhausting herself, she responds that she is offering her efforts on behalf of another nun who is threatening to leave the convent.

For Thérèse, these gifts of bodily pain are understood as gestures of affection for a God who is good and caring. When the young saint's sister encourages her to sleep without a mattress or blanket, observing, "Suffering is the key," Thérèse asks, "Not love?" It is clear that even though she takes her sister's advice and imitates her ascetic practices, she does it not out of guilt or servitude. She does it rather with the passion of a suitor. At one point she encourages a nun who feels that her prayers to Jesus are unheard, advising, "Fondle him. That's how I snared him!"

Sacrificial asceticism in Thérèse's case is playful and affectionate, but it does not always manifest itself quite so benignly. At times, sacrifices become bargaining chips in a desperate gambit for salvation. Such a view of asceticism is portrayed with disturbing intensity in Maurice Pialat's *Under the Sun of Satan* (*Sous le Soleil de Satan*), a movie released in 1987 and based on Georges Bernanos's novel of the same name. Starring Gerard Depardieu, the film portrays the life of a poor young parish priest named Father Donissan. Donissan is unintelligent, we are told; his manners are crude, and his way of interacting with the villagers in his parish makes them uncomfortable and shy. More than one character remarks that Donissan is not really fit to be a priest, and yet as the film progresses, we come to see him as burning with a religious fervor that drives him nearly mad at times and that leads others to call him a saint.

Part of Donissan's spiritual regimen is to inflict pain on his body. We watch him whipping his own back with a chain until he nearly faints. His pastor, unaware of the extremes to which the young cleric is prone, is horrified to discover one day that Donissan has been wearing a coarse hair shirt under his cassock. The garment has turned the skin on his chest into an open and bloody wound, and when he sees it the pastor backs away in horror. "God is not displeased with you," he attempts to convince the young priest.

It is not until later in the film that we learn the reason for Donissan's austerities. As he is packing to leave for an extended retreat in a Trappist monastery, he has a conversation with the pastor who is sending him away. Donissan tells the older man, "So many souls possessed by sin. That enraged me. To save them, I offered all I had. My life, first; it's not much. My salvation, if God wants it." Along with his life and his salvation, he offers his bodily pain. He has taken on himself the burden of others' sins in such a way that he can feel no joy himself and must inflict as much agony on himself as he can stand. He has condemned himself to despair so that others might experience salvation.

Donissan's character embodies a type of thinking called Jansenism, which the Catholic Church has condemned as heresy. Simply put, Jansenism is the belief that people are helpless to do good apart from the grace of God and that God offers this grace only to some and not to others. Apart from God's offer of assistance, according to the Jansenists, people are totally depraved, and even when they try to do good they will only fall more deeply into the traps of evil. If God wills that they will be saved, then nothing they can do will prevent their salvation. If God does not so will, then nothing they can do will prevent their damnation. These beliefs were condemned in the seventeenth century as contrary to the teachings of the Catholic Church.

Part of what was at stake for the Church in denouncing Jansenist ideas was the role of Jesus in the forgiveness of sins. If only some are offered the grace of redemption, the Church reasoned, then Jesus died only for some. In that case, Jesus could not truly be called the savior of the world. In contrast to Jansenism, the Church taught that all people are offered the opportunity of salvation through the merits of Jesus, but that not all choose to avail themselves of this grace.

Donissan's character, believing that most people are irredeemably possessed by sin, is clearly influenced by Jansenist tendencies. However, he departs from Jansenist theology in one significant way. He cannot resign himself to the notion that so many people are simply lost to Satan. Instead, Donissan makes a gamble. He makes an offer that he hopes cannot be refused: his own pain and torment in exchange for the souls of the people under his care. Note that he does not urge his parishioners themselves to change their sinful ways. As far as he is concerned, they are so far lost that they are not really responsible for their actions. They are merely puppets abandoned to the will of the Devil. Instead, Donissan believes with a kind of spiritual arrogance that he can offer something so valuable that it is worth the freeing of a multitude of souls. Apparently concluding that Jesus' death was not enough to open the gates of heaven, he hopes to open those gates himself with the promise of his own blood.

The spiritual danger of the priest's sacrifices is shown in a conversation he has one night with someone whom he takes to be Satan. Donissan, on his way to visit a parish some distance away, has become lost and is wandering aimlessly when night begins to fall and shadows start to obscure the surrounding countryside. At this point he meets up with a man who claims to be a horse trader and who offers to show him a shortcut to his destination. The two walk men walk side by side along the dark road speaking of this and that, but after some time the priest becomes tired and ill and has to stop to rest. As he does, it occurs to him, exhausted and feverish as he is, that his companion is not really a simple tradesman but is rather the Evil One. As if reading his thoughts, the horse trader kisses him tenderly on the mouth ("I sought you—hunted you ardently. None of you escapes me!") and tells him that if he looks him in the eye, he will see himself.

The horse trader warns Donissan that his soul is in jeopardy, saying gleefully, "You will often fondle me, *thinking* you're fondling *the other*!" He tells him that the two of them are alike in that both have rejected the grace and peace of God. Crows the trader, "We alone are not fooled!" "We chose his hate, not his love." The man's observations are echoed later when Donissan's superior cautions the priest, "You risk damnation by straying from the path, as you've done. Hope is almost dead in you!" The implication is that Donissan's sacrifices are not offerings of love but are rather born of resentment and despair.

For the fact is that Donissan does not really believe that God is able to save humankind. He declares at one point, "Satan is prince of this world. He holds it in his hands. And God is conquered with us." His belief in the unopposable power of Satan accounts for the title of the film. We do not live in a world of grace, attests Donissan; rather, we live under the glare of evil, under the sun of Satan. We are simply the playthings of a malevolent power whom we desperately hope to escape but whom we are doomed to serve.

A scene near the end of the film makes vivid the troubling nature of Donissan's sacrifices. A young boy in the village has fallen ill with meningitis, and the boy's father fetches the priest hoping that his prayers can cure him. When father and cleric arrive at the family's house, however, they discover that they are too late; the boy has died. Refusing to accept the loss of her child, however, the boy's mother pleads with Donissan for help. After an internal struggle, the priest agrees to pray at the boy's bedside. He does not approach the deathbed with the confidence of a servant of God, but rather with dread. He holds the child, who is quite clearly dead, in his arms and prays, "Say who is master, him or You! Show yourself before abandoning me forever!" Looking into the face of the lifeless child, he continues, "O Father, I would have sacrificed even eternal life." At that moment the boy's eyes flutter open, and Donissan drops him to the bed in horror. As the child's mother screams, "He's alive! You are a saint!" Donissan rushes from the room. "I hope for your forgiveness," he cries. "Forgive me!"

This scene is puzzling and can be interpreted in at least two different ways. On the one hand, perhaps God really has intervened to restore the dead boy in an act of divine power. In this case, Donissan exhibits a pathetic misunderstanding of what has happened to him. Determined to believe that he is in the clutches of Satan, he runs from God and believes himself the victim of an evil trick. Stubbornly clinging to a Jansenist pessimism regarding human nature, he cannot convince himself that God really does love the world and would intervene to spare a mother the death of her son. What he thinks he needs to be forgiven for is his hope that the world might be loveable after all: that God might actually care about it.

On the other hand, perhaps the child's resuscitation is, as Donissan believes, the work of evil. Later, in the solitude of his room, he speaks softly to Satan: "When did I first yield? *You* suffered. *You* prayed with me. Even that miracle…." In this case, the film seems to offer no hope of redemption for the tortured cleric. He truly is under the sun of Satan and will find no rest because of it. All of his ascetic rigors have enriched Satan rather than God, and his brief hope that God might somehow prove to be the master of the world is extinguished in the mockery of Satan's laughter.

It should be noted that regarding the child's recovery, the film diverges significantly from the book on which it is based. In Bernanos's novel, when Donissan holds the dead child in his arms he believes that he feels the boy's body grow warm for an instant, but in the end, there is no return to life. In the film, on the other hand, the child opens his eyes, and, though he closes them again in a way that would suggest death, slight movements of his hand in the next few frames indicate that the mother's joy is not misplaced. The child really has recovered.

This difference between the book and the movie has important implications. By choosing to alter the plot of the novel, the film eliminates one explanation for Donissan's behavior. That is, up until the time of the "miracle," it is possible for viewers to think that all of the priest's spiritual torments are simply the result of a deluded mind. Even the conversation with Satan on the dark country road could be dismissed as illusion; after all, it occurs at night and at a time when Donissan has been weakened by his austerities. Moreover, the day after it takes place, the priest has an exchange with a villager who claims to be well acquainted with the horse trader, having bought a filly from him the previous year. Was he then really the Prince of Darkness, or was he simply an itinerant salesman? It is impossible for viewers to tell. However, the fact that later on Donissan is truly able to raise a child from the dead lends credence to the cleric's belief that something supernatural is afoot.

What remains unclear in the film, though, is whether that "something" is God or Satan. The movie leaves the holiness of Donissan's life as an unresolved question. Is he a saint as several characters in the movie claim him to be? Are his self-inflicted tortures good and pleasing offerings to the divine? Or is he rather a pawn of evil, succumbing to the dangerous fantasy that he can, through his pains and his prayers, become a savior and redeemer for his people? In the end, to whom are Donissan's sacrifices actually made? Are they enticements for God to relent and to allow the poor banished children of Eve into glory? Or are they offerings to Satan, the one who seems to rule both this world and the next? *Under the Sun of Satan* does not answer, and we are left only with the uneasy feeling that whatever holiness is, it is perilously close to madness on the one hand and to the demonic on the other.

Do This in Memory of Me

Still another motivation for ascetic behavior is the desire to imitate Jesus. As we saw in the last chapter, the earliest Christians remembered and retold over and over again the story of the death of Christ. When in later centuries some of their own members were executed for professing faith in Jesus, they fashioned the accounts of those martyrdoms in accordance with the gospels' accounts of the Passion. The implication was that since the martyrs had died in imitation of Jesus, they would, like him, have a share in heavenly life.

As Christianity became the dominant religious force in Europe, however, occasions for martyrdom grew scarce. No longer was it likely that an ardent lover of Jesus would be called upon literally to offer her or his life in the hopes of being raised to Easter glory. Thus Christians felt a need to develop new ways of being "crucified" for God. While they could not be martyred for Jesus, they could put to death their sinful natures by embarking on long journeys of prayer, self-denial, and self-mortification. Moreover, they, like the early martyrs, saw their suffering as participating in the redemption wrought by Christ. Asceticism became a way for Christians to identify with Jesus so as to enact in themselves the salvation that he made possible.

Historian Caroline Walker Bynum makes this point in her landmark study entitled *Holy Feast and Holy Fast: The Significance of Food to Medieval Women*. Bynum notes that in the Middle Ages, an emphasis on the physical sufferings of Jesus during the Passion became more and more prominent in Christian piety. It was, after all, in the thirteenth century that Saint Francis of Assisi became the first recorded "stigmatic"—the first person to be mysteriously afflicted/blessed with wounds in his hands and feet like the wounds of the crucifixion. Other medieval saints began to re-enact the Passion of Christ by having themselves whipped or by piercing their own bodies with spikes.

During this time also the faithful placed a renewed emphasis on the body of Christ as received in the Eucharist. According to the Christian gospels, on the night before Jesus died, he held a meal with his disciples. At that meal, he took bread in his hands and said to those gathered at the table, "Take this and eat it. This is my body." Then he took wine and said, "Take this and drink it. This is my blood." Christians ever since have reen-acted that gesture in what is called the Eucharist (from a Greek word that means "thanksgiving") or Communion or the Lord's Supper or, in the Catholic tradition, the Mass.

According to Bynum, in the Middle Ages, women in particular were likely to express their piety in terms of the body of Jesus in the Eucharist. This was so for many reasons. First, the Eucharist is a kind of food, and women traditionally are responsible for the making and serving of food. Moreover, women often *are* food. They feed babies with their bodies just as Jesus was believed to feed the faithful with his body at the Mass. Medieval biology taught that breast milk was a form of transmuted blood, and so women were thought to offer their life-blood just as Jesus offered his blood to the disciples.

But if women developed a strong devotion to the Eucharist, they were also likely to identify their physical suffering with the physical suffering of Christ. Bynum explains that medieval philosophy identified male nature with spirit and female nature with matter. Thus women were thought to be more "physical" than men were. One might imagine that women would feel devalued by being linked to matter as opposed to spirit, but Bynum argues that this was not the case. She explains, "The goal of religious women was…to realize the *opportunity* of physicality. They strove not to eradicate body but to merge their own humiliating and painful flesh with that flesh whose agony, espoused by choice, was salvation. Luxuriating in Christ's physicality, they found there the lifting up—the redemption—of their own."[94]

In this case, then, asceticism is not an escape from the body but rather its opposite. It is a way of glorying in the body so as to conform more closely to Christ. We can see this in the case of medieval mystic Blessed Angela of Foligno, who, during one Maundy Thursday, visited lepers in a hospital near her home. After bathing the feet of the lepers, Angela drank the water with which she had washed them. She reports that the water tasted sweet; moreover, she did not even mind when a scab from one of the lepers' sores became stuck in her throat: "My conscience would not let me spit it out, just as if I had received Holy Communion," she remarks.[95] Sharing in the leper's suffering became a way of sharing in the suffering of Christ.

Precisely this story from the life of Angela of Foligno is invoked by one of the sisters in the film *Thérèse*. The incident is related by Sister Lucy, a young nun who adores Thérèse and who cannot bear the thought that her beloved friend is about to die. After describing the event from Blessed Angela of Foligno's life, she steals into Thérèse's room and lifts the cup that contains the patient's bloody sputum. Drinking it is her way of imitating the holiness of the saints. However, it is also a means of becoming one with Thérèse whom she cherishes. More than this, it is a ritual of communion that binds her more closely with Jesus. As the disciples drank the wine that Jesus called his own blood, Lucy drinks the blood of Thérèse's suffering. In one gesture she mingles the pain of Jesus, the pain of Thérèse, and her own willingness to suffer out of love.

The Power of Suffering

It's possible that such suffering can bring about spiritual power? Every year in the Philippines, a ritual is enacted that to many of us might seem not just strange but downright macabre. On Holy Thursday (which commemorates Jesus's last meal with his disciples) and Good Friday (commemorating Jesus's crucifixion), groups of devout Christians walk along highways and dusty roads, through both modern cities and rural villages, whipping their own backs bloody and raw. Other Christians, both men and women, opt for a more grueling ordeal: crucifixion. They willingly have their hands, and sometimes their feet as well, nailed to a cross. The volunteers, called *kristos*, remain on their crosses for only a short period of time and do not sustain serious or long-lasting injuries; still, for the few seconds or minutes that they spend on the cross, they come as close as anyone could to imitating the sufferings of Jesus.

The Catholic Church officially frowns on these reenactments of the crucifixion, pointing out that Jesus' suffering two millennia ago already redeemed the world from its sins. Still, the practice continues and has even become something of a tourist attraction. Travel brochures list the time and place when each town will hold its crucifixions, and the curious are invited to watch as the *kristos* are nailed to their wooden crosses.

As social anthropologist Nicholas H. Barker points out, undergoing the crucifixion is thought to be a source of spiritual power. He observes, "By voluntarily inflicting suffering upon oneself in public, and then, by controlling and conquering pain, the negative experience of suffering is transformed by flagellants (and *kristos*), both metaphorically and sensorily into a positive act or encounter."[96] According to Barker, Good Friday is the most potent day of the year for faith-healers to acquire supernatural powers. On this day shamans venture into "dangerous" places such as cemeteries or caves so as to confront and harness the powers of malevolent spirits. Undergoing crucifixion is another way of coming into contact with the dark side of the supernatural and at the same time overcoming it. Notes Barker, "The more literal the reenactment of the passion of Christ, the greater the risk involved, the more potent the power available. If spiritual power is efficacious, the likelihood of healing is obviously enhanced."[97] A *kristo* might enact a cure by smearing his or her bloody palms over the sick or by dripping blood over ailing spectators.

The notion that power can be gained through suffering is not unique to the Philippines, of course. According to musical lore, only someone who has lived the blues can really sing the blues, and people who have been sick themselves are sometimes said to make the best doctors. Psychoanalysts must venture into the dark recesses of their own ids and egos before they can help others to mental health, and conventional wisdom holds that no artist or writer can become truly great without undergoing some torment in life. The connection between suffering and power can also be seen in a film biography of the Christian stigmatist Padre Pio called *Night of the Prophet* (*La Notte del Profeta*).

Padre Pio was born in Italy in 1887 and baptized Francesco Forgione. At the age of fifteen he entered a Franciscan religious order; several years later he was ordained, and in 1907 he professed perpetual vows of poverty, chastity, and obedience. The Catholic priest became famous not only for his piety but also for his allegedly miraculous powers. His followers claim that he had the ability to peer into people's souls, to heal the sick, and to bilocate, or to be present in two places at once. He was most famous, however, for the stigmata that afflicted him most of his adult life. "Stigmata" is simply the Greek word for signs or marks; the stigmata are thought to be wounds inflicted by God in imitation of the wounds of Jesus and given as a special, albeit painful, grace. Padre Pio's cause for sainthood has advanced steadily since his death in 1968, and he was beatified on 2 May 1999.

Night of the Prophet (1995) features Sergio Fiorentini as Padre Pio and Rodolfo Corsato as a journalist named Ettore Rossi who, in 1946, investigates the life of the Franciscan mystic. Rossi, who is told by a cardinal in Rome that 98 percent of people who claim to have mystical visions have psychological problems, travels to San Giovanni Rotondo, a town in the Gargano Mountains of Italy, to meet Padre Pio and to speak with his followers.

There he meets a woman who converted to Catholicism from a Protestant faith and who lives at the monastery where Padre Pio resides. After listening to the woman's story, Rossi asks her what it is that moves her most about the priest. She answers, "His capacity to bear so much suffering." She then lists the types of suffering that Padre Pio undergoes: physical pain, the moral pain of being able to read the sins in people's hearts, and the spiritual pain of seeing the Church and society moving away from God. She continues, "It was through this suffering that Father attained the miracles that the Lord granted him." The miracles, as depicted in the film, are numerous. Padre Pio heals a man on crutches and a girl who cannot see. When the journalist Rossi approaches him, the priest looks at him intently and tells him what he already knows: that he hasn't been to confession in three years. It is through his pain, attests the movie, that Padre Pio's spiritual powers grow. Suffering brings divine potency.

"Love Still Unknown, Why Do You Leave Me?"

Thus far we have looked at several motivations for asceticism (mental illness, spiritual discipline, penance, sacrifice, identification with Christ, and spiritual power) as well as at their manifestations in film. There is one further reason why saints have practiced ascetic behaviors, however, and this one seems to have no cinematic counterpart. The final topic we must address is asceticism born of desire: desire for God.

Blessed Angela of Foligno, the medieval mystic who drank scabs from a leper's feet, made a pilgrimage to Assisi in the thirteenth century. There she underwent a strange and intense spiritual experience. Looking at a depiction of Jesus holding Saint Francis in his arms, she heard Christ telling her, "Thus I will hold you closely to me and much more closely than can be observed with the eyes of the body." When she turned to see who was speaking, she observed "something full of immense majesty" that she could only describe as "the All Good." As it began to fade, Angela felt her joints becoming dislocated, and she began to scream, "Love still unknown, why do you leave me? Love still unknown, why? why? why?"[98]

It may seem strange that Angela would describe the object of her love as "still unknown." After all, she was a Christian who had been praying to Jesus all her life. Moreover, Jesus had just spoken to her and had called her "sweet daughter" and "my temple" and "my delight."[99] She seems to have been on more intimate terms with Jesus than most Christians could ever hope to be. Yet when she cries out, it is to someone whom she describes as "still unknown." How can this be?

There are many ways of understanding mysticism—probably as many as there are mystics. However, we might be able to group these understandings loosely under two different models. In the first, God is something (or someone) "out there" that the mystics are fortunate enough to encounter. Through prayer or fasting or sheer good luck, mystics come into contact with the Divine in a way that eludes the rest of humankind. In this model, there is no inherent connection between God and human beings. We might stumble onto divinity as we go through our lives, or we might not. God might reveal Godself to us, or God might not.

In the second model, however, God and human beings are always already intimately related to one another. God is always at the heart of humans' experience of themselves and of their world. The Catholic theologian Karl Rahner expresses this concept with his notion of the "supernatural existential," or the structure of grace that permeates all human beings. Grace is "supernatural" because it comes from God. It is "existential," however, because it is a fundamental part of who we are.

For Rahner and others like him, mystical experiences are not encounters with a God who is otherwise unknown. It is not as if the mystics travel to a distant land and bring back tales of what is forever alien to the rest of us. Instead, mystical events are simply vibrant and psychologically intense manifestations of what all of us already experience in our daily lives. We are all of us, each one of us, graced by God. Mystics simply realize this more fully than the rest of us do. Or, as Rahner (in his typically abstruse fashion) puts it, "…mystic experiences sustained by the Spirit, which make God's spirit accessible, do not differ from normal Christian existence because they are of a higher nature simply by virtue of being *mystical* experiences of the Spirit. They are different because their natural substratum (for example, an experience of suspension of the faculties) is as such different from the psychological circumstances of everyday life."[100]

If we understand mysticism in this way, then we can see that the kind of events that Blessed Angela describes (visions, voices, etc.) are not a privileged access into Divinity. They are psychologically distinct and no doubt personally powerful, but they do not tell us something different from what all of us already experience in our capacities as free, loving, and intelligent human beings.

This is, from a Catholic theological perspective, as it should be. Catholic theology has a long tradition of affirming that God is essentially a mystery. God cannot directly be the object of our knowledge or experience because to be an object is essentially to be limited. God, according to this tradition, is beyond all limitation. God is more than any word or concept or imagining ever could be. Thus no matter how intimate we may feel our knowledge of God to be, God must always in some sense remain "still unknown." No matter what the mystics report that they hear or see or feel in their raptures, God in Godself cannot be known directly but only indirectly: "through a glass darkly," as Saint Paul says.

When Angela realizes this, she says that she feels as if her joints are coming apart. We can observe that often in the writings of the mystics, the most intense experiences of grace are followed by the most painful bodily sensations. Saint Teresa of Avila, describing her anguish when she feels her distance from God, notes that at times "the pain becomes so severe that the soul can do neither penance nor anything else, for the whole body is paralyzed. One is unable to stir with either the feet or the arms."[101] It is almost as if pain is used as a form of expression, articulating something that words seem inadequate to convey.

Moreover, when the spiritual pain of God's being "still unknown" becomes too intense, many of the mystics deliberately inflict physical pain on themselves in order to soothe their spiritual agonies. Again, Teresa of Avila writes, "When this thirst is not too severe, it seems it can be appeased somewhat; at least the soul seeks some remedy—for it doesn't know what to do—through certain penances.... They can relieve it somewhat, and the soul can get along in this way while at the same time begging God to provide a cure for its sickness."[102] Thus another reason that mystics might pursue the pains of asceticism is to alleviate the spiritual torment that afflicts them. Causing anguish to the body can block, if only temporarily, the more agonizing pains of a spirit that feels separated from what it loves.

In some ways, this type of asceticism mirrors that discussed by the psychiatrist Favazza. Instead of soothing mental anguish, however, self-harming behavior in this case soothes the spiritual anguish of being far from God. It is not something that filmmakers have managed to bring to the big screen, however. We can speculate as to why this might be. Perhaps filmmakers fear that audiences would misinterpret such ascetic behavior as pathological. Or perhaps they simply find it too difficult to convey on film the spiritual power of mystical experience and the psychological dynamics that accompany it. In any case, it seems a fruitful area of exploration for actors and directors interested in portraying the ascetic practices that so often accompany saintly life.

5

Make Disciples of All Nations

Introduction

From the first moments of *The Mission* (starring Jeremy Irons and Robert De Niro), viewers know they have entered a world not for the faint of heart. Brazilian Indians tie a missionary priest to a cross, carry him through the forest to a river, and watch as his body is swept over a tremendous waterfall. When the missionary's battered corpse is found at the base of the falls, his brother priest does not run in fear. Instead, he removes his shoes and scales the cliffs of the waterfall himself, hoping to find and minister to the very people who killed his friend.

Since its earliest days, Christianity has been a missionary tradition, attempting to spread its message to the very ends of the earth. The Gospel of Matthew ends with the resurrected Jesus urging his followers, "Go therefore and make disciples of all nations, baptizing them in the name of the Father and of the Son and of the Holy Spirit, and teaching them to obey everything that I have commanded you. And remember, I am with you always, to the end of the age" (28:19–20). Whether or not those words were actually uttered by Jesus cannot be verified; what is indisputable, however, is that Christians have understood themselves as having a responsibility to preach and to teach the good news of Jesus Christ, and that they have gone about this task with vigor.

They have done so with a variety of motivations and with varying results, and film reflects this diversity. For example, the movie biography of

California missionary Blessed Junípero Serra, *Seven Cities of Gold,* portrays Serra as both minister to and defender of the Native Americans whom he has come to serve. Serra preaches to the natives but also protects them from the soldiers who are seeking gold rather than souls. Similarly, *The Life of Charles de Foucauld* shows the Venerable Little Brother of Jesus protesting against the slavery he sees in Algeria and living a life of simplicity and love for others. On the other hand, though *The Mission* is unabashed in its admiration for the priests who brought the gospel to Brazil in the eighteenth century, it does not hesitate to show the tragic consequences of Christianity's intrusion into the lives of the Indian peoples. *Black Robe*, based on the lives of Jesuit missionaries to Canada, goes even further, suggesting that Christians would have been better off adopting the beliefs and practices of the very people whom they were trying to convert.

What Is the Mission?

The meaning of missionizing has changed significantly during the course of Christian history. When the Gospel of Matthew challenged its readers to "make disciples of all nations," it meant something far different from what nineteenth-century explorer-missionary David Livingstone intended when, reflecting on the spread of Christianity in Africa, he wrote, "Those two pioneers of civilization—Christianity and commerce—should ever be inseparable...."[103] By the time Livingstone was writing, European Christianity understood itself as bringing not just spiritual but also cultural and economic salvation to the "dark continent." To be Christianized meant to be reformed into the likeness of a European, and winning converts to Christ often meant tearing people away from their native language and traditions. Since Livingstone's day, several shifts have taken place in people's understanding of what it means to spread the Gospel, and undoubtedly new interpretations will emerge in the decades to come.

Let us look briefly at a few examples of various theologies of evangelization (or "missiologies") that have characterized Christianity's two-thousand-year history; then we will be ready to look at how they have found their way to the big screen.

The Gospel of Matthew offers one of the earliest expressions of a missionary theology. Many scholars believe that the author of the gospel was a Jew, part of a newly-emerging group that was struggling to integrate its commitment to Jesus with the covenant it had inherited from Abraham and Moses. At the time the Gospel was written, most likely towards the end of the first century (possibly in Syria),[104] a strict division between "Christians" and "Jews" had not yet taken place; many followers of the Christ attended synagogue services as they always had, and they followed Jewish law. Thus, when Matthew presents Jesus's Great Commission to baptize and make disciples, he does not mean that followers should bring in converts to Christianity in the way that we in the twenty-first century might think of it. The Church in our contemporary sense didn't yet exist. Instead, what Matthew seems to have in mind is simply that the good news that was preached by Jesus is to be shared with everyone. That good news is that God is with us and will continue to be so, "to the end of the age." Evangelism here doesn't mean getting people to join a particular congregation. Instead, it means bringing about a conversion of life. It means getting people to commit themselves to God's reign and to God's will: namely, justice, and love for everyone.[105]

As time went on, however, the meaning of missionizing began to change. For one thing, Christians started thinking less and less about the Kingdom of God that Jesus had promised. Or, rather, they adopted the Greek distinction between body and soul, and they began to equate the Kingdom of God with a spiritual afterlife in heaven. Instead of looking forward to a time when God's will would be done "*on earth*, as it is in heaven" (see Matt 6:10), they thought about their own individual after-lives and the fate that their souls would undergo at death.

At the same time, Christianity was coming into its own as a religion separate from Judaism, and in Europe it gained so much power that Church and state became virtually indistinguishable. The pope came to be seen as the successor to Saint Peter, keeper of the keys to heaven, and salvation was thought to depend upon one's being a member of the Catholic Church. The Council of Florence in 1441 summed this idea up this way: "Not only pagans but also Jews, heretics, and schismatics will have no share in eternal life. They will go into the eternal fire which was prepared for the devil and his angels, unless they become aggregated to the Catholic Church before the end of their lives."[106]

In this context, evangelization meant gathering souls into the Church, by force if necessary. Often this brought Christian missionaries into conflict with the traditions of the people whom they had left their home-lands to serve. A famous story from the life of Saint Boniface illustrates this point. Boniface, who lived in the eighth century, was sent to bring the pagan tribes of Germany into the one true faith. To prove the falsehood of the Germans' ancient native religion, he took an axe and cut down an oak tree that they held sacred. To the tribes' astonishment, no punishment descended upon Boniface's head, and, according to the story, the people realized that their native gods were in truth impotent. From then on, "the work of evangelization advanced steadily."[107]

An engaging version of this conflict between the old gods and the new appears in the French Film *The Sorceress* (*Le Moine et la Sorcière*, 1987), written by medievalist Pamela Berger and directed by Suzanne Schiffmann. The premise of the movie is this: in a town near Lyons, village people venerate Saint Guinefort, a greyhound who once saved a child from a deadly snake.[108] When a Dominican friar[109] representing the Church's Inquisition comes to town, he is outraged by what he sees as a mockery of the Christian institution of sainthood. The friar destroys the grave of the holy dog and cuts down a tree nearby that the townsfolk believe to have healing powers. Later, however, he comes to regret his actions. As a sort of compromise with the villagers, the friar builds a chapel on the site of the sacred tree, and he reinvents Saint Guinefort as a man-saint with a canine companion. One can see in the film how Christianity often merged with the cultures that it encountered, both changing them and being changed by them.

In the sixteenth century the Protestant Reformation called into question the power and authority of the Catholic Church that had marked the European Middle Ages, and during the Enlightenment the Church lost even more of its control. Though Europeans still overwhelmingly identified themselves as followers of Jesus, they began to see their Christianity less in terms of institution and dogma, and more as a moral code that stressed love for all people. The Enlightenment especially gave birth to great optimism about human nature and about what progress humans might achieve if they were freed from the trappings of religious superstition. Of course, this movement had its down side: "human" often meant "European male," and "progress" meant the adoption of the customs, languages, technologies, and beliefs of European culture. Christianity thus came to be seen as the equivalent of civilization; evangelism went hand in hand with colonization. Missionaries understood themselves not just as saving souls but as bringing the light of culture to dark and primitive lands. It was for this reason that David Livingstone could urge in 1860 that the two pioneers of civilization, namely, Christianity and commerce, should always be conjoined. At roughly the same time, the American

Presbyterian James Dennis wrote a three-volume work entitled *Christian Missions and Social Progress*. The implication of the title was that Christians are obliged to evangelize not just for the sake of the faith, but also for the advancement of human culture.

In the present day, there are a number of different opinions about just what it means to evangelize. Some missionaries take an exclusivist approach to missiology similar to that held by the Council of Florence.[110] Exclusivists hold that Christianity is the one and only salvific religion and that unless one is a follower of Jesus, one cannot enter the kingdom of God. They find justification for their belief in various biblical texts, including the following from the Gospel of John:

> For God so loved the world that he gave his only Son, so that *everyone who believes in him* may not perish but may have eternal life. (3:16, emphasis added)

> Jesus said to [the apostle Thomas], "I am the way, and the truth, and the life. No one comes to the Father except through me." (14:6)

> [Jesus said,] "I am the vine, you are the branches. Those who abide in me and I in them bear much fruit, because apart from me you can do nothing. Whoever does not abide in me is thrown away like a branch and withers; such branches are gathered, thrown into the fire, and burned." (15:5-6)

An exclusivist missionary would see the salvation of others as the single most important reason to spread the Gospel. Loving others entails converting them to Christianity lest they be cast into the fires of hell.

An example of this approach to evangelization appeared a few years ago in a newspaper article with the headline, "Southern Baptists Take Heat for Saying 46 % in Alabama Are Bound for Hell." According to the story, the Southern Baptist Convention had done a county-by-county study of the population of Alabama, subtracting the number of Baptists from the total population and then using a formula to estimate how many people from different denominations and faiths were going to heaven based on how closely those denominations' beliefs approximated Southern Baptists'. A spokesman for the church's Home Mission Board is quoted in the article as saying, "We don't know who's lost and who's saved. All we know is that as we understand the doctrine of salvation, a lot of people are lost." The purpose of the study was not to damn these people but rather to assess where evangelization was most needed. As one minister put it, the study had "a good motive behind it, and that is not one of judging, but of reaching."[111]

In contrast to exclusivists, another group of missionaries can be called inclusivists. Inclusivists hold that there may be many true religions in the world but that Christianity remains the norm against which all of them must be judged. Some inclusivists claim that Jesus Christ is the most direct path to God and that other religions offer only dim and tortuous routes. Others hold that no matter which religion a person follows, be it Hinduism or Buddhism or Shinto, that person is in the end always and only saved by the grace of Jesus. You don't have to be a Christian to enter the Kingdom of God, say these inclusivists, but Jesus is the only one who can, as it were, validate your passport.

Why would an inclusivist engage in missionary work? After all, if people can be saved no matter what their religious preference, why should anyone bother them with the message of the Gospels? Two answers come to mind. First, one might become a missionary simply to learn about other religions and to see where God is already at work in them. The Catholic document entitled "Declaration on the Relationship of the Church to Non-Christian Religions" (also called "Nostra Ætate"), issued in 1965, has this to say: "The Catholic Church…looks with sincere respect upon those ways of conduct and of life, those rules and teachings which, though differing in many particulars from what she holds and sets forth, nevertheless often reflect a ray of that Truth which enlightens all men."[112] Learning about other religions can be a way of basking in the world's various "rays of Truth."

Second, an inclusivist might wish to show members of other religious traditions a "truer" or "clearer" manifestation of God: namely, Jesus the Christ. Armed with the conviction that Christ is present in all people through the grace of the Holy Spirit, a missionary might wish to introduce non-Christians to the source of that grace.

Aside from exclusivists and inclusivists, there is another category of missionaries who would identify themselves as pluralists. Catholic theologian Paul Knitter, for example, contends that there may be many other universal, decisive, and indispensable manifestations of the divine besides Jesus.[113] In Knitter's estimation, Christians need not think of Jesus as God's full, definitive, and unsurpassable revelation. Since God is a mystery who can never be fully comprehended, there is always more to God than can be learned from any one person, even if that person is Jesus.

Nonetheless, says Knitter, there is a need for Christians to be missionaries because Jesus offers a message that is universal, decisive, and indispensable.[114] While Christians do not have the only truth, they have a truth that is worth sharing and that is important for others to hear. Moreover, Christians need to be in contact with other religions because they themselves need to hear the truth of others. Knitter notes, "As much as Christians…feel that Buddhists might be included or fulfilled in what Jesus has to offer, so must they be ready to be included and fulfilled in Buddha's message."[115]

In summary, then, what evangelists understand themselves as doing has varied throughout history, and even today there is considerable disagreement about what "the mission" that they are to accomplish might be. Before moving on to cinematic versions of missionizing, however, there is one more question we should consider: namely, what it is in human beings that makes us seek out what is different from ourselves? While it is true that Christianity historically has urged its adherents to evangelize, it is also true that many of them have needed little urging. There is something in us that thrives on encounters with what is different from ourselves or with what we perceive to be exotic.

For example, Junípero Serra, whom we will have occasion to discuss shortly, recorded in the eighteenth century his first encounter with the California Indians whom he had come to serve. Explaining that some of his companions had summoned him to meet with these strange new people, Serra wrote, "I came out at once, and found myself in front of twelve of them…. I saw something I could not believe when I had read of it, or had been told about it. It was this: they were entirely naked, as Adam in the garden, before sin."[116] For Serra, the "pagans" of California represented the possibility of starting over, of beginning history anew, of watching the development of civilization all over again. They offered him a kind of innocence that Europe could never hope to recover.

Likewise, contemporary Jesuit priest Daniel Berrigan notes that when he first met the indigenous women actors who would play the Guaraní tribe in Roland Joffe's *The Mission*, they were all wearing matching t-shirts. Apparently the film company had given the shirts as gifts so that the women would have something to cover their normally uncovered breasts. After meeting with these native people, Berrigan wrote a poem in which he exults, "O the dance, the stifled heart/set free/the vowels of birds in a vocal reed,/the body's splendor,/the momentary lost and found/ blaze of the human!"[117] There is something that fascinates in what we perceive to be the "primitive" or "unspoiled" nature of people different from ourselves: the stifled heart set free, the splendid body released from all artificial trappings. As we look at cinematic portrayals of evangelization, we should keep in mind that perhaps missionaries act out of their own desires as much as they act for the glory of Christ. We should also be careful to ask ourselves what draws us to such films: what we believe we have lost, and what we think we might find in cinematic portrayals of "primitives" or "heathen" or "pagans."

Seven Cities of Gold: God, Guns, and Savages

The movie *Seven Cities of Gold* (1955) tells the story of Junípero Serra, a Spanish Franciscan priest who in the eighteenth century founded several Catholic missions along the California coast. In reality, Serra was able to evangelize the native peoples who were living in the area only with the help of the Spanish army, but *Seven Cities of Gold* praises Serra by telling us, "While the conquering army carried muskets, he carried a cross. Where they sought treasure, he sought salvation."

Based on the novel *The Nine Days of Father Serra* by Isabelle Gibson Ziegler, the movie presents itself as being true to the evidence of history. A voice at the beginning of the movie assures us that what we are about to see is a faithful depiction of Serra and his companions: "The only change we have made is to set their words in English." As we will see, however, what the film leaves out may be as important as what it includes. Serra was beatified in 1988, but his cause for canonization is controversial. Critics point out that the priest participated in the devastation of Indian cultures, and they allege that calling him a saint would be to justify Christian triumphalism at the expense of the native peoples who were destroyed.

Seven Cities of Gold opens in 1769 in what was then New Spain and what is now called Mexico. Spain has decided to colonize the upper California coast and is sending expeditions of soldiers both to claim that territory for the Spanish empire and to search for the cities of gold that legend says can be found there. Along with soldiers, the Spaniards send priests to attend to the religious needs of the armies and to establish missions among the native populations. Father Junípero Serra, a native of Mallorca who has lived in New Spain for twenty years despite chronic lameness in one leg, is charged with the spiritual welfare of the expedition that is traveling by land. According to the plan, that company will meet up with another traveling by sea, and together they will establish a mission/fort in San Diego.

Serra, according to the film, is a staunch defender of the Indian peoples of New Spain. As the soldiers prepare to march northward, he offers his blessing to the troops. The prayer is not, however, quite what the soldiers were expecting:

> A long time ago we came to Mexico. We took a group of simple Indians, Indians of childlike love. We turned them into a race of slaves. Their skin was darker than ours, and because of that they were beneath us. And so we told ourselves that it was just. So a handful of soldiers like yourselves stripped them of their gold, their love and their freedom. Now in the dawn of a wonderful mission, you're starting out in the same way. You plan to walk across their fields—to take their gold and leave them nothing. You plan to pillage and plunder and loot and lust, and all because their tongue is strange and their skin is colored. In the name of Saint Joseph and all the saints who surround the throne of God, I say, "How dare you!"

The commander of Serra's company is Captain Gaspar de Portola, played by Anthony Quinn. He is, quite understandably, reluctant to take Father Serra with him on his journey, and he attempts to use the priest's lameness as an excuse to send him back. Serra persists, however, and soon the entire company is headed towards San Diego.

At one point on the journey north, Serra and one of the Spanish soldiers become separated from the rest of the troops and get caught in a dust storm. Seeing a light ahead of them, they follow its beam and find themselves welcomed into a small hut by a beared man wearing a robe, his beautiful wife (dressed in blue) and their infant child. The man and woman silently feed the weary travelers and then smile as the exhausted pair falls asleep at the table. The next morning, Serra and his companion awake under a cactus.

The people in the hut are obviously the Holy Family, an interpretation confirmed by Serra as he discusses the "dream" that both he and the soldier had had during the night. Serra assures his companion that they will soon be rescued, as God would not have preserved them during the storm only to have them die in the desert. Within seconds of his saying this a search party appears, and the two lost travelers are reunited with their compatriots. The clear implication of the scene, in a film that purports to present only "the truth," is that Serra's mission is the work of God.

After several other trials and tribulations, the company that had set out by land finally reaches San Diego, only to find that their sailor counterparts are dying of scurvy, typhus, and hunger; it seems that a drought has plagued the area for quite some time. Eager to begin his work, Serra blesses the ground with holy water. He then hangs a church bell in a tree and strikes it, listening as the peals ring out across the newly-Christianized land. Immediately the rains that have not fallen for six months begin to pour down, and Serra falls to his knees in gratitude. Once more, the movie tells us that God is on the side of Serra and his missions.

It is this claim, that God willed the Spanish colonization of California, that many Native Americans find troubling, to say the least. Historian George Tinker, a Lutheran minister and a member of the Osage Nation, writes, "That Serra was both pious and courageous cannot be doubted." However, he observes, Serra was responsible for founding the California mission system, a system with an ugly legacy:

> The legacy includes forced conversions of native peoples to Christianity and the enforcement of those conversions by imprisonment; physical violence in the form of corporal punishment; the imposition of slave labor conditions on Indian converts…; a living environment that was akin to a concentration camp and cycles of famine and constant poor nourishment that were both unprecedented among these native peoples; an extraordinary death rate among converts; and the devastation of many California native cultures.[118]

Tinker backs his assessment of Serra's work by pointing to the priest's own letters and diary. It is true that at times Serra seems oblivious to the dynamics of power that characterized Spanish interactions with Native Americans. At one point in his journal, Serra records that several of the company's Indian guides had deserted: "We had no notion why. And so, little by little, we find ourselves deprived of the services of these men, who are more useful than people realize, for only a person who is right on the spot can form a proper idea of how hard they have to work—on poor food and no salary."[119] The fact that Serra cannot fathom that native guides might resent working in such poor conditions shows a blindness that could not help but impair his ability to serve them.

Tinker's primary charge against Serra is that the priest acted as an extension of the Spanish government and the Spanish army. Indeed, Serra describes himself as being part of the conquest (*conquista*) of California, and he notes that, upon reaching the site of Monterey, he and his compatriots erected at one and the same time a large cross and the Royal Standard. After Serra had celebrated the Mass, he tells us, "the officers performed the official act of taking possession of the country in the name of the King, our Lord, whom God keep."[120]

This interdependence of God and guns in the conquest of California is deliberately minimized by *Seven Cities of Gold*, however. Over and over again in that film, Father Serra is depicted as defying the army's desire to conquer by force. When the soldiers wish to shoot a small band of native men whom they encounter on the trail, Serra instead approaches the group and offers them beads in exchange for safe passage. When the captain takes a native man prisoner in a skirmish at the fort, Serra treats the man's wounds and sets him free. Far from being an agent of Spain, the Franciscan is depicted as actually subverting the Spanish soldiers' intentions.

Moreover, there is nothing in the movie that would suggest that Serra's efforts at conversion were anything but laudatory. The native Californians are depicted as creatures less-than-human; they walk with a hunched-over gait and stare up at Serra with what can only be described as bestial stupidity. They do not speak so much as grunt, and they seem to have no religious beliefs or traditions of their own. When the priest gathers some of them into the mission to cut their hair and give them European-style clothes, they do not react with outrage but rather with the delight of children. If one knew nothing of the complexity and dignity of native traditions, one might be convinced by this film that Christianity offered the natives both spiritual and cultural enlightenment. Seeing how they are portrayed, it is easy to believe that they were truly far better off under the tutelage of the kindly priest and his soldiers.

As history shows, however, this was not the case. *Seven Cities of Gold* ends with Serra ringing a brand-new mission bell that has been brought to him by a supply ship from Mexico. As he listens to its timbre, he muses to himself, "A voice clear and loud—one my Indians will love. I can hear them coming. I can hear them coming!" Unfortunately, the more Indian people came to the missions, the more they died. One scholar estimates that in the sixty years between 1770 and 1830, roughly three-fourths of the native population living on the missions died; annual death rates approached 10 percent for adults and 15 percent for children.[121]

Moreover, those living under the direction of the Franciscan priests faced cruel treatment. Serra himself demanded of the local officials that his Franciscans be given the power to punish the Indian people, requesting that "no chastisement or ill-treatment should be inflicted on any of them whether by Officer or by any soldier, without the Missionary Father's passing upon it. This has been the time-honored practice of this kingdom ever since the conquest; and it is quite in conformity with the law of nature concerning the education of the children, and an essential condition for the rightful training of the poor neophytes."[122] History tells us that such punishments included whipping with a barbed lash, mutilation, branding, use of stocks, and execution.[123] Moreover, once native people entered the mission, they were not free to leave. They were required to attend Catholic worship services and were discouraged from consorting with family members who had not yet come under the control of the missions. For peoples used to relying on the support and affections of an extended family, such isolation was a particular hardship.

Given this historical evidence, it is difficult to watch *Seven Cities of Gold*. The movie asks its audience to cheer when Father Serra is finally able to establish his missions for the salvation of God's Indian children, and yet we know that those missions will have a devastating effect on the tribes that they touch. It is one thing to believe that people must be converted in order to be saved. It is quite another to say that bringing such salvation is worth any risk at all, even the destruction of tens of thousands of lives.

In contrast to *Seven Cities of Gold*, *The Mission* (whose screenplay was written by Robert Bolt) makes every effort to portray native people on screen with dignity and complexity. The Guaraní tribespeople in the film are neither savage monsters nor simple-minded children. They speak their own language and wear their own clothing. They are human beings with their own traditions and ways of relating to the world, human beings who find themselves caught up in forces of history beyond their control. Those forces, as the film makes clear, exact a terrible toll.

The Short-Lived Mercy of Men: *The Mission*[124]

When Father Gabriel climbs the cliffs that will lead him to the Guaraní, he does so with the conviction that these native people living in what are now Argentina, Paraguay, and Brazil are truly God's children. Unfortunately, the Portuguese government that is about to gain power over the territory is not of the same mind. To that government and to the slave-traders rubbing their hands in anticipation of the fortunes they will make, the Guaraní are fit for nothing more than servitude: "These creatures are lethal and lecherous. They will have to be subdued by the sword and brought to profitable labor by the whip," one of them declares. At issue in *The Mission* is whether or not the Jesuit missionaries who have been working with the Guaraní will submit to the orders of the Vatican and allow those people now to be enslaved.

The history of the Jesuit missions in South America is complicated and fascinating. The missions were first founded in the seventeenth century as a response to the miserable conditions to which native peoples had been subjected under Spanish rule. According to the law of Spain, colonized people in the New World could be forced to labor for a local Spanish official who in turn was charged with their protection and religious instruction. Though Spain officially forbade slavery, this *encomienda* system that it had established in South America was in practice just as bad.

Seeing the deplorable conditions in which native peoples were kept, the Jesuits by contrast set up what were called reductions (*reducciones*) that emphasized cooperative labor for the benefit of all. On the reductions, land was owned communally and tools came from a common supply. The Indian peoples cultivated wheat, rice, cotton, and fruit, among other crops, and the yields were distributed among the workers according to their needs. The Guaraní, whose lives and history are featured in *The Mission*, were adept at trades such as carpentry, stone-cutting, and weaving, and they had artistic skill in painting, calligraphy and music. The reductions developed plumbing systems that rivaled anything available in Europe, and their residents enjoyed a level of health that had never been possible under the *encomienda* system.[125]

The Reductions were not utopias; the Jesuits there instituted corporal punishments for people who committed infractions of the rules just as the Franciscans did on their missions in California. However, by all accounts such punishment on the reductions was used sparingly, and capital punishment was not permitted. Moreover, governance of the *reducciones* was less in the hands of the Jesuits than in those of the native residents. Leaders were elected on a regular basis, and the Jesuits encouraged communal decision-making. Unlike the Franciscans in California, the Jesuits had no army with which to enforce their rule over the native people; on the contrary, the reductions developed their own armies to defend themselves against hostile neighbors and against the Portuguese.

The reductions in *The Mission* reflect the high level of technical and artistic sophistication that marked the real-life *reducciones*. When in the film a Vatican official named Cardinal Altamirano goes to visit one of the missionary communities, he is greeted by a children's choir singing in Latin and accompanied by violinists. As he walks through the mission's fields he is impressed by the systems of irrigation and cultivation that he finds there. Moreover, the cardinal is fascinated by the cooperative spirit of the Guaraní. Expressing his surprise that the fruits of the people's labor are held in common, he is told by one of the workers, "It was a doctrine of the early Christians."[126]

Despite his amazement at the abilities of the people whom he had expected to be primitive and savage, however, Cardinal Altamirano orders that the reductions be closed and that their residents either be transferred to Spanish territory or face enslavement at the hands of the Portuguese who are taking control. He does this, he explains, for the good of the Church; the Vatican cannot afford to anger the Portuguese government. Father Gabriel and his fellow Jesuits are outraged at the decision, but the cardinal remains resolute. If the missionaries resist, he warns, then the Jesuit order of priests and brothers will be expelled from Portugal. For the sake of the universal Church and for the sake of the Jesuits, the missionaries must comply with the Vatican's orders.

What follows in the film is a series of conversations between the Jesuits and the Guaraní, on the one hand, and among the Jesuits themselves on the other. Father Gabriel, a judicious man who is reluctant to disobey the cardinal's orders, attempts to convince the Guaraní to return to the forests in which they used to live. True, there they will be preyed upon by slave traders, but at least they will not be easily caught. The Guaraní object to this plan, however. They remind the priest that, in the words of one of them, "The Devil lives there."

Here we see one of the most tragic aspects of Christian missionary efforts in South America. No matter how beneficial the reductions were in the lives of the native peoples, and the evidence is overwhelming that they were amazingly beneficial, they nonetheless were part of a process of colonization that ended in the destruction of those people's cultures and traditions. The Guaraní had formerly been a nomadic group with little interest in stabilized agriculture. They had relied primarily on hunting and fishing for their livelihood rather than on the cultivation of crops. When the Spanish and Portuguese took control of their territories, however, the native people were encouraged, often at the point of a gun, to restrict their movements and to work for the good of their overseers. The reductions, though they operated on the principle of communal cooperation and though they respected the Indian peoples as free human beings, nonetheless contributed to the end of the Guaraní's earlier way of life. Thus, when the reductions were threatened, there could be no simple return to the forests.

With that option gone, the Jesuits in the film must decide how they will respond to the Vatican's orders. Two divergent paths emerge. Father Gabriel, relying on the power of non-violent resistance, will lead his people in prayer as heavily armed slave-traders and mercenaries invade the mission. He declares, "If might makes right, then love has no place in the world." His friend and spiritual son Mendoza, however, opts for violent resistance, insisting that he cannot simply leave the Guaraní to be slaughtered or enslaved. In the end, neither strategy is vindicated by the film. Both Gabriel and Mendoza are killed in the battle that destroys the mission, and only a few Guaraní children are left at the end to carry on the memory of the Jesuits' work. Reflecting on the role that he has played in the destruction of the *reduccion*, Cardinal Altamirano remarks bitterly, "So it was that the Indians of the Guaraní were brought finally to account to the everlasting mercy of God—and to the short-lived mercy of men."

The Mission was released in 1986 and must be understood not simply as a historical drama but also as a commentary on the politics of its time. Peace activist Daniel Berrigan, a Jesuit priest who plays a small role in the film, remarks that the movie "is an accurate image of Nicaragua and Afghanistan and Northern Ireland and South Africa." It is about our human history of oppression and bloodshed, he says, "that trackless world of pain and disappearance, of hope deferred and heroism unquenched."[127] *The Mission*, like *Romero*, is best read in light of the liberation theologies that had come to the fore in Latin America. Unlike *Romero*, however, this movie refuses to take a stand on the question of violence; neither Father Gabriel nor Mendoza is held up as the best model to follow. Instead, that choice is left for viewers to ponder for themselves.

While *The Mission* raises issues about the proper role of the missionary, it cannot quite bring itself to ask if the missionary endeavor itself should be called into question. That is, the film is unabashed in its admiration for the evangelical zeal of the Jesuits. When in the opening scene Father Gabriel scales that rocky cliff in his bare feet, clinging precariously to the tiny crevices that mark the cliff's face, we cannot help but be awed by his determination. When he ventures into the Amazon Forest to met the Guaraní armed with nothing other than his flute, we are overwhelmed by his courage. Though the movie does not hesitate to show the tragedy that followed the Jesuits' efforts to evangelize the native peoples, there is no sense in the film that the priests should have stayed in Europe or that the Guaraní would have been better off if they had never encountered Christianity.

By contrast, such pessimism about Christian evangelization is precisely the message of another movie about Jesuit incursions into the New World. *Black Robe*, which takes its title from the distinctive garb worn by Jesuit priests, asks why Christians should ever feel it necessary to convert people who already have their own religious traditions, traditions that may be superior to the missionaries' own. *Black Robe* is a bleak and violent movie, and, as we will see, it forces us to ask if missionaries are saints or terrible fools.

"Do You Love Us?:" *Black Robe*

Black Robe (1991) is based on the novel of the same name by Brian Moore. Moore was inspired to write his book after reading about the life of Saint Noel Chabanel, a seventeenth-century Jesuit missionary to the Huron people native to what is now Canada. Chabanel was apparently not the most successful of evangelists. After several years of practice he could not learn even the rudiments of the Huron language. As one of his brother Jesuits wrote, "This was no little mortification to a man who burned with desire for the conversion of the Savages...." Chabanel detested the Hurons and the conditions in which they lived: "There, one must always sleep on the bare ground, and live from morning to night in a little hell of smoke; in a place where often, of a morning, one finds himself covered with the snows that drift on all sides into the cabins of the Savages; where vermin abound; where the senses, each and all, are tormented both night and day." Despite his aversion to the native people, or, more precisely, because of it, Chabanel made a sacred promise not to give in to what he saw as the temptations of the Devil to return to France. On the Feast of Corpus Christi (the day that honors the body of Christ) in 1647, he declared, "I, Noel Chabanel,—being in the presence of the most holy Sacrament of your Body and your precious Blood, which is the tabernacle of God among men— make a vow of perpetual stability in this Mission of the Hurons."[128] His desire to complete his life as a missionary was fulfilled. He was murdered in 1649 by a member of the Huron tribe, a man who had abandoned his earlier conversion to Christianity.

What are we to make of Chabanel, a missionary who despised the very people whom he had come to serve? Why would he persist in living in what was for him an intolerable situation? What drove him to bind himself ever more tightly to what he simply could not love? These are the questions that drive both Moore's novel and the cinematic version of *Black Robe*, whose screenplay Moore also wrote. In the end, we will have to decide for ourselves whether Father Laforgue (Chabanel's cinematic counterpart) was saintly or arrogant, exceptionally holy or merely stubborn. The film itself raises these questions about the value of missionary activity, and it answers them by suggesting that the Jesuits may have been better off being converted by the Huron rather than trying to convert that people to Christianity.

Black Robe opens in Quebec in 1634. Father Laforgue (Lothaire Bluteau) is being sent by his superior to the Jesuit mission in the land of the Hurons. At the request of Samuel de Champlain, a group of Algonquin families has agreed to escort Laforgue to his destination. The trip will be arduous: 1500 miles by canoe, much of it in hostile territory. Despite the fact that he speaks Algonquin and Huron only imperfectly, Laforgue is eager to venture to the mission outpost. He is anxious to win the Huron over to God, reminding his young companion Daniel, "If we do not change them, how can they enter heaven?" Though two other Jesuits have been living for some time at the remote mission, they have not been heard from in some time, and it is not clear if they are even still alive.

Daniel, a Frenchman who is contemplating joining the Jesuit order and who has mastered several indigenous languages, is not convinced by Laforgue's fervor. On the contrary, as he sees it, the native people are more generous and kindhearted than are their European counterparts. When Laforgue declares, "The Devil rules here. He controls the hearts and minds of these poor people," Daniel protests: "But they are true Christians. They live for each other. They forgive things we would never forgive." Daniel, who has agreed to accompany Laforgue on his journey to the Hurons, clearly appreciates the culture of the Algonquins. He smokes with the Indians and eats with them, and he manages to catch the eye of a young Algonquin woman named Annuka, daughter of Chomina, the expedition's leader.

In contrast, like Noel Chabanel, Laforgue can barely hide his disgust with the Indian people's way of life. He detests their food and their smoky dwellings. He is scandalized by their scatological jokes and by what he sees as an immorally loose sexuality. As the movie shows, Laforgue himself is not above the temptations of the flesh. One night, unable to sleep because of the smoke of the fire, he ventures outside into the dark night. There he stumbles upon Daniel and Annuka making love in the forest. The priest is aroused by the uninhibited coupling of the two, but he is also horrified by his own arousal. Mortified by his fleshly weakness, he desperately rips a branch from a nearby tree and whips himself until his temptation has passed. Unlike the Algonquin, he is frightened by and ill at ease with his own bodily needs.

With his dour demeanor and his unyielding piety, Laforgue is clearly an enigma to the Algonquin. They cannot understand why the Blackrobe's God would demand that he have no women in his life, or what he is doing when he paces up and down reading his breviary. They do not see why he grows hair on his face or why, when he tries to speak their language, he sounds so ridiculous. They laugh when he must relieve his bowels by squatting over the edge of the canoe, but they resent the fact that though he has tobacco in his pack, he will not share it with them. When the Algonquin party meets up with a group of Montagnais people along the way, they discuss Laforgue with the local shaman, a dwarf named Mestigoit. Mestigoit convinces the Algonquin that the priest is a demon and that no good can come from his presence. Taking his advice, the Algonquin (and Daniel as well, who decides to pursue his love of Annuka) abandon Laforgue.

As it happens, however, the leader Chomina comes to regret his decision and decides to turn his canoe around; after all, he had promised to make sure that the priest reached his destination safely. He, his family, and Daniel return to the spot where they had left Laforgue, only to be ambushed there by a small band of Iroquois. Chomina's wife is killed instantly, and his son is killed before his eyes when the group is taken back to the Iroquois camp. (Here the movie spares us some of the details of Moore's novel which involve cannibalism.)

Aware that they will be tortured the next morning, Chomina warns Daniel and Laforgue not to cry out during their ordeal; if they do, he says, when they die the Iroquois will take possession of their spirits. Laforgue answers that when he dies he will go to Paradise, and he begs Chomina to allow him to baptize him so that he can go there as well. Chomina responds, "Why would I go to your Paradise? Are my people there? My woman? My boy? It is only Blackrobes." This is one of several conversations in the film about the afterlife. Earlier, Laforgue had explained to a group of skeptical Algonquin men that there would be no tobacco in heaven and no sex with women: that they would be happy just to be with God. When Daniel tells Laforgue that the Algonquin believe in an afterlife in which the souls of men hunt the souls of animals, Laforgue dismisses this idea as childish. Daniel challenges him: "Is it harder to believe in than a Paradise where we all sit on clouds and look at God?" Laforgue has no answer.

As it turns out, Chomina's warnings about torture are not necessary, as the captives manage to escape from the Iroquois. Chomina, however, falls ill soon after. When the time comes for Chomina to die, Laforgue attempts to baptize him once again but is refused: "Leave, my friend," Chomina tells him. He prefers to wait alone for the She-Manitou to come to take him to the place of the dead.

When Laforgue, who has ordered Daniel to take Annuka back to her people, finally reaches the Huron mission, he finds that one of the Jesuits is dead and the other nearly so. The mission is snow-covered and bleak; only black branches and a huge wooden cross stand out against the icy landscape. Laforgue himself is a changed man. His face is haggard and his spirit is weary. He is no longer sure of his mission or what he ought to believe. When shortly after his arrival the one remaining Jesuit dies, Laforgue asks, "Lord, why is Father Jerome with you in heaven? While Chomina lies forever in outer darkness. Help me."

Father Jerome dies of a fever that is raging through the mission. In fact, his companion priest had been murdered only shortly before Laforgue's arrival by a man whose child had died and who blamed the sickness on the priests. There are some at the mission who resent the Christians' incursions into their land: "The Blackrobes want us…to stop killing our enemies. If we obey them we will no longer be Hurons. And soon our enemies will know our weakness and wipe us from the earth." They plan to torture and kill Laforgue.

The only thing that stops them from carrying out their plan is a rumor that those who are baptized will be spared the sickness. A group approaches Laforgue and asks him to help them—to baptize them and thus preserve their lives. The priest is hesitant. He knows that a baptism will not heal them, and he is reluctant to baptize those who are not truly converted. The group persists, however. One man looks straight into the eyes of Laforgue and asks, "Do you love us?" Instantly we see flashback scenes from Laforgue's life with the native peoples: shots of Chomina and of the faces of the Iroquois torturers, of Mestigoit and of an old Algonquin woman. Laforgue summons every ounce of strength that he has left and answers, "Yes." He agrees to baptize them. As the baptisms take place, we see the dark wooden cross outlined against the bleak landscape, lighted only by the departing sun. A few men stand outside the chapel, refusing to take part in the ritual going on inside. Slowly, all but one turn and walk away.

There are at least two ways of interpreting the final scenes of *Blackrobe*. One interpretation is offered by Peter Fraser in his book *Images of the Passion: The Sacramental Mode in Film*. Fraser argues that the film is about "the triumph of God and the Church." He explains, "What the Indians' animistic world lacks is love, a God who is personal and compassionate, and whose messengers are likewise. The dwarf Mestigoit becomes in this context an excellent representative of the great lack of love at the heart of the Indian world-view."[129] The cross at the end of the film, in Fraser's view, signifies redemption through suffering borne in love.

Several factors militate against such an interpretation, however. First there is the fact that the native people in the film are for the most part far more attractive than any of the Europeans. Chomina in particular is a man of integrity and wisdom who clearly loves his family. He is also a man of great courage and strength, as we see during the scenes at the Iroquois camp. By contrast, Daniel, though well-intentioned, is naive; he romanticizes life among the Algonquin and cannot believe that they would ever treat people the way the Iroquois do, despite Chomina's assurances to the contrary.

For his part, Laforgue is a thoroughly unattractive character. He is courageous, to be sure, but his courage seems born more of resignation than of hope. He cannot bring himself to appreciate the warmth and humor of the Algonquin, not even of the children who attempt to climb onto his lap or who steal his black hat and toss it about in play. Convinced that they are in the grip of the Devil, he sees the Algonquin solely as potential converts rather than as people to be enjoyed and appreciated as they are. When he is abandoned by his escort party, he comforts himself by praying, "Thou has given me this cross for Thy honor, and for the salvation of these poor barbarians. I thank Thee." In truth, Laforgue's only truly human moment comes when the Huron ask, "Do you love us?" When he answers, "Yes," we have the impression that he loves them in spite of his Christian beliefs and not because of them. He has had to stop clinging to his dogmas and laws in order to come to a simple recognition of the Hurons' humanity.

In addition to showing the priest in a less-than-sympathetic light, the movie goes out of its way to show that the Europeans are in no way superior to the Algonquin. A striking sequence near the film's beginning makes this point. As Champlain and Chomina prepare for the ceremony in which Laforgue will be entrusted to the care of the Algonquin, we see the two leaders dressing themselves. One puts on a medal, , the other puts on paint. One dons a hat with a plume, the other arranges feathers in his hair. Both put on robes of furs. They approach the ceremony as Algonquin men beat drums and dance, and as French traders play something akin to an accordion and dance. The encounter of the French with the Algonquin, the movie indicates, is not a case of civilization meeting barbarity but rather of competing civilizations and competing barbarities.

The second factor that should lead us to question Fraser's interpretation is the fact that Chomina's beliefs about death and the afterlife are vindicated by the film. As he lies dying in the cold, Chomina sees a beautiful woman appear in the woods; it is the She-Manitou who has come to take him to the place where men's souls hunt the souls of animals. Of this scene, Fraser writes, "How this should be interpreted—as dream or vision, hallucination, fact or strange intervention of God Himself—is left open."[130] However, there is no reason to question the reality of the She-Manitou. There is even less justification for believing her to be an intervention of the Christian God. The fact that this scene is included, and that there is no comparable scene at the death of Father Jerome, should lead us to wonder if Fraser's interpretation isn't simply a bit of wishful thinking or, worse, an example of Christian imperialism akin to Laforgue's.

The third reason to question the idea that *Black Robe* is about the triumph of Christianity is that the film ends on an exceedingly somber note. As the sun sets and the Algonquin men turn their backs to the chapel, the following words appear on the screen: "Fifteen years later, the Hurons, having accepted Christianity, were routed and killed by their enemies, the Iroquois. The Jesuit mission to the Hurons was abandoned and the Jesuits returned to Quebec." It is difficult to interpret this as a positive message about the role that Christianity played in the lives of the Huron. On the contrary, it bolsters the prediction that the men on the mission had made earlier: that Christianity would make them weak and that their enemies would then destroy them. Moreover, the fact that the

Jesuits eventually abandoned the mission would indicate that there was no final triumph. The Christians simply retreated from what they saw as their mission and returned to the relatively safer world from which they had come.

Rather than being about the victory of God and the Church, *Black Robe* is an exploration of one man's faith and of the consequences of that faith. It does not ask us to admire Laforgue. It asks only that we acknowledge his stoic commitment to his mission as extraordinary. Why did he feel it necessary to leave his home in France and live his life among people whom he despised? The film hints at two reasons: fascination with "the savages" and a desire for saintly glory. Are these enough to justify imposing his beliefs and his culture on the natives of the New World? The film suggests that they are not. While it recognizes Laforgue's faith, it leaves viewers with a sense that that faith is tragically misplaced. Critic Roger Ebert summarizes his reaction to the movie this way: "...when it was over, I sat there in a state of depressed suspension, wondering if that could possibly be all there was.... It was as if the entire story of *Black Robe* was a prelude to nothing."[131] The film asks us to consider that perhaps the same might be said about the missionary endeavor itself.

Making Disciples of All Nations

There can be no doubt that many of the men and women who left their homes and families to preach the Gospel in foreign lands were heroic in piety and devotion. Reflecting on Jesuit Noel Chabanel's promise to remain with the Algonquin despite his aversion to them, the author of the novel *Black Robe* muses, "*A solemn vow. A voice speaks to us directly from the seventeenth century, the voice of a conscience that, I fear, we no longer possess.*"[132] It is difficult for most of us to imagine the kind of courage it would take to leave home, family, language and the comfort of all that is familiar in order to venture into an unknown and often dangerous world.

Clearly it can be said of missionaries that there were and are many saints among their number. Clearly there have also been many scoundrels, and at times missionary efforts have brought nothing but sorrow and bloodshed. What this chapter has tried to do is to show how movies have dealt with this complexity in evangelization. Some films simply ignore that complexity altogether and portray their protagonists as unambiguously holy and uniformly beneficent. Others wrestle with it quite openly, acknowledging that those who brought God sometimes brought tragedy in their wake.

There are hints in all of the movies that we have discussed here of the role that wonder-working has played in the spread of Christianity. For example, in *Seven Cities of Gold*, Serra is able to lure one of the Indian leaders to the mission with a promise that he will teach him how to make the mission bell ring. The Algonquin in *Black Robe* sit for long periods of time watching Champlain's timepiece tick, until to their amazement "Captain Clock" finally rings out. Many early missionaries gained reputations for the miracles that they performed. Saint Joseph Anchieta, for example, one of the first Jesuit missionaries to Brazil, is remembered primarily as a wonder-worker. It was believed that Joseph could tame wild birds and that he could prophesy the future. A touch of his cloak, it was said, could heal the sick. He was able to perform his duties as a missionary in part because of his talent for miracles. As we will see in the next chapter, wonder-working has long been part of Christian tradition. As we will also see, it is a phenomenon that has found no little treatment in film.

6   The Miracle Worker

Introduction

Jonas Nightengale can work miracles. From twenty paces, he can tell exactly what a woman hopes God will do for her. He can just look at a man and know what disease afflicts him. He can make the mute sing and the deaf hear—or at least so he says. What the movie audience knows as they watch Preacher Nightengale (played by Steve Martin) on the screen is that he is a fraud. He cannot read people's minds. He knows what the faithful are wishing for only because his accomplices have been out in the congregation making small-talk with the crowd, and they feed their information to the "miracle-worker" through a tiny transmitter in his ear.

In Richard Pearce's *Leap of Faith* (1992), Jonas Nightengale is a con man who has no qualms whatsoever about duping the faithful out of their hard-earned money. Under cover of darkness, he repaints the huge crucifix that dominates his revival tent so that the statue of Jesus seems to open its eyes miraculously. He offers an elderly but able-bodied woman a wheelchair to sit in, and then at the height of his performance he brings her up on stage, prays over her, and commands her to walk. When she rises from her chair, the crowd erupts in jubilation.[133] All of this Nightengale does in the name of free enterprise and good entertainment. When questioned by a suspicious small-town sheriff, he defends himself: "I give my people a good show. Plenty of music. Worthwhile sentiments. And most of them go home with a little hope in their lives that wasn't there before."

The trouble comes when Jonas discovers that he is a little too good at what he does. Among the faithful at the revival meetings is a crippled adolescent named Boyd who pins all his hopes on Nightengale's healing powers. The irony of the film, of course, is that in the end, Boyd's dream of walking without his crutches is fulfilled. When the preacher confesses that he is not really a man of God, the boy asks, "What difference does it make if you get the job done?" Jonas looks at him steadily and says, "Kid, it makes every difference in the world." That night Jonas leaves his traveling road show behind, observing sadly, "The one thing you can never ever get around is the genuine article."

Was Boyd's cure really "the genuine article"? Was it really an instance of divine intervention? Did it come about because Nightengale's tricks somehow freed the boy from the psychological obstacles that prevented his walking, and if that is the case, was the cure any less miraculous? The film leaves all of these questions open, asking viewers to come up with their own answers. But before we could even begin to respond, we need to come to a clear understanding of just what a miracle might be. Definitions of the term have ranged from divine intervention to mass hypnosis of the gullible. How movies have portrayed miracles and miracle-workers depends to a large degree on what sort of definition they adopt.

Miracle: What a Coincidence!

Any number of saints have been remembered as working miracles while they walked the earth. One need only think of Saint Patrick driving the snakes from Ireland, or Saint Blaise healing the child with a fishbone stuck in his throat, or Saint Thecla taming the wild beasts in the arena. However, saintliness and miracle-working are related not only because some saints have been said to work miracles while they lived. Most saints, according to Catholic tradition, have worked miracles after their deaths. Since at least the sixth century, posthumous miracle-working has been a preeminent factor in deciding who qualifies for sainthood. Moreover, in the last four centuries, miracle-working has come to be an actual prerequisite for canonization.[134] No matter how holy a person may have been, he or she still needs God's seal of approval before being declared a saint, and that seal is believed to be the working of miracles.

Yet, we must come to grips with the fact that for many contemporary people, the idea that the dead can intercede with God to perform favors for the living seems ludicrous at best. The Enlightenment heritage that many of us share assures us that the world works according to regular laws and predictable processes. In this context, miracles can seem nothing other than literally in-credible. Since that is the case, we need to approach the subject of miracles with care, with as few assumptions as possible, and with as open a mind as we can muster.

Imagine, then, the following scenario: a toddler is in the path of an oncoming train. There is a curve in the railroad tracks such that it would be impossible for the engineer to see the child in time to prevent the train from hitting him. Suddenly, just a few feet from the boy, the train comes to a stop, and the toddler is spared.

The events in this scenario, offered by philosopher R. F. Holland [135], would for many people constitute a miracle. How else to account for the fact that the child does not perish under the crushing steel of the locomotive? Indeed, many would hold to their conviction that the occurrence is miraculous even were they told that the train stopped for perfectly natural reasons. As Holland develops his scenario, he explains that some distance down the tracks, the engineer had fainted due to a sudden rise in blood pressure about which the man's doctor had warned him but against which the man had not taken proper precautions. When the engineer's hand stopped exerting pressure on the control lever, an automatic brake system kicked in, and the brakes happened to stop the train just short of where the child was playing. Divine intervention or natural occurrence?

In his discussion, Holland distinguishes between two meanings of the word "miracle." The first is what he calls the "contingency concept," in which a miracle is a coincidence of events regarded as significant and impressive enough that those who witness it feel moved religiously. Under this interpretation, the fact that the train stopped before it hit a child could indeed be called miraculous. Holland explains that "the kind of thing that, outside religion, we call luck is in religious parlance the grace of God or a miracle of God."[136] If the train had stopped before hitting a paper cup left lying on the tracks, no one would have thought twice about it. It is the fact that a *child's* life was spared that we interpret as divine providence, or as God's action on humans' behalf.

Most people, however, think of a miracle as something impossible, something that simply could not happen at all without the intervention of God. This second concept of the miraculous has numerous cinematic incarnations, and so we will spend a fair amount of time examining it.

Miracle: Violating the Laws of Nature

Holland contrasts his contingency concept of miracles with what he calls the "violation concept," or a definition in which something is miraculous to the extent that it disrupts the natural order of events. According to this second definition, a miracle "must at least be something the occurrence of which can be categorized at one and the same time as empirically certain and conceptually impossible."[137] For example, Holland asks us to "suppose that something happened which was truly bizarre, like my rising slowly and steadily three feet into the air and staying there."[138] If we could satisfy ourselves that his hovering off the ground was due to no trick or natural cause, then we would be on our way towards verifying a miracle in Holland's second or "violation" sense of the term.

It is interesting that Holland chooses the example of his rising into the air, because levitation is precisely what is at issue in the 1962 film *The Reluctant Saint: The Story of Saint Joseph of Cupertino.* Joseph of Cupertino was born in 1603 in Italy, the rather doltish son of poor peasants. According to his biographers, after he was accepted as a brother in the Franciscan Order and subsequently ordained a priest, he acquired the gift of flight. It is said that on one occasion when he caught sight of a statue of the Virgin Mary, Joseph flew about a dozen paces over the heads of witnesses in order to arrive at the foot of the statue.[139] On another occasion he is reported to have flown seven or eight feet into the air to kiss a statue of the infant Jesus.

Joseph is not the only saint whose biography includes episodes of levitation. Saint Christina the Astonishing (d. 1224) is said to have awakened in her coffin and flown to the rafters of the church in which her funeral was being held. She refused to come down because she was repulsed by the smell of sinful human bodies.[140] Teresa of Avila records in her autobiography that on one occasion the nuns in her convent had to hold her to the floor to prevent her body from rising up during Mass.[141] Levitation is reported to have occurred in the lives of over two hundred saints and holy persons in the Catholic tradition. It is also a phenomenon attested to by other religions.

The Reluctant Saint accepts reports about Joseph's extraordinary abilities at face value. The movie begins with this assurance to viewers: "The story you are about to see is true in its essential details." It takes us to 1623 Cupertino where Joseph, aged twenty, bumbles about the village as a clumsy but good-hearted oaf. After his mother convinces her brother, a

Franciscan priest, to take Joseph in, the young man is admitted to the religious brotherhood and is set to work in the stables. Through a series of unlikely events he manages to pass the exams necessary for ordination, and in his gratitude he prays to a statue of Saint Mary, the mother of Jesus. As he prays he rises slowly off of the ground, a phenomenon that is repeated when he celebrates his first Mass. At this point his fellow Franciscans report his behavior to their superiors, and an investigation begins.

In Holland's second definition of the miraculous, recall, a miracle "must *at least* be something the occurrence of which can be categorized at one and the same time as empirically certain and conceptually impossible." The phrase "at least" means that for something truly to be a miracle in this sense, a further criterion would have to be met: namely, that the event can be attributed to a deity. Unless that condition is satisfied (and it is unclear in Holland's writing precisely how one might verify it), rising three feet into the air cannot be called a miracle. Observes Holland, "From a religious point of view it would either signify nothing at all or else be regarded as a sign of devilry; and if the phenomenon persisted I should think that a religious person might well have recourse to exorcism...."[142] This is precisely what happens to poor Saint Joseph. Not everyone is convinced that his flights come from God; some accuse him instead of witchcraft.

One of the priests who is most disturbed by the flying Joseph is a Franciscan priest named Don Raspi, played by Ricardo Montalban. Don Raspi argues that Joseph is not holy but is rather "the Devil's genius" who is playing tricks on his brother priests. Through his "sorcery" he has duped and bewitched them all. Thunders Raspi, "I charge that Lucifer himself is working through this young man!" Note the double-sided charge that is levied against Joseph. On the one hand, Joseph is not an instrument of God but rather of the Devil. His powers come from Satan, and he must be tried by the Inquisitional Court. On the other hand, he is not really flying at all and has merely deceived the others into thinking that he has miraculous powers.

This ambivalence is common in the history of Christians' encounters with non-Christian wonder-workers. Suspicion of fraud mingles with fear that devilish powers are at work; the tendency to scoff is tempered by caution, lest one offend the all-too-real forces of darkness. For example, we can read testimony from the Acts of Peter, a Christian text that was recorded some time after the second century. In this book, the apostle Peter engages in contests with a man named Simon the Magician (who also makes an appearance in the New Testament's Acts of the Apostles) to see which of the two is truly a servant of God. One round of the tournament has Simon trying to raise a man from the dead. In a scene that could serve as inspiration for the popular film *Weekend at Bernie's*, the magician holds the dead man's head in his hands and makes him open his eyes and bow to Peter. The crowd is astonished, but Peter sees through the hoax; as soon as Simon's hands are removed from the corpse, it falls back to the ground in a heap, and thus Simon is shown to be a fraud. In another scene, the magician astonishes the crowds by rising into the air and flying over the temples and hills of Rome. Peter, gazing at his rival, prays, "Make haste, Lord, with your grace; and let him fall down from this height." Immediately Simon falls and breaks his leg in three places. A few days later, we are told, "Simon, the angel of the Devil, ended his life."[143] Was Simon a clever con man along the lines of Jonas Nightengale, or was he powered by Satan? Was he merely deceptive or was he allied with the forces of evil? The Acts of Peter isn't interested in the distinction; deception is assumed to be demonic. Likewise, *The Reluctant Saint* doesn't consider the possibility that the saint's flights are simply harmless entertainment. Trickster or demon, Joseph is taken into custody, imprisoned in the bowels of the Franciscan monastery, and subjected to an exorcism.

Interestingly, Joseph himself accepts this treatment without protest. When a friend asks why he is being imprisoned, Joseph replies, "It's for my own good." He endures an all-night ceremony while chained to the ground (Satan, we are told, is unable to break strong metal bonds), and when morning comes, Don Raspi pronounces Joseph "no longer possessed by the Devil." Nonetheless, poor Joseph is left chained up to ponder his sins. As the cadre of priests prepares to leave the penitent to his meditations in the dungeon, the inevitable occurs. Joseph's chains fall away, and he flies out the window of his cell into brilliant sunlight. Don Raspi falls to his knees in adoration, and Joseph's holiness is finally confirmed. He is canonized, the movie informs us, in 1767.

Anyone watching *The Reluctant Saint* (anyone, that is, except the most credulous) will come away from the movie with a number of questions. First of all, how could someone ever verify that the event in question really took place? Maybe Joseph accomplished his flights with nothing more than smoke and mirrors. Maybe he was simply a good athlete along the lines of basketball player Michael Jordan, who often seemed suspended in air as he slam-dunked two points for the Chicago Bulls. Or maybe the whole episode is the product of superstitious imaginations, embellished to the point of absurdity. In *The Reluctant Saint*, one priest claims that Joseph hovered two feet above the ground, another swears that it was five feet, and still another testifies to three times that. Who knows what actually took place?

Further, even if we could determine that the flights really took place, how could we conclude beyond a shadow of a doubt that they were not due to some process known at the time but lost to modern science? In other words, how do we know that what is "conceptually impossible" to us was impossible to our ancestors or will be to our descendants? Just a century or two ago it would have been conceptually impossible that I could speak into a small device in my hand and be heard by someone on the other side of the globe, and yet today cell phones are taken for granted by much of the world.

These kinds of questions have been asked about miracles since at least the eighteenth century, when the skeptic philosopher David Hume published his famous work *An Enquiry Concerning Human Understanding*. In that book, Hume considers the possibility of miracles (which he defines as violations of the laws of nature) and concludes that there is no good evidence to believe that they have ever taken place. His arguments are more practical than theoretical. He observes, for instance, that "there is not to be found, in all history, any miracle attested by a sufficient number of men, of such unquestioned good sense, education, and learning, as to secure us against all delusion...."[144] He adds that reports of miracles seem to abound chiefly among people in "ignorant and barbarous nations" who cannot be believed by those in more civilized societies, and he notes that for every claim that a miracle has taken place, one can find testimony to the contrary as well. For Hume, it is only our inherent desire for the marvelous and the extraordinary that makes us believe in miracles rather than resign ourselves to our ordinary everyday experience. In sum, he concludes that "no testimony for any kind of miracle has ever amounted to a probability, much less to a proof."[145]

Hume's opinions are anything but obsolete. A contemporary organization called the Committee for the Scientific Investigation of Claims of the Paranormal (CSICOP) publishes a magazine called the *Skeptical Inquirer* featuring such articles as "Fears of the Apocalypse: The Escape from Reason," "God Is Dead, After Weather and Sports," and "Miracles or Deception?: The Pathetic Case of Audrey Santo."[146] Author Joe Nickell contributes a column to the magazine entitled "Investigative Files" in which he exposes such hoaxes as the autopsy of an alien that supposedly took place in Roswell, New Mexico, and a case of spontaneous human combustion in Pennsylvania.

Nickell is particularly interested in what he believes to be fraudulent religious phenomena such as weeping icons, faith healing, and stigmata. As we saw in chapter 4, the stigmata are wounds that appear mysteriously on people's hands, feet, head, back, and torso, mimicking the wounds of Jesus. Of this phenomenon, Nickell writes, "Indeed, I feel that hoaxing—the proven explanation in numerous cases—provides the most credible overall solution to the mystery of stigmata."[147] He points out that numerous stigmatics have admitted to inflicting their injuries on themselves. Other cases, in which the afflicted person denies any such responsibility, Nickell chalks up to unstable personality, a propensity for self-mutilation, or a pious desire to promote the example of Christ to others.[148]

The most famous stigmatic, and the first in recorded history, was the thirteenth-century Italian Saint Francis of Assisi. According to his biographers, Francis prayed one day that he might feel in himself the pain that Jesus sustained during the crucifixion. All at once, a Seraph appeared to him in the likeness of a crucified man, saying, "I have given you the Stigmata which are the emblems of My Passion, so that you may be My standard-bearer."[149] After this, Francis's feet and hands "seemed to be pierced through the center with nails, the heads of which were in the palms of his hands and in the upper part of his feet outside the flesh, and their points extended through the back of the hands and the soles of the feet so far that they seemed to be bent and beaten back...."[150] Likewise, Francis developed a wound on his right side that dripped blood onto his habit and breeches, causing him intense pain. These sores remained until his death.

A noteworthy interpretation of Francis and his wounds can be found in the film *Stigmata* (1999) which stars Gabriel Byrne as Father Andrew Kiernan, a priest who investigates paranormal phenomena for the Vatican. (In reviewing his performance, the *Washington Post* called Byrne "the best-looking, best-dressed priest in the movies since Montgomery Clift in *I Confess*.... One studly man of the cloth."[151]) Before looking at *Stigmata*'s use of Francis- imagery, though, we must observe that the movie's plot is entirely fictional. That is, the plot of *Stigmata* revolves around the discovery of a "secret" gospel thought by the Church to be so threatening that those who have seen it must be killed, lest they divulge its contents. The movie ends with this stern notice: "In 1945, a scroll was discovered in

Nag Hammadi [Egypt], which is described as 'the secret sayings of the living Jesus.' This scroll, the Gospel of Saint Thomas, has been claimed by scholars around the world to be the closest record we have of the words of the historical Jesus. The Vatican refuses to recognize this gospel and has described it as heresy."

In point of fact, the Gospel of Thomas is hardly a secret; copies can be found in any good bookstore.[152] Moreover, scholars disagree about the dating of the gospel, and they disagree about its relation to the actual words of Jesus. While some believe it to contain accurate transcriptions of Jesus' sayings, others think it reflects instead the ideas of one particular early Christian community. True, the Vatican refuses to "recognize" the Gospel of Thomas in that it does not believe the text to have been divinely inspired in the same sense that it believes the four gospels in the Bible were. However, the Vatican does not discourage scholars from studying it, and numerous Catholic thinkers use insights taken from the gospel in their own writings.

That having been said, *Stigmata* is nonetheless significant for its use of saintly wounds as a vehicle for criticizing Church practice. The wounds in question appear on the body of a character named Frankie Paige, a young woman who lives in Pittsburgh and who makes her living as a hair-dresser/manicurist. Frankie is hardly a stereotypical saint. In the movie's opening scenes we see her having enthusiastic sex with her drunken boyfriend, and when she first meets Father Kiernan she offers to pierce his nipples for him. She has no religious affiliation and describes herself as an atheist.

Yet Frankie is the one chosen to receive the stigmata: wounds on her wrists, feet, head, and back serious enough to threaten her life. Naturally, her unusual affliction has come to the attention of the Vatican, and Kiernan has been dispatched to investigate. He is at first reluctant to take the case. Upon learning that Frankie does not believe in God, he declares, "Throughout history, only deeply devout people have been afflicted with these wounds.... To say that a self-confessed atheist exhibits the wounds of Christ is a contradiction in terms." He becomes convinced of the super-natural origin of Frankie's wounds only when he sees the young woman fall into a trance and begin to write in ancient Aramaic (the language spoken by Jesus) on the wall of her apartment.

What she writes is these words from the Gospel of Thomas: "Split a piece of wood, and I am there. Lift a stone, and you will find me. The kingdom of God is inside you and all about you." As noted above, the

Gospel of Thomas is widely available and is not a "secret" at all. In the plot of the movie, however, the gospel has since its discovery been kept carefully hidden by the Vatican because of its revolutionary message. After all, if the kingdom of God can be found anywhere by anyone, then there is no need for all of the trappings of religion, and Catholicism is thus obsolete. One Vatican official named Cardinal Houseman (Jonathan Pryce) is so afraid of the gospel's implications that he attempts to murder Frankie, raging, "You will not destroy my Church!"

How is it that Frankie was chosen to be the herald of this explosive text? According to the movie, when the Gospel of Thomas was first discovered, its contents were known only by the murderous Cardinal Houseman and by three other priests who had been charged with its translation. Houseman warned the three translators to keep silent about what they had read, and two of them complied. The third, however, a monk, stole the gospel and went into hiding. He was, as it turns out, an intensely holy man who suffered from the stigmata. When he died, his spirit chose an equally holy person to proclaim the Gospel of Thomas's version of the good news of Jesus: that the kingdom of God was everywhere, and that the rules and practices of the Church can only get in the way of God's work.

But why Frankie? Why a party-loving, club-hopping, platform-sandal-wearing beautician from Pittsburgh? The answer is that Frankie is unspoiled by the dogmas of the Church. She is simply a good person: someone who rushes into the street to save an infant in danger, who loves flowers, and who gives money to homeless men. She stands in contrast not only to the evil Cardinal Houseman but also to Father Kiernan (with whom, by the way, she has fallen in love). In one of her trances, she reveals in the voice of the dead monk that Kiernan became a priest out of pride and out of fear that women would complicate his life too much. His vow of celibacy prevents him from knowing what true holiness is. He belongs, bellows the dead monk's spirit, to "a Church of virgins and eunuchs." Moreover, even though he is a priest, Kiernan does not pray and does not really believe the words he says at Mass. Charges the dead monk, "The messenger believes. The messenger has faith. You have only doubt." Father Kiernan, the man of God, does not believe. Frankie, the atheist, is the true person of faith.

The film expresses the young woman's holiness most clearly through imagery related to Saint Francis of Assisi. First, notice the character's name—Frankie, short, one assumes, for Frances. Second, Frankie is shown feeding by hand the doves that congregate on her windowsill. The dove is, of course, a traditional Christian symbol for the Holy Spirit, but the birds in the movie also remind us of the saint from Assisi. According to legend, Saint Francis was so gentle that even the animals of the forest were drawn to him, and he is frequently shown in art with a bird perched on his shoulder.

The connection between the saint and Frankie comes to fulfillment in the movie's final scene. With a statue of Francis in the background, Frankie appears in a garden reaching out to a dove. Not only has she defeated the villainous cardinal, but she has also apparently convinced Kiernan of the futility of his vow of celibacy. The two engage in a passionate kiss, and as the movie comes to an end, Frankie walks slowly through a garden, her white garment a sign of her purity and holiness.

Stigmata, in other words, uses the traditional marks of Catholic sanctity as a way of criticizing Catholicism itself. It is not those who follow the rules of religion who are holy, says the movie. Such people are, in the words of the dead monk who speaks through Frankie, "blind men." True holiness is found not inside the walls of the Church but in the world around us: Split a piece of wood, and it is there. Lift a stone, and you will find it. It is no accident that the movie evokes the example of Saint Francis to make its point. Francis refused to be ordained a priest, and he lived not in a church building but in the countryside around Assisi, sleeping under the stars and preaching to the animals he loved.

Though Francis was the first and the most famous stigmatic, he was not the only one to bear the wounds of Jesus. A stigmatic second in fame only to Saint Francis was the Italian priest Padre Pio, who was beatified by Pope John Paul II in 1999. His story is told in several film biographies as well as in an Italian docudrama entitled *The Night of the Prophet*. This film, as we saw in chapter 4, takes for granted that the unusual phenomena associated with the priest were both authentic and supernatural in origin. It depicts without hesitation visions that Padre Pio is said to have had as a boy: of his guardian angel, for example, and of Jesus on the cross. At various times throughout the film, the saint exhibits his prophetic powers by looking intently into the faces of the faithful and revealing to them their most secret sins. He heals a blind girl and commands a lame man to throw down his crutches and walk. Admirers report that he has the power of bilocation, or appearing in two places at the same time. As an adult, Padre Pio claimed to have been beset by evil spirits, and the movie includes a scene in which an inanimate object moves itself across a room, flames leap of their own accord out of a fireplace, and evil-sounding laughter fills the air. Of course, the film also shows us the saint's bleeding palms, sign of his devotion to God.

What should we make of these astounding phenomena? Even if we accept that the events in question actually occurred and are not simply the product of willful deception or pious gullibility, we might explain them without recourse to the supernatural. For example, any child might "see" things that no one else sees; it is not unusual for children to confuse dreams and fantasies with reality. As for looking into people's souls, it is fairly easy to trick subjects into giving away more information than they realize they are providing; skilled magicians can convince even the most skeptical that they are able to read minds. While healing the blind and the lame is impressive, we need not assume that Padre Pio's cures were super-natural in origin. Increasingly, medical practitioners are coming to understand the power of suggestion and the influence of the mind on the body. Evidence shows that if a patient believes a doctor's promise that he or she will get well, a cure is far more likely.

Likewise, claims of bilocation can be dismissed as instances of wishful thinking or of mistaken identity. As for moving objects, we have no reason to assume that such reports are accurate. In 1985 in Ireland, a statue of Mary was said to be moving in a roadside grotto. Thousands of spectators flocked to the scene, and several people at various times claimed to see the statue move. However, scientists from the department of Applied Psychology at University College in Cork explained the claims by observing that if you visit the grotto at twilight, "you haven't got visual contact with your immediate surroundings. As is usual you are going to start swaying on your feet, perhaps your neck will start trembling, as you might have been looking up for too long, and on the back of your eye you will see the image of that little lit statue on top of the hill. You will see that image moving."[153] In short, if we are predisposed to believe in miracles, we are likely to interpret purely natural phenomena as miraculous.

But what about those holes in Padre Pio's hands, his stigmata? The blood was real. Several doctors examined the priest and attested to the fact that there were real wounds on his body. Surely the wounds should give us pause. In *Night of the Prophet*, a man confesses to Padre Pio that he knows a doctor who believes the stigmata to be the product of autosuggestion: evidence of the mind's influence on the body. Padre Pio instructs the man to tell the doctor to "think hard about a bull. We'll see if he grows horns." Yet the possibility of autosuggestion cannot be so easily dismissed. An article in the medical journal *Lancet*, for example, relates the case of a thirty-five-year-old man who was prone to sleep-walking. While in a hospital in India, the man had been forcibly restrained by having his arms tied behind his back lest he hurt himself in the night. Eleven years later, the man was admitted to a hospital in London for sleepwalking and aggressive behavior. During his time in the London hospital, his doctor injected him with a narcotic and then kept watch while the man thrashed about in his sleep, his arms held behind himself. The doctor reports, "I watched him writhing violently for at least three-quarters of an hour. After a few minutes weals appeared on both forearms; gradually these became indented; and finally some fresh petechial hœmorrhages [small red spots] appeared along their course."[154] A photograph accompanying the article shows the man's arm deeply ridged with what appear to be rope marks.

In the same article, the doctor also refers to the case of a woman who at the age of ten had been in a riding accident. In remembering the event under the doctor's care twenty-five years later, the woman developed hemorrhages, bruising, and acute pain on her right side, the side on which she was said to have fractured her ribs in the accident. Does all this mean that we can discount the stigmata of Francis of Assisi and Padre Pio as simply the result of an as-yet poorly understood but perfectly normal psycho-physiological process? Are they merely the bodily results of a psychologically intense piety? David Hume asserts, "Nothing is esteemed a miracle, if it ever happens in the common course of nature."[155] If we believe that stigmata are unusual phenomena but nonetheless phenomena rooted in the common course of nature, we may be inclined to agree with Hume that the wounds of Francis and Padre Pio are simply not miraculous.

This might put an end to the question of miracles were it not for the fact that other reports of inexplicable events continue to surface even in this age of science and technology and even in "civilized" (by which Hume presumably meant Westernized) cultures. There is, for example, the case of Benedicta McCarthy who, in 1987 at the age of two, swallowed the equivalent of sixteen lethal doses of a common painkiller in her home in Massachusetts. As the girl lay in a coma with her liver and kidneys failing, her family began to pray to Edith Stein. Stein had been a Jewish philosopher who converted to Catholicism and had taken the name Teresa Benedicta when she became a Carmelite nun. The toddler's parents had named their daughter after this intellectual whom they admired, and so it was natural that they should turn to Stein, who had died at Auschwitz in 1942, for help. They asked everyone they knew to pray for Blessed Edith's intercession, and within days, their small daughter made a full recovery. Her cure was accepted as a miracle by the Congregation for the Causes of Saints, and eventually Edith Stein was canonized as a saint of the Catholic Church.[156] Clearly, phenomena that cannot be explained by science continue to occur, and thus the existence of miracles cannot be dismissed outright.

The reasoning behind the use of miracles to substantiate a person's sanctity is that presumably only denizens of heaven could intercede with God to effect cures on earth. In other words, if a person's life had ended in eternal damnation, it would seem unreasonable that that person could ask for God's favors. Wonder-working thus appears to be a sure sign that a person deserves the designation "saint."

And yet, there are some involved in the saint-making process who would just as soon dispense with the requirement that a candidate for sainthood produce a miracle in the sense of an event that occurs outside the ordinary course of nature. Jesuit theologian Paul Molinari stresses that in the earliest centuries of the Church, saint-making occurred without reference to the working of miracles. He finds it neither historically nor theologically necessary that miracles be required for canonization.

In developing his case, Molinari writes, "From time to time we come across a reputation for holiness which has an exceptional and lasting quality.... Is not such a phenomenon an evident sign of the presence of the supernatural, a valid argument for the claim that God wishes the beatification and canonization of this servant of God?"[157] His conviction is that authentic holiness is in itself a divine sign and not merely a "natural" phenomenon. We do not need to search for events that defy the laws of science, says Molinari, in order to find evidence of God's presence in the world.

Miracle: Transforming Reality into Revelation

Molinari's conviction that holiness itself is evidence of the divine takes us close to the ideas of Protestant theologian Paul Tillich. For Tillich, religion makes a serious mistake when it equates "miracle" with the violation of a natural law. He discards entirely the notion that God could or would contradict the natural order of things. Since he understands God as the ground of being, it is unthinkable for him that this ground would contradict the very structure of being; if it did, "God would be split within himself." Moreover, Tillich does not believe that we should think of God as "acting," in history at all. To speak of God as someone who acts in the universe, whether in accordance with its laws or in violation of them, is to turn God into one being among others. For Tillich, God is the ground of being, not *a* being.

Tillich seeks to recover the origins of the word "miracle" as simply "that which produces astonishment." His definition of a miracle includes three elements. First, a miracle is an astonishing event that *does not contradict* the rational structure of reality. Second, it is an event that somehow points to the meaning of our lives or to what Tillich calls "ultimate concern." We all long for something to devote ourselves to unconditionally, he says, something to love without counting the cost. A miracle reawakens us to that fundamental desire for something that is, in the end, "worth it." Third, a miracle is an event that is received as revelatory of God. It shows us that our being and our love are not merely transitory phenomena but are rooted in the ground of being and love.[158]

In other words, think again of the train example offered by R. F. Holland. For Tillich, the astonishing occurrence might very well count as a miracle, not because a being named God somehow stepped in and caused the train to stop (whether in accordance with natural law or in violation of it), but because it is received by those who witness it as what he calls a "sign-event." In Tillich's thinking, there is no such thing as an "objective" miracle. Something can only be called a miracle if it somehow brings people before the mystery that pervades our lives: the power of being which is also the power of love.

In summary, then, we are presented with three very different understandings of the miraculous. The first, Holland's "contingency concept," imagines that God acts in history but in such a way that the natural order is not disrupted. The second, which Holland calls the "violation concept," is a divine suspension of or interference with the laws of nature. The third definition disentangles the miraculous both from the actions of a divine being and from the impossible. A miracle is defined by its capacity to make manifest the mystery of God, a God who is not one being among others, but who is the power of love at the heart of all being.

Putting It All Together: *The Third Miracle*

A complicated mixture of these three interpretations can be found in Agnieszka Holland's *The Third Miracle* (1999), which stars Ed Harris and Anne Heche and is based on the novel of the same name by Richard

Vetere. Harris plays a street-wise Chicago priest named Frank Shore whose job is to investigate reports of miracles. Heche plays Roxane, the agnostic daughter of a woman thought by many to be a saint. As Shore delves into the life of Roxane's mother, Helen O'Regan, he grapples with his own wavering faith and with the faith of simple, ordinary people to whom miracles offer a ray of hope in an otherwise hopeless world.

Shore is not a disinterested investigator. The very meaning of his life hinges on whether or not miracles really do happen. As he explains to Roxane, when he himself was a boy, his father, a police officer, had been gravely wounded in the line of duty. Shore prayed by the dying man's bedside and promised that if God allowed his father to recover, he would become a priest. The father was healed, and Frank kept his promise; he was ordained. Three months later, his father died. Was Frank a fool for interpreting his father's recovery as divine intervention? Is his vocation to the priesthood simply the result of wishful thinking and lucky coincidence? Has he wasted his life serving a God who may not even exist? These are the questions that drive the priest and, at the same time, the plot of the movie.

If Shore is not disinterested in his investigations, he is nonetheless very good at what he does—so good, in fact, that he has earned the name "Miracle-Killer" for his expertise in exposing frauds. His most recent case, we learn through a series of flashbacks, involved reports of there being healing waters in a lake in which another priest had drowned. Shore visited the site and saw for himself that the cures reported to be taking place at the lake were genuine. At night, alone under the moonlight, he waded into the quiet waters and lifted his arms imploringly to the huge crucifix that someone had planted there. It came as a serious blow to him when he discovered that the dead priest who was supposedly responsible for the miracles lived a less-than-exemplary life and in fact committed suicide by drowning himself.

This brings us to the caution that philosopher R. F. Holland offered in his attempt to define a miracle. According to Holland, an extraordinary event in and of itself is not sufficient evidence of God's interference with the laws of nature. The event also has to be attributable to a deity, and this is what Shore's investigation called into question. Why would God intervene at the behest of a priest who, as we learn, had drawn lewd pictures of demons with the caption, "The darkness calls: I answer"? Shore admits that the cures he saw were both real (in Holland's terms, "empirically certain") and unbelievable ("conceptually impossible"). However, he cannot accept or ask the Church to accept that they were performed by God. It simply doesn't make sense that God would heal people in the dead priest's name. So what brought the cures about? Says Shore dismissively, "Belief is powerful. Ask the doctors." He appears satisfied with himself for having exposed yet another fraudulent case of the miraculous. Inside, however, he is devastated: "You don't understand," he tells a friend. "This one was supposed to be real."

As a result of this last investigation, Shore has become reluctant to take on any more cases. He feels that his work has destroyed too many people's faith, including his own. He takes a sudden and unapproved leave from his priestly duties, setting up residence in a flop house and eating his meals in a nearby soup kitchen. Nonetheless, when his bishop hunts him down and orders him to look into newspaper accounts of a bleeding statue in a nearby parish, he complies. The statue, at least according to the reports, began bleeding at a memorial Mass offered in November for Mrs. Helen O'Regan, a kindly woman who lived quietly on the grounds of a convent and who worked for her local Catholic parish. It has bled every November since then, but only when it is raining as it had rained during the first memorial. Moreover, the blood is believed to have healed a little girl named Maria who was dying of lupus.

The fact that the statue bleeds only in the rain leads Shore to suspect fraud. He enlists the help of a local chemist to determine if the "miracle" isn't simply someone playing a joke—for example, smearing the statue with pig fat so that in the rain the fat would melt and appear as blood. The movie is wise to include this chemist, for the fact is that numerous apparent miracles have been exposed as clever tricks or at least as scientifi- cally explainable. Perhaps the most famous of these is the thrice-yearly liquefaction of the blood of Saint Januarius, a fourth century Catholic martyr. The supposed blood of the saint is stored in two vials in Naples, and on various feasts it is removed from the vaults in which it is kept, and it "miraculously" liquefies. Occasionally the transformation fails to take place, as is supposed to have occurred in the year when the city elected a Communist mayor. Various studies have shown, however, that the apparent miracle can be re-created in a chemist's laboratory. What seems to be blood is most likely an iron-based compound with the property of thixotropy: turning to liquid when it is shaken.[159] Though the Church has not allowed the vial to be tested, the fact that the same phenomenon can be observed under perfectly natural conditions might lead us to suspect that no miracle is taking place.

No such simple answer emerges in *The Third Miracle*. The liquid pouring from the statue of Mary is found to be human blood of the same type as Helen O'Regan's. Shore remains skeptical; he still must investigate the life of the woman said to be responsible for the statue's behavior and for Maria's cure. During the course of the film, we learn that Helen's daughter Roxane is disgusted by the effort to canonize her mother. She is still furious with the supposed saint for having abandoned her by going to live in a convent, and she lives an aimless life guided primarily by this anger. As she explains her position to Shore over the course of several days, Roxane finds herself attracted to the priest. Frank is only too happy to fall in love with the young woman, as he is convinced that he has too many doubts to be a priest anyway.

As his investigation continues, though, Shore finds to his own surprise that he believes that the miracles attributed to Helen are genuine. He ends the romance and presents Helen's case to Church officials. Then a showdown occurs. How is it possible, asks an archbishop from the Congregation for the Causes of Saints, that God would entrust the cause of a saint to a priest who has so obviously been lacking in faith? "God has given me doubts, yes," says Shore. "But he has also given me Helen." The movie seems to agree. When Shore goes to pray at the bleeding statue, he holds his arms out to it just as he had before the crucifix in the lake. The very next scene is a flashback in which Helen appears, gently wiping fog from a convent windowpane. What this might mean, we shall consider presently.

Up until the end of the film, the word "miracle" is used exclusively in the two senses laid out by Holland. The first sense, recall, is that a miracle is a providential coincidence of events. Such coincidences occur twice in *The Third Miracle*. The first time is when little Maria is cured from her lupus. This is not in itself a violation of the laws of nature; people who suffer from the disease sometimes experience remissions that can last several years. The second time is when Maria, now a young woman, lies badly beaten in a hospital bed. She is in a coma, and doctors predict that no recovery is possible. ("God wasted a miracle," her mother observes sadly, recalling the first time her daughter was cured.) When the doctors disconnect her respirator, however, not only does she survive, but she awakens and is released from the hospital. Again, her recovery is not really conceptually impossible; people in comas do sometimes wake up even after virtually everyone has given up hope. The point is rather that these two events are each about as likely as a train stopping in its tracks just inches from a two-year old boy.

The second definition describes a miracle as the violation of the natural law. This type of event also occurs twice in *The Third Miracle*. One instance is when the statue of Mary begins to bleed. There is no reasonable way to explain how a stone carving could emit human blood. The second example (and here is one of those instances where I must, alas, reveal a movie's surprise ending) has to do with bombs that failed to explode when Helen O'Regan was a child. *The Third Miracle* actually begins not in Chicago but in Slovakia in 1944, where the village of Bystrica is being attacked by Allied forces. As the entire town rushes towards an underground shelter, a little girl breaks free from her father's grip and instead runs toward a statue of Mary that stands outside a church. She falls on her knees and begins to pray as Allied planes pass overhead and drop their deadly cargo. The little girl grows up to be Helen, and the bombs, we come to find out, never landed on the town. Instead, according to one eyewitness, they turned to birds. "Pigeons," the witness recalls. "I never saw so many pigeons."

Again, it is conceptually impossible that bombs should turn into birds. It simply cannot happen. Yet, the movie insists, it did happen. It happened, and it happened because a little girl asked the mother of God to make it happen. It was, in other words, a miracle.

But what of the "third miracle" of the movie's title? In the movie's final moments, a third definition of the term emerges. The setting is several years after Shore first began his investigation of the life of Helen O'Regan. Frank appears in priestly garb shepherding a flock of children during their First Communion Mass. He looks happy and at ease in his role as the pastor of a parish. As he stands in front of his church, a woman passes by who turns out to be none other than Roxane, smiling and radiant as she cuddles her baby daughter in her arms. She asks Frank about the process of her mother's canonization, and Frank informs her that thus far two miracles (Maria's recovery, and the bombs that did not drop) have been accepted by the Vatican, but that they are waiting for a third. "And you're a priest," observes Roxane. Replies Frank, "Yes. And you're a mother."

The implication here is that the third miracle of the movie's title has already taken place. Frank has been transformed from a faithless skid-row derelict into the priest he was meant to be. Roxane has turned her hurt and anger into love for her newborn daughter. Neither of these events is conceptually impossible. Neither is an event as unlikely as that train stopping for the toddler or Maria's waking up from her coma. Yet, the film implies, the changes wrought in these two people are nonetheless miraculous.

What "causes" such miracles? Tillich might explain them by pointing to the state of estrangement in which human beings live. We are all estranged from ourselves, he believes, and estranged from other people and from God (the ground of being). He describes three different types of estrangement. The first is hubris, in which we make ourselves the center of the universe. The second is concupiscence, in which we treat other people and the world solely as resources for our own satisfaction. Finally, we suffer from what Tillich calls un-faith, or a refusal to acknowledge that anything really matters.[160] Both Roxane and Frank, like all of us to some degree, have participated in these three types of estrangement.

However, Tillich believes that we only know we are estranged because we also know moments when estrangement is overcome: moments of revelation. He writes, "This is what revelation means, or should mean. It is an event in which the ultimate becomes manifest in an ultimate concern, shaking and transforming the given situation in religion and culture."[161] When Frank and Roxane are transformed, Tillich would say, it is not because some divine being has stepped in and "zapped" them. It is rather that the power of love that is the basis of all our lives has become clear to them, as clear as the convent window was after Helen wiped its fog away.

During the First Communion ceremony over which Frank is presiding at the end of *The Third Miracle*, a small boy with an angelic voice sings the following words: "Before Your eyes the world unfolds. Let me dissolve my hatred so I can know You. Let me sacrifice my fear so I can see You." This dissolution of hatred and fear is precisely what happens to Frank and Roxane. The two of them are no longer tempted to throw their lives away as if nothing matters. They no longer put their own hurts and doubts at the center of their lives. Instead, they have turned outwards in love and service to others. In sum, what was once only reality has taken on the character of revelation.

Do Miracles Happen?

So where does this leave us? Do miracles really happen or are they, as Hume argued, simply the result of fraud or wishful thinking? At the very least, we can say that events continue to occur that are, given our current level of knowledge, unexplainable. This fact alone does not mean that miracles take place, as we have seen. It may mean simply that we have much more to learn about the world we inhabit. It may mean that some extra-normal force is at work in the universe, but not a god: perhaps ghosts or fairies or aliens instead. After all, there are literally thousands of horror films in which strange events take place due to the intervention of a super-natural being other than God.

In the end, the choice of whether or not to believe in divine miracles may come down to a kind of picture-preference. Novelist Madeleine L'Engle puts the matter this way:

> There are three ways you can live life…. You can live life as though it's all a cosmic accident; we're nothing but an irritating skin disease on the face of the earth. Maybe you can live your life as though everything's a bad joke. I can't….
>
> Or you can go out at night and look at the stars and think, yes, they were created by a prime mover, and so were you, but he's aloof perfection, impassible, indifferent to his creation….
>
> Then there's a third way: to live as though you believe that the power behind the universe is a power of love, a personal power of love, a love so great that all of us really *do* matter to him. He loves us so much that every single one of our lives has meaning….

L'Engle concludes, "That's the only way I can live."[162]

7

Blessed Are the Poor

Introduction

According to the Gospel of Luke, Jesus spent forty days in the wilderness before beginning his ministry as a preacher. After those days, having been filled with the Holy Spirit, he began to teach in the synagogues in Galilee, and all those who heard him praised him. Luke does not tell us what Jesus said in those first few sermons of his new career. We do not know what impressed his hearers so much. However, Luke does offer an account of what happened shortly thereafter when Jesus came into his own home town of Nazareth. According to the Gospel, Jesus went to the synagogue on the Sabbath. He stood and was handed a scroll to read: a scroll containing the ancient words of the prophet Isaiah. He unrolled the parchment until he found this passage: "The Spirit of the Lord is upon me, because he has anointed me to bring good news to the poor. He has sent me to proclaim release to the captives and recovery of sight to the blind, to let the oppressed go free, to proclaim the year of the Lord's favor" (Luke 4:18–19. See Isa 61:1–2). Rolling the scroll back up, Jesus said, "Today this scripture has been fulfilled in your hearing" (Luke 4:21).

Whether the story as it is related by Luke is historically accurate or not is difficult to say. Some scholars, doubting that Jesus could either read or write, would say that the event never took place. Others would speculate that perhaps something like this event occurred, but that the details are subject to question. Virtually all scholars, however, would agree that the story told by Luke in this passage nonetheless illustrates a fundamental truth about Jesus: that his life and teaching were seen as bringing "good news to the poor."

Working with and on behalf of the poor has been a consistent theme in the history of sainthood. Many of the holy have taken into their own hearts the advice Jesus gave to the rich man in the Gospel of Mark who desired eternal life: "Go, sell what you own, and give the money to the poor, and you will have treasure in heaven; then come, follow me" (10:21). According to the Gospel, the man to whom Jesus spoke went away sad because he didn't want to give up his possessions. Many of the saints, on the other hand, have willingly embraced poverty even as they have worked to lift the poor out of their misery.

This chapter will examine the lives of some of those saints as they have been presented in film. Our exploration will take us into some of the most controversial aspects of Christianity, including its critique of wealth, its apparent glorification of poverty, and its frequent collusion in the economic and political systems that oppress the poor. As we have seen in earlier chapters, saints often make choices that run counter to common sense. At times their actions seem to spring more from pathology than from sanctity. However, as we have also seen, saintly motivations are varied and complex, and they resist over-simplification. In this chapter, saintly desire for poverty and service on behalf of the poor will prove to be no less perplexing than was their cultivation of suffering or their welcoming of martyrdom.

Who Are the Poor?

Before we can discuss sainthood and poverty, we must come to some understanding of just what it means to be "poor." The word itself is confusing. On the one hand, poverty is an evil to be overcome. All of us hope that some day everyone will have food to eat and clothes to wear, a meaningful job and a decent place to live. Every year, the United States spends billions of dollars to alleviate poverty both here and abroad. On the other hand, however, there is a long history of Christian saints seeking out poverty and extolling its virtues. How can we make sense of this?

Christian theologian Leonardo Boff offers a typology of poverty that will be helpful to us as we examine the relationships between being poor and being holy.[163] He discusses five different understandings of what it means to be poor. The first kind of poverty that Boff identifies is simply the lack of the means necessary to live and reproduce. This lack may be due to natural disaster or inadequate natural resources or general technical backwardness. While Boff describes this kind of poverty as an evil, he notes that it does not necessarily involve sin; it may be nobody's fault that people are poor.

The second kind of poverty in Boff's typology is due to what he calls "sins of injustice." In this case, people are poor not "naturally" but because they have been exploited by the wealthy and the powerful. These poor lack material resources because of unfair wages, laws that discriminate, corrupt political processes, biases in education and so on. It is these people, according to Boff, whom the Gospel of Luke has in mind when it records Jesus as saying, "Blessed are you who are poor, for yours is the kingdom of God" (6:20). It is these poor who will benefit first from the goods of God's reign.

The third type of poverty in Boff's schema refers not to material lack but rather to a spiritual state: total availability for and trusting surrender to God. The poor in this case are not the materially destitute but rather those who are detached from material goods and who live lives of simplicity. They are the "poor in spirit" who Jesus says are blessed in his Sermon on the Mount (Matt 5:3). They are the *anavim*, the poor and humble ones of God spoken of in the Hebrew Bible.[164] Their opposite are the proud, those who call attention to themselves and who imagine that they depend on no one, not even on God.

Fourth, Boff notes that poverty is sometimes thought of as a virtue associated with asceticism. It involves a moderate use of goods and wise restraint in one's affection for possessions. Its opposite is irresponsible waste and disrespect for the value of material things.

Finally, Boff speaks of a love for the poor that leads to sharing the lot of the poor. In this case, people may opt for poverty not because it is good in itself but rather because they are in solidarity with those who suffer from it. Such people may do nothing more than offer companionship in the poor's struggle for survival. Or, they may choose to help organize the poor and search with them for ways of overcoming their poverty. Either way, this type of poverty is chosen for the poor and against their condition. It is born of a "holy anger" against the destitution that keeps people from living fully human lives. It is, says Boff, the poverty practiced by Jesus.

The Courage to Be Poor: *Francesco*

It is also the poverty practiced by Francis of Assisi as portrayed in Liliana Cavani's *Francesco* (1989). Francis is one of the most beloved of the Catholic saints, second in popularity perhaps only to the Virgin Mary. Venerated for his humility, simplicity, and gentle good humor, Francis has captured the imaginations of several filmmakers including Franco Zeffirelli, whose 1973 film *Brother Sun, Sister Moon* portrays the saint as a kind of medieval flower-child. Cavani's Francis (played by Mickey Rourke), by contrast, is a man tormented by a passion for God that wracks his body and his mind.

Francesco follows Francis's transformation from wealthy son of an Assisi cloth merchant to poor man of God: from aspiring knight to beggar. We see him go off to war in the year 1202, only to be taken captive and held as a prisoner in Perugia. There, according to the film, Francis acquires a copy of the Gospel written not in Latin but in his own spoken language. He reads it incessantly, and, after he returns home, what he has read continues to bother his conscience. Eventually he abandons his dream of becoming a soldier and instead begins to live among the poor and the lepers.

Why does he make such a radical change in his life? What is his motivation? The movie offers several answers. First, Francis is simply following the commands of Jesus. The saint reads from the Gospel of Matthew to his friends: "Take nothing with you. No purse, no money, no sandals" (10:9); "He who would follow me must renounce himself and take up his cross and follow me" (16:24).[165] As Francis understands it, by sleeping in the woods and wearing nothing but rags in the wintertime, he is doing nothing other than what Jesus demands.

On another level, however, Francis seems to have very personal reasons for withdrawing from the wealth of his earlier life. He tells his friends that through his detachment from worldly goods he has discovered a sense of freedom: "There's nothing to fear. I hardly have any fear now." Preaching to his brother friars, Francis observes, "Nobody obligates us. We are the brothers without anything. We do not judge those who are above us. All I say is that we have chosen to be lower, with nothing, and therefore those without fear. Free." This freedom from attachment is not absolute, however. At one point, Francis confesses to his friend and disciple Saint Clare that her safety is his one remaining worry: "The only fear I have left is for you."

Being free of material wealth is, for Francis, being free of obligation and anxiety. It is also, however, identification with Jesus. This point is made with startling clarity early in the film. Francis has yet to leave his father's house, but he has taken to sleeping in a ruined chapel near his home. It is there that Clare finds him one day, huddled against the cold stones. When she asks him what is wrong, he lifts a huge wooden cross with the image of Jesus painted on it, and he stands it upright in front of the altar. Then, as if it were a lover, he embraces the cross and presses his body against it, gently caressing it with his face. He stretches his arms out to mirror the arms of Jesus, and he lays his head against the wood. Clearly he is a man in love, and he wants to be as near as possible to his beloved.

This entails more than simply an emotional commitment, however. Francis comes to believe that by living with the poor he will learn more about Jesus. He preaches to the faithful in Assisi's cathedral, "It is easy to worship wooden images. They never suffer hunger or cold." Loving Jesus, though, entails loving those whom Jesus loved. Declaring that it is the poor who have the courage of saints, he leads the assembly in a litany: "Blessed Elena, paralyzed and peaceful, pray for us. Blessed Mateo, orphan full of hope, pray for us." He invokes the prayers of the leper who does not curse, the blind man who sees the sun and the stars, and the mother of a dead child, a mother "without milk, but with faith." Turning to the wealthy of the city, he asks, "Will you help us? Will you pray with us?"

By the end of the film, Francis's commitment to poverty has taken its toll on his health. Abandoned by many of his friars because of his insistence that they live without security, he has grown weak and despondent. Indeed, when several of the brothers come upon him one day in the woods, he has the aspect of a lunatic, wearing a burlap sack for a hood and peeking out at the interlopers from behind a tree. Realizing that his vision is not shared by all ("Don't you think the practice of the Gospel should be more accessible?" asks a papal representative), he goes off by himself to pray.

It is there, in the rocks and hills of the countryside, that Francis is touched by God. After a period of several days' intense prayer, Francis awakens to find that his hands, feet and side are bleeding. He has been given a share in the suffering of Christ by bearing in his own body the marks of the crucifixion, and when he realizes what has happened to him, he begins to laugh. Later, when asked what she thought about this extraordinary occurrence, Clare remarks, "I thought that love had made his body identical to the Beloved's. And I asked myself whether I would ever be capable of loving that much."

In *Francesco* we see all five of the types of poverty that Boff identified. First, we see people who are poor because of their vulnerability to the forces of nature: the snows that blow through the hills of Assisi, for example, and the mud slides that accompany the spring rains. However, the movie makes it clear that these poor are also oppressed by the wealthy of Assisi. Because they do not even appear in the city's census, officially they do not even exist; they are not truly "people." When beggars do wander the town, they are chased away by the merchants who fear for their wares and by the aristocrats who find them a nuisance.

Third, in Francis we see someone who has given up his material goods as a way of living out his commitment to spiritual simplicity and trusting surrender to God. When asked by one of the pope's counselors if it is important to dress like a beggar, Francis replies that it is a good first step: "Dress as a new man," he explains, and spiritual transformation will follow. This does not mean, though, that Francis is immune to the needs that pressure all of our bodies. On the contrary, he recognizes the value of a moderate use of material goods (Boff's fourth type of poverty). When one night the friars cannot sleep for the rumbling of their stomachs, Francis takes a bit of bread and distributes it among them: "Eat in peace," he tells them.

However, what comes across in the film most clearly is Francis's sense of solidarity with the poor. When a thief is about to be hanged, Francis tries frantically to rescue him, explaining that the thief is his "brother." He does not romanticize poverty but lives in the hope that one day no one will have to be poor. When he realizes that his death is near, he confides to a friend, "I see so many. So many faces. And what have I been able to do to help them? Nothing. Nothing. Nothing."

The Poor Are Our Masters: *Monsieur Vincent*

In the movies, people are believed to speak most truly when they are about to die. Knowing that his own death is near, Saint Vincent de Paul (played by Pierre Fresnay) summons a young novice nun to his room. He wishes to instruct her before she goes out to meet the indigent people whom she is to serve for the first time. What he offers is the wisdom he has accumulated from his more than forty years of helping the ones most neglected by society. Of these poor, he tells the novice, "They are your masters, masters who are terribly sensitive and demanding.... It is only for your love, for your love alone, that the poor will forgive you for giving them bread."

Giving bread was the lifelong project of Saint Vincent de Paul (1580–1660). The film *Monsieur Vincent*, directed by Maurice Cloche, tells the story of Vincent's first encounters with poverty, the enormous energy he spent founding institutions to aid the hungry and the sick, and his struggles with the French nobility whose reactions to him ranged from amused toleration to hostile opposition. Winner of an Academy Award for most outstanding foreign language film released in the United States during 1948, *Monsieur Vincent* is a powerful depiction of the life of an extraordinary man.

The first thing we must note, however, is that the life of Vincent de Paul as it is presented in the film bears only a passing resemblance to the life of the actual man. While the broad outlines are the same (e.g., Vincent lived in seventeenth-century France, he cared for the poor, he founded shelters and hospitals) several episodes in the movie either never actually took place or happened quite differently. For example, there is a scene in the film in which Vincent, appointed chaplain to galley slaves on a ship, is overcome by the wretchedness of their condition. Moved by pity and outrage, he lifts the exhausted body of one of the rowers aside and takes the man's place at the oars. The basis for the episode is a story related by one of the first biographers of Saint Vincent, Louis Abelly. However, virtually all historians since have agreed that the event never occurred. The fact that these historians' assessments were available well before the film was produced leads one to wonder why the scene was nonetheless included.

Likewise, one of the sources of dramatic tension in the movie is a struggle between Vincent and the ladies of the French nobility; these latter are portrayed as well-meaning but silly, cowardly, and self-indulgent. The tension between the priest and the ladies comes to a head when Vincent wishes to open a home for foundlings. He brings to the ladies an infant left at the door of the church, and he lays the child on the table between them. The ladies are horrified and refuse even to look at the child who was presumably born to an unwed mother. They call the infant "the wages of sin." Vincent begs them to reconsider, but they remain unmoved. Even Mademoiselle de Marillac (later Saint Louise de Marillac) refuses to meet the priest's eyes, and Vincent sadly removes the baby from the ladies' midst. In point of fact, however, though an argument did take place between Vincent and the Ladies of Charity regarding foundlings, it was merely regarding whether to take control of an existent home for children or to establish a new foundation. Vincent favored the latter option and put his plan into operation. He did so with the cooperation of the ladies and with the enthusiastic support of Louise de Marillac.[166]

In short, there is a conflict between historians' accounts of Vincent de Paul and the picture presented by *Monsieur Vincent*, and viewers should keep this fact in mind as they watch the film. It will be interesting to speculate about reasons for the discrepancies; for the moment, however, we shall confine ourselves to the cinematic version of the saint's life. *Monsieur Vincent* begins in 1617 in the small French village of Châtillon-les-Dombes. Vincent arrives as the town's new priest, and his first act is to rescue a girl whose mother has just died. Fearing the plague, townspeople had shut the girl up in her small hovel and left her to what they assumed would be her own horrid demise. Outraged, Vincent carries the girl from her shack and finds her bread and soup to eat. He builds a coffin for her mother who, it turns out, had not died of plague at all but rather of some other illness.

As Vincent digs a grave for the dead woman and presides at a Christian burial, curious onlookers gather, and it is to these that the priest turns after the funerary rite is finished. Putting his arm around the forlorn daughter of the dead woman, he asks, "Who'll care for her? I'm not speaking to those who have plenty. I'm speaking to the poorest of you, someone who has just enough to feed her own. I want that one and only that one to come forward. And the Lord will smile on her." Out of the crowd emerges a woman with several children of her own, and she offers to take the girl into her home.

There is something disturbing about this scene. Why would the priest burden the poorest of the poor with yet another mouth to feed? Why would he put such a responsibility on this woman's shoulders when the rich could surely bear it much more easily? Later, when talking to the count who acts as lord of the town, Vincent rhapsodizes about the hardships that the peasant woman caring for the girl will face. She will have to work a little later into the evening, he says, and she will have to get up a little earlier in the morning. Yet, he concludes, "It is she who is rich." One can't help but feel that Vincent, who until recently had been tutor to the children of a wealthy family in Paris, is indulging here in a kind of sentimentalism that the poor can ill-afford. This feeling is only partly mitigated when, the next day, the priest arrives at the peasant woman's home with a large loaf of bread to help feed the orphaned girl. Bread for a day is hardly enough to shield the woman's family from its newly-exacerbated poverty.

We are justified in concluding at this point that Vincent has confused two types of poverty. He has confused spiritual humility (Boff's third way of being poor), which is good and praiseworthy, with material destitution (Boff's first and second types), which is an evil to be overcome. Adding another mouth to the peasant woman's household will not necessarily make her humbler or more detached from material goods. Indeed, it may make her even more desperate, leaving no room for what Boff calls "the higher activities of the human spirit, such as intellectual, moral, artistic creativity."[167] It is difficult even to think, much less to pray or worship, when one is fainting from hunger and overwork.

In his glorification of poverty, Vincent is drawing on a very old tradition in Christian thought and practice. In the third century, at least according to legend, the prefect of Rome demanded to be given all the treasures that the Christian Church owned. In response, the deacon Laurence (soon to be Saint Laurence, martyr) gathered up the decrepit, the blind, the lame, the maimed, lepers, widows, and orphans whom the Church supported. "These," he told the prefect, "are the treasure of the Church."[168] Nearly two millennia later, a Catholic bishop caught up in the US government's debates about Social Security argued, "The poor belong to us. We will not let them be taken from us!"[169] Characterizing the poor as "treasures" or as having value precisely because of their poverty gives the impression that the poor should remain poor so that the rich will be able to benefit by caring for them. Indeed, Monsieur Vincent urges a young priest who wishes to help him in his mission, "Take care of the poor—your poor. If you can only find one, comfort him. Don't allow anything to come between you and him. Believe me, you have as much need of him: as much as he will have need of you."

Though it does depict the poor as objects of the wealthy's largesse, *Monsieur Vincent* does not allow us to dismiss saintly concern for the poor as merely a form of spiritual slumming. In extolling the worth of indigent people, Vincent is actually fighting against his society's disregard of those people's humanity. In the seventeenth century, Catholics were likely to equate poverty with sin; begging was considered a form of "disbelief."[170] By affirming that society's cast-offs have worth in the eyes of God, Vincent echoes the prediction of Jesus that when the Son of Man comes, he will judge people according to how they treated the hungry, the thirsty, strangers, the sick, the naked, and prisoners. "Truly I tell you," the Lord will say, "just as you did it to one of the least of these who are members of my family, you did it to me" (Matthew 25:40). If Vincent is misguided in imposing more material burdens on the needy, he is nonetheless heroic in his recognition of the dignity of the poor.

Nor does the film allow Father de Paul to sentimentalize poverty for very long. In what is perhaps the film's most memorable scene, Vincent spends his first night in a wretched tenement of Paris. He is joined in his room by a drifter who has no place else to stay. As the two men lie awake in the dark, they hear various sounds of poverty: the howls of a madwoman, the screams of a woman being beaten by her jobless husband, the thump of a loom being worked far into the night, the cries of a baby with nothing in its stomach, the blood-stained coughs of the sick. The drifter tells him that after a while he will become used to the noises and will fall asleep easily: "The rich can afford to have feelings," he says. "The poor have none left."

In *Monsieur Vincent*, Father de Paul vacillates between accepting the caste system of rich-versus-poor, on the one hand, and undermining it on the other. That is, at some points he does not seem to question the fact that some are born to nobility and others to lowliness; all he asks is that the wealthy give of their means to assist the poor who remain dependent on them. At other times, however, he comes close to questioning why the distinction between "rich" and "poor" should exist in the first place. Early in the film there is a scene in which the local lord, the Count de Rougemont, is grumbling about the low estate into which he has recently fallen. Vincent reminds him that there are many people poorer than he, but the count shrugs off this concern. After all, he says, that's just the way the world is. With fire in his eyes, the priest retorts, "Because we make it so!" When the count refuses to see how privileged he is when compared to the peasants in his village, Monsieur de Paul tells him, "They're all worse off than you. *You owe them everything.*"

The notion that what the rich own rightfully belongs to the poor may sound shocking, but it is actually a very old Christian conviction, at least within some theological circles. We can see it clearly in the writings of Saint John Chrysostom, bishop of Constantinople in the fourth century. Chrysostom (the name means "golden-mouthed" and was given to him because of his skill in preaching) instructed his followers that "not giving part of one's possessions to others is already a kind of robbery," and that "wealth is not a possession, it is not property, it is a loan for use." Furthermore, Chrysostom declared, "So destructive a passion is greed, that to grow rich without injustice is impossible." Even people who have inherited wealth are culpable, said the saint, because they receive what was gathered through injustice. "God in the beginning made not one man rich and another poor." Thus, if there are inequities, it is because someone has begun to usurp what God intended for all, "using those cold words 'mine and yours.'"[171]

On the other hand, Chrysostom was willing to allow people to possess private property if they used it for the good of others. After all, he said, if everyone had as much money as he or she needed, then there would be no opportunity for almsgiving. All people have been given some portion of riches and talents, and all are called upon to share them: "In this way, impelled by our needs we communicate with one another, give to others what we have overmuch and receive what we lack. Thus we increase our love for our brethren."[172] In sum, Chrysostom displayed an ambivalence about the distinction between wealth and poverty similar to that found in *Monsieur Vincent*. Wealth is suspect but not completely to be done away with lest charity become impossible and its spiritual fruits disappear.

It will perhaps be helpful at this point to consider why the makers of *Monsieur Vincent* altered so significantly the life of the saint. Two such changes have already been noted: Vincent's taking over the oars of a galley-slave, and his battle to save foundling children. It is also the case that Vincent's entrance into the small village of Châtillon-les-Dombes had nothing of the drama that occurs in the film. In point of fact, the church that is portrayed in *Monsieur Vincent* as dilapidated and abandoned was actually in quite good repair, and there were already six ecclesiastics living in the town. Moreover, plague came to the village some months after de Paul had already been established there, and when it did, the townspeople did not abandon its victims. Instead, they helped erect sheds where food and medicines could be prepared, and they tended to the sick.[173]

Why then the portrait of a lonely Vincent struggling against all odds with neither support nor sympathy? Why is he depicted as a voice in the wilderness whose spiritual genius goes unappreciated? The answer could lie in the fact that the film was co-written by Jean Anouilh, a French playwright whose characters tend to be brooding heroes who rise above the mediocrity that surrounds them and who are "condemned to a solitude which admits of neither love nor friendship."[174] As a tragic figure in the tradition of Anouilh, Monsieur Vincent must transcend the fools and idlers of his day and pursue his ideal, whatever the cost: hence the scenes in which he is frustrated by his constant struggle to get the women with whom he works to do and to give more and more. In reality, Vincent de

Paul often wrote to Mme. Louise de Marillac begging her not to work too hard and to take good care of herself when she was ill.

However, there may be another reason behind the film's portrait of the saint. Reading Vincent's de Paul's correspondence, one can see how much of his time was taken up with the tedious details of everyday life, including finances and building plans, personnel issues and travel itineraries. Perhaps we simply do not like to think of our saints as enmeshed in these quite ordinary routines. Perhaps we prefer that their lives be written with large print and bold colors so that there is no mistaking who is holy and who is not. It spares us from thinking that sanctity might be found in our own dull worlds. When someone suggested to Dorothy Day (1897–1980), co-founder of the Catholic Worker movement, that she might one day be canonized, she snapped, "Don't dismiss me so easily!" In other words, calling her a saint could be a way of making her life irrelevant to our own. Day wished to resist the kind of veneration evident in *Monsieur Vincent* that lifts its subjects out of their ambiguities and banalities. She protested against being turned into a holy card. It seems that she got her wish, as all the messy complexities of her life are featured prominently in the film biography *Entertaining Angels: The Dorothy Day Story*.

The Poor As Meeting-Place With God: *Entertaining Angels*

The saint of *Monsieur Vincent* is only a tentative critic of the economic, social, and political structures that contribute to poverty. In contrast, the subject of *Entertaining Angels* makes criticizing those structures the center of her mission. Long before her conversion to Catholicism, Dorothy Day (played by Moira Kelly) appears in the film marching on behalf of women's suffrage and writing exposés of poor laborers' working conditions. In fact, her devotion to the oppressed and outcast nearly prevents her from pursuing her growing fascination with Catholicism. Convinced that religion is an opiate that keeps the poor from improving their lot, she dismisses it, scoffing, "Hypocrisy. Morbid escapism. Cowardice in the struggle for justice. That's your Church."

Entertaining Angels presents a picture of Day that is quite close to the one offered in the reformer's autobiography called *The Long Loneliness*, though it devotes considerably more time than that book does to Day's relationships with men and to the abortion she underwent in her early twenties. In the film (and indeed in the book as well), Day comes across as a restless wanderer who searches for something to devote her life to:

"I have something to give," says the cinematic Dorothy to her friend, playwright Eugene O'Neill, after a night of drinking in a seedy Greenwich Village bar. "But I don't know what it is. I know that I want to live fully. I want to do things that no one has ever done before." What exactly it is that Dorothy has to give, however, remains unclear for quite some time. She writes stories that go unprinted and starts essays that remain unfinished. She falls in love with a man who loves no one but himself, and she has an abortion in hopes of convincing him to stay in her life. Instead of comforting her, her lover abandons her at the illegal practitioner's door, and when she returns home to find him gone, she smashes the mirror in her bedroom. (In her later life, Day deeply regretted the abortion.) Gazing into the broken glass, she sees her own face peering back at her, distorted and incomplete.

The setting for the next section of *Entertaining Angels* is Dorothy's beach house on Staten Island. It is here that she falls in love with Forster Batterham, a fisherman and intellectual who despises convention in general and religion in particular. The two of them enter into an easygoing relationship that self-consciously asks no commitment of either but seems fulfilling for each. Something of the transcendent seems to live in the love they share; after one session of love-making, Dorothy gazes upward and whispers, "Thank you." Who or what she is thanking is not quite clear, either to audiences or to Dorothy herself. An ardent atheist, Day at this point characterizes Christianity as being an enemy of the poor.

It is during a playful bicycle race with Forster that Dorothy first encounters the nun who, at least according to the film, changes her life. (This segment of the movie compresses significantly the long period during which Day became more and more acquainted with the Catholic Church.) Impressed by the nun's work with the poor of the area, Dorothy begins going to Mass and reading the New Testament. When she gives birth to Forster's daughter Tamar and insists on having the infant baptized, Forster leaves her life for good. Daughter and mother are baptized together, and thus begins Dorothy's life as a Christian.

After several years, mother and daughter move to New York City to take up residence in the home of Dorothy's brother John and his wife Tessa. The year is 1933, the height of the Great Depression, and poverty and sickness are everywhere. Dorothy has still not discovered how best to use her talents and her zeal on behalf of the poor. She kneels before a statue of Jesus and prays, "Lord, you've got to tell me what you want— what I'm supposed to do. I write, but that's not enough. I've got to do.

What? I don't know. Please show me how. Please." The answer to her prayers is waiting for her when she returns to her apartment. Peter Maurin, French thinker, writer, and poor man for Christ (played for comic effect by Martin Sheen) greets her as she walks through the door and does not stop talking for the rest of the evening. He is reading to her from the "Prayer of Saint Francis" (which legend has attributed to the saint from Assisi) as she, exhausted, finally hands him his hat and shuts the door in his face.

Their association does not stop there, however. Soon, at Peter's instigation, Dorothy is feeding and sheltering all the drunk, derelict, and desperate people who show up at her door. She and Peter also begin publishing the *Catholic Worker*, a newspaper devoted to changing the lives of the poor through the teachings of Jesus. When the cardinal of the New York archdiocese comes to Dorothy, he complains about her opposition to General Franco's regime in Spain and about her support of labor unions which, in his opinion, are run by communists. Dorothy responds in the words of famed Brazilian Archbishop Dom Helder Camara: "If you feed the poor, you're a saint. If you ask why they're poor, you're a communist." She refuses to take the name "Catholic" off of the newspaper, and she justifies the *Catholic Worker*'s stands on social issues: "We believe that the Sermon on the Mount means what it says.... Justice and peace go together. You can't have one without the other."

The conviction that helping the poor entails not just giving aid but also changing the structures that contribute to their poverty marked a new era in Catholic social teaching. The first stirrings of this idea can be found in the papal encyclical *Rerum Novarum*, or "On the Condition of the Working Classes." Issued in 1891 by Pope Leo XIII, the letter encouraged workers to form unions, though it discouraged strikes, warning that "such paralysing of labor not only affects the masters and their work people alike, but is extremely injurious to trade and to the general interests of the public."[175] The letter made clear that employers were not at liberty to exploit workers as they pleased but rather were responsible for providing fair wages and safe working environments. Forty years later, Pope Pius XI reiterated the ban on strikes in his *Quadragesimo Anno* ("On Reconstruction of the Social Order"), but he too called for employers to pay enough so that a working man could support his family.

These ideas would come to fruition at the Church's meeting called the Second Vatican Council (1962–1965). There, Catholic bishops gathered from around the world and declared that people have rights to food, clothing, and shelter; that they are entitled to education, employment, and liberty of conscience; that they must be free to live out their religious beliefs and commitments, and that they deserve the respect of their fellow human beings. Attending to these matters, said the council, is not the responsibility of only a few: "Let everyone consider it his sacred obligation to count social necessities among the primary duties of modern man, and to pay heed to them."[176]

For Dorothy, the poor were not merely people to be helped but were, as for both Francesco and Monsieur Vincent, mediators of divine grace. When in the movie her fellow Catholic Workers complain about the drunks and prostitutes that are turning their home into a flop house, Dorothy reflects back on the trajectory her life has taken:

> It's been a very lonely life, and I've been looking to fill the emptiness. Now I see—it begins with these people. The ones that nobody else wants. The ones that are hurt and are angry and have nothing left to give. They are my meeting-place with God, and if I would just give him a chance, I know God will fill me with love, fill me through these people. I don't think that God will judge us on how successful we are at changing the world. I do think he will judge us on how faithful we are serving his poor.

This is not to say that Dorothy romanticizes poverty or the poor. At one point in the film she tells God angrily that too much is being asked of her: "These brothers and sisters of yours, the ones that you want me to love? Let me tell you something. They smell."

Entertaining Angels does a very good job of portraying Day's solidarity with the poor (Boff's fifth type of poverty). What it leaves out, however, is the breadth of her commitments. Day did not only lobby for workers' rights, but she was also a pacifist who opposed the Second World War and the War in Vietnam, and she protested against US involvement in the nuclear arms race. She spoke out frequently on behalf of African-Americans' civil rights and was a founding member of the Committee of Catholics to Fight Anti-Semitism. Arrested numerous times, she was jailed for the last time in 1973 at the age of seventy-five; her crime was participation in an illegal protest on behalf of farm workers.

Dorothy Day is not a saint. Her cause for sainthood, however, was officially opened in March 2000, when Day was declared by the pope to be a Servant of God. Much debate surrounds the move to canonize her. As the Catholic Worker organization that she founded observes, "Voices opposing the process say that Dorothy Day shunned the suggestion she was a saint and believe she would rather have any money spent on her canonization given to the poor. Others are concerned that her radical vision will be sanitized and spun to support Catholic traditionalism and a narrow anti-abortion stance, neutralizing her ardent pacifism, radical critique of society, and love of the poor."[177]

Whatever comes of the canonization process, it is clear that the Christian attraction to poverty is as controversial now as it ever was. When Jesus told one of his admirers that if he wanted to be perfect he should give all he had to the poor, the young man "was shocked and went away grieving, for he had many possessions." Figuring out how or if it is possible to follow Jesus without divesting oneself of material goods is an ongoing challenge. As is clear from the films discussed in this chapter, the idea of voluntarily committing oneself to a life of poverty continues to fascinate even as it repels. As the films also make clear, however, those who choose to follow that road often find it to be a very lonely one indeed.

8

Saints and Auschwitz

Introduction

Every year on the twenty-seventh day of the Hebrew month of Nissan, sirens ring out in every city in Israel. All work stops. Traffic stops. Radio and television broadcasts fall silent. The entire country stands still for a moment to remember the six million lost in what has come to be known as the Holocaust.

It is important to remember the Holocaust. To remember is to revolt. To remember is to break through guilty conspiracies of silence. It is to demand accountability in a world that would rather forget what it has done. There are reasons to remember: but there are also reasons to be wary of our remembrance.

This is especially true when film confronts the Nazi attempt to slaughter all of the world's Jews. Because film has the ability to depict horrors in full color and with slow-motion precision, because it can fool us into a literalistic mentality that believes that "the camera doesn't lie," it has both enormous potential and enormous responsibility in presenting this darkest of human undertakings. The risks are many: trivialization, sensationalism, and the self-satisfaction of feeling that one has "dealt with" the Holocaust because one has seen it depicted on screen.

With regard to *saints* and the Holocaust, one other risk must be mentioned: the possibility that cinematic versions of Christian sanctity will obscure or replace altogether the troubling memory of Christians' involvement in Hitler's Final Solution.

Before we can look at specific movies about saints and the Holocaust, we must address one prior issue. The question to consider is this: is film an appropriate medium for depicting the horrors of the *Shoah*?[178] Documentary maker Claude Lanzmann contends that dramatic movies, which rely on a coherent plot, sympathetic characters, and a satisfying ending, cannot hope to do justice to Auschwitz or Buchenwald. For Lanzmann, films such as *Schindler's List* (1993) and *Life Is Beautiful* (1997), both of which have "happy" endings, are unforgivable distortions of what happened to the vast majority of Jews. He contends, "The truth is extermination. Death wins.... This is not digestible. It is not a fairy tale."[179] Perhaps film is simply not capable of coping with those years between 1933 and 1945, the years in which Germany offered the world a final answer to its "Jewish problem."

Film and the Holocaust: Images of the Impossible

Jewish novelist, philosopher, teacher, and concentration-camp survivor Elie Wiesel has devoted much of his life to the problem of how to convey the horror of the Holocaust. Wiesel asks rhetorically, "But how is one to say, how is one to communicate that which by its very nature defies language? How is one to tell without betraying the dead, without betraying oneself? A dialectical trap which leaves no way out."[180] There is no way out. That is, speaking is not acceptable because words are inadequate to their subject. On the other hand, silence is unacceptable because it leads to forgetting. Referring to the rich tradition of Jewish story-telling, Wiesel asks, "How is one to explain the inexplicable? I prefer the Midrashic legends or the Hasidic tales. But my students insist."[181]

His students, many of them children and grandchildren of Holocaust survivors, insist on painfully accurate, excruciatingly detailed information about the horrors of the camps. If language is inadequate, it seems nonetheless necessary, and for a number of reasons. First, there is the distressing fact that the Holocaust itself is in continual danger of being "revised" out of history. When Wiesel received his Nobel Prize, protesters outside the building where the ceremony was held distributed leaflets declaring the Holocaust to be a fraud. There is a need, incredibly absurd, to defend the very factualness of the events. Language must fight amnesia.

The fight is a moral necessity. Says Wiesel, "The executioner often kills twice, the second time when he tries to erase the traces of his crimes."[182] Remembering and making public that remembrance are acts of defiance against murder and death. Philosopher Emil Fackenheim, another camp survivor, describes what he calls "The Commanding Voice of Auschwitz." That voice commands that Jews survive as Jews: "Jews are forbidden to hand Hitler posthumous victories."[183] But the Voice also commands that the victims of Auschwitz be remembered. The victims are to be remembered in a way that forbids despair, for to despair would also be to hand victory to the oppressors. The victims are to be remembered in a way that makes clear the immensity, profundity, and radicality of the *Shoah*.

Language is also necessary, despite its inadequacy, for the simple reason that humans need it in order to engage reality. The post-Holocaust world cannot hope to understand or even describe itself without language of some sort. Tentative, halting, always incomplete, language provides a way to think about and struggle with the momentous events that have so changed history and humanity. Film critic Annette Insdorf describes her reaction to seeing the film *Night and Fog*, a French documentary about the death camps this way: "…for the first time, I had an inkling of what my parents—among others—had endured. The film provided a shape for, and a handle on, abstract fears. It occurred to me that if I, the only child of Holocaust survivors, needed a film to frame the horror and thus give it meaning, what about others?"[184] Note Insdorf's language: the film "provided a shape for" her fears about the Holocaust. It "framed" the horror and was thus able to "give it meaning." Silence alone, no matter how powerful, cannot articulate the experience. Words, images—these too are necessary if people hope to remember and come to grips with the event. Precisely what kinds of words and images, though, is the question of this chapter.

The Meaning of Auschwitz

Many Catholics have never heard of Saint Maximilian Kolbe. If they know anything at all about him, it is simply this: that while he was in a Nazi concentration camp in Auschwitz, Poland, he offered to take the place of a condemned man. He was thrown into a starvation block with several other prisoners, and he perished.

The story is true. On 31 July 1941, ten men were chosen to die as punishment for another prisoner's escape. When Polish army sergeant Francis Gajowniczek was selected, he began to sob: "My wife and children!" Hearing his lament, Kolbe stepped forward, identified himself as a priest, and asked to die in his fellow prisoner's place. After enduring two weeks of starvation, he was given a lethal injection. His body was cremated in the ovens of Auschwitz.

However, Kolbe's story is not quite so simple. As a point of entry into its complexities, let us look at the film biography entitled *Maximilian: Saint of Auschwitz* (1995). This one-man drama stars Leonardo Defilippis, a Catholic actor also known for his roles in *St. Francis: Troubadour of God's Peace* and *John of the Cross*. It opens with Saint Maximilian praying the rosary, a common form of Catholic devotion in which praise is offered to the Virgin Mary. Kolbe's dedication to the mother of Jesus was the guiding force in his life. Virtually everything he did, he did in the name of "The Immaculata," the woman who Catholics believe was born without sin.

Maximilian relies on several different devices to tell the saint's story. First, DeFilippis portrays Kolbe at various stages of his life: ten-year old visionary to whom Mary offers the twin crowns of purity and martyrdom; young seminarian unsure if he should become a soldier or a priest; energetic founder of the "Militia Immaculata," a society dedicated to Mary; and, finally, prisoner at Auschwitz, victim of the Nazi machine.

Second, DeFilippis appears as a variety of other characters, including a Nazi guard, a leader in the Masonic movement, and a satanic figure who dresses in red and who is framed by eerie lighting suggestive of flames.

Third, the plot of the movie is often advanced through the "recollections" of an unnamed Franciscan friar (also portrayed by DeFilippis) who speaks directly into the camera. The effect of these scenes is to give the film the feel of a documentary, interpreting the events of the past through the lens of the present. Many of our insights into the motives of Kolbe are provided by the reminiscences of this character.

Fourth, actual footage from pre-war Poland and from Nazi Germany and its concentration camps is used. Anyone familiar with the classic Holocaust documentary *Night and Fog* will recognize a number of these scenes, a point we shall address further on.

Finally, other devices in the movie include voice-overs that both advance the story and contextualize it through reference to Scripture, and background music, often hymns of praise to the Virgin Mary.

The picture of Kolbe that emerges from *Maximilian* is that of a loyal son of Poland who is dedicated to both his homeland and its Catholic faith. When Kolbe is wavering in his vocation and considers abandoning his plans to join the Franciscan priesthood in order to join the military, his mother (who is not seen, but whose voice is heard from off-camera) tells him, "Trust in the Immaculata always, and she will defend our country and the Church in battle." The cause of Poland is understood as the cause of God, and the enemies of Poland are portrayed as deluded atheists at best, and as children of Satan at worst.

It is to fight these enemies that Kolbe begins his "Militia Immaculata" and the newspaper *Rycerz Niepokalanej*, or "Knight of the Immaculata"; of the latter, he tells his off-screen Franciscan Superior, "Father, I will not write anything that could not be signed by the Virgin Mary herself!" When the newspaper's circulation grows rapidly, Kolbe founds a new monastery at Niepokalanów ("City of the Immaculata") with space enough for printing presses and the monks who keep them running. Dedicating the new foundation to Mary, he declares, "Everything that is already there and will be there is her possession." This includes, presumably, one of the monastery's other publishing ventures, the *Maly Dziennik* ("Little Daily"), as a brief shot of that newspaper is included in the documentary footage of the film. That Kolbe bears responsibility for the daily is confirmed when he declares, "I am the director of these publications and of this priory."

It is an affirmation that does not serve his memory well. The fact is that the *Maly Dziennik* routinely published vicious attacks against Jews, whom it saw as the allies of Communists, Masons, secular free-thinkers, and liberals. Kolbe himself did not edit the newspaper, and he contributed to it only rarely. Nonetheless, as head of the monastery where it was published, he had an indirect supervisory role regarding its contents. The influence of the newspaper was enormous if one can judge by its circulation. By 1938 it sold 300,000 copies each day and had the largest readership of any daily newspaper in Poland.[185]

The *Maly Dziennik* took the position that there was an international conspiracy, headed by Masons and Jews, to overthrow the Catholic Church and to subject the world to its evil plans. This opinion was fairly widespread in the 1930s and had been encouraged by the publication of the bogus *Protocols of the Elders of Zion*, the supposed plan of Jewish leaders to gain dominion over the globe. The *Maly Dziennik* published articles in 1935 stating that German persecution of Jews had been brought on by those Jews' own megalomania and that the Nuremberg laws restricting marriage between Jews and non-Jews were enacted to put an end to Jewish domination of German life. When Italy enacted similar laws in 1938, the paper's headline declared that the action had been an "act of self-defense by Italians against Jews."[186]

As the economy in Poland worsened, the Franciscans' newspaper supported a boycott against Jewish businesses, encouraging its readers to ask about the religion not just of the retailers whom they patronized but of the manufacturers as well; it regularly printed a banner over its list of advertisers that proclaimed, "A Pole buys only from other Poles." A cartoon in the daily depicted a Polish hostess serving rolls purchased at a Jewish bakery, and her guests then becoming sick from food poisoning.[187] One article in 1937 contended that the rest of Europe ought to feel indebted to Poland for taking in the Jews whom other countries had driven out, and that Poland had been "too hospitable" for too long.[188] In hindsight, the words are chilling.

None of this material is included in *Maximilian: Saint of Auschwitz*. The publications that Kolbe oversees are depicted there solely as giving honor to the Virgin Mary and to God. Indeed, when one machine breaks down as Kolbe is walking among the presses, the saint muses that the Devil must have caught his tail in it. He advises the monk tending the machine to say a prayer, and within seconds it is up and running again. Knowing what we know, the scene is anything but humorous.

The point is not to indict Kolbe personally as an antisemite. By many accounts, he was not. Though he was eager to convert Jews (as well as other groups) to Catholicism, he felt that the best way to do this was through love. Regarding the boycott, he advised that editorials not discourage readers from buying from Jews, but simply urge them to patronize Polish stores. Perhaps most significantly, he and his monastery cared for every refugee who came their way, including an estimated 1500 Jews.

Again, the aim here is not to incriminate Kolbe, but rather to make clear that by the time *Maximilian* was made, the nature of the *Maly Dziennik* and the controversy over its contents had been well-documented. That the newspaper's history, and Kolbe's role in it, are omitted or distorted by the film cannot be construed as a mere oversight. This point gains significance when we look at the movie's last few scenes, in which Maximilian is arrested and taken to Auschwitz. The descriptions of that concentration camp as a "Golgotha" and a "modern-day Calvary" take us into the heart of an ongoing controversy about the meaning of Kolbe's death and his subsequent canonization.

Here is the text of the commentary offered by the unnamed Franciscan priest (played by DeFilippis) in the movie as he informs the audience of Maximilian's fate:

> I cannot tell you what Auschwitz means to the Polish people. Oswiecim: even today I cannot hear this name without a deep sense of panic and horror. Auschwitz is forever a symbol of the slaughter of the defenseless of all times and places by those under the Devil's command to choose death rather than the gift of life given by the Creator. The purpose of Auschwitz was the mass destruction of especially Jews and Poles and other groups and persons Hitler and his servants considered threatening or detestable to their sight. Indeed, not only Jews were imprisoned and died in this modern-day Calvary, but people of many different nationalities and religions.

There is much that needs to be said about this speech. First, we must clarify the fact that "Auschwitz" was not a single camp but contained three separate facilities. The first of these, sometimes called Auschwitz I, was built prior to World War I as a barracks for soldiers of the Austro-Hungarian Empire. From 1940 on, it was used as a concentration camp for Polish political prisoners, including some Jews and some Roman Catholic priests. Auschwitz II, also called Birkenau, was established to hold Russian prisoners of war but soon became simply a death camp. Its sole purpose was to kill. Auschwitz III was a labor camp housing slaves used by the I.G. Farben company to produce synthetic rubber.[189]

It is estimated that more than 140,000 Poles were imprisoned at Auschwitz I and that more than half of them died there.[190] Thus the film accurately reflects the fact that, in the words of one historian, "In the collective memory of the Poles, Auschwitz is primarily the camp set up to destroy the most prominent elements of the Polish nation...."[191] If *Maximilian* were a straight-forward historical drama attempting simply to present Polish interpretations of the camp, then the Franciscan's reminiscences about "what Auschwitz means to the Polish people" would be appropriate; most Poles during the war and many still today think of the camp as directed against Polish nationals. However, the fact that his is the only voice that speaks from the present makes that voice authoritative for viewers. The Franciscan does not provide simply *one* interpretation, but rather *the* interpretation, of Auschwitz.

This is extremely problematic in view of the fact that approximately one million Jews were murdered at Auschwitz, their ashes scattered to the winds by the crematoriums there. Jews in fact accounted for about 90 percent of the total number of victims.[192] To say, as *Maximilian* does, that "the purpose of Auschwitz was the mass destruction of especially Jews and Poles" is to mislead. The purpose of Auschwitz I was to imprison (harshly, in ways that often led to death) political prisoners. The purpose of Auschwitz II was to murder Jews. Jews were targets regardless of their political views or affiliations. They were targets regardless of their religious beliefs. Under German law, anyone with at least three, and in many cases two, Jewish grandparents was eligible for extermination.[193] Jews were killed not because of what they did or believed but because of who they were.

The second element of the Franciscan's speech that we must consider is the declaration that "Auschwitz is forever a symbol of the slaughter of the defenseless of all times and places"; in other words, the Holocaust is a universal tragedy with universal meaning. One can understand why such an interpretation is attractive and, indeed, important to contemplate. If murder matters only to the victims—if we cannot identify ourselves with them or ask what responsibility we might have for their and others' suffering—then we are truly lost. However, if we move too quickly from the particular to the universal, if we interpret *this* murder as *any* murder, then we risk losing sight of the very specific causes and circumstances of the victims' deaths.

This is the criticism that has been levied against Alain Resnais's classic movie *Night and Fog*. Resnais' little film, widely regarded as one of the best cinematic records of the Holocaust, presents the crimes committed in the camps as crimes committed against "humanity" rather than against specific people. The word "Jew" is mentioned only once in the script, and it does not appear at all in the English subtitles. One could easily watch the entire movie without understanding why the Holocaust occurred or who its victims were.

Apparently this was the intention of the director. When asked why he made the film, Resnais replied, "The whole point was Algeria."[194] Rather than being a film about the Jewish genocide, *Night and Fog* (1955) was really a cry against then-mounting atrocities caused by French involvement in Africa. The Holocaust served simply as an example of humans' inhumanity, and the film, rather than focusing on violence against a particular group, offered a universal message of vigilance.

This movement towards universalizing human suffering can be dangerous, particularly when we are dealing with the Holocaust, in which Jews were the one group specially marked by the Final Solution[195] and which took place in the heart of Christian Europe. The relationship between Nazism and Christianity is hopelessly complicated, and it is doubtful that a satisfactory account of the religion's role in the murder of six million Jews will ever be provided. It is true that Hitler once declared, "One is either a German or a Christian. You cannot be both."[196] On the other hand, it is also true that many of the laws passed by the Nazis had parallels in earlier Catholic Church law. For example, the Church's Fourth Lateran Council in the year 1215 decreed that Jews wear special markings on their clothes, and its Synod of Breslau in 1267 made ghettos for Jews compulsory.[197] Moreover, Protestant reformer Martin Luther's tract "On the Jews and their Lies," published in 1543, sounds like it was taken straight from a Nazi manual of action, as it calls for the destruction of Jews' houses, schools, and synagogues. All of this brings into question any attempt to generalize the meaning of the Holocaust. The genocide was not a "universal" tragedy. It was perpetrated by particular people, virtually all of whom had been raised as Christians, and it was perpetrated against anyone of Jewish faith or ancestry.

Night and Fog includes footage from a variety of sources, including the Nazi propaganda film *Triumph of the Will* and photographs taken by the Allies when concentration camps were liberated. Even though it seldom mentions the word "Jew," it contains material in which refugees and prisoners are wearing the yellow stars that identify them as Jews. However, *Maximilian*, which incorporates much of the same documentary footage as does *Night and Fog*, includes not a single frame that would identify victims of the Holocaust as Jews. There are no stars on people's clothing. There are no synagogues with broken windows. Whenever the word "Jew" is mentioned, it is always as part of a list, e.g., "Jews, Poles, and other groups and persons Hitler and his servants considered threatening," or "Communists, Social Democrats, Catholics and Jews."

As we have seen, this tendency towards universalizing suffering is problematic. *Maximilian* does not stop with universalizing, however. It goes one step further, so that Auschwitz becomes not a Jewish tragedy, not a human tragedy, but a specifically *Christian* tragedy. The friar compares the camp to Golgotha, the site where Jesus was executed. In and of itself, the comparison does not seem troubling. After all, Kolbe did suffer as Jesus suffered, and he offered his life for another, as Christians believe Jesus died on behalf of others. It must be noted, though, that historically, the primary charge that Christians have used to rationalize violence against Jews is that Jews killed Jesus. Saint John Chrysostom, for example, wrote regarding Jews, "You did slay Christ, you did lift violent hands against the Master, you did spill his precious blood. This is why you have no chance for atonement, excuse, or defense."[198] Likewise, Saint Augustine wrote, "The Jews held Him, the Jews insulted Him, the Jews bound Him, they crowned Him with thorns, they dishonored Him by spitting upon Him, they scourged Him, they heaped abuses upon Him, they hung Him upon a tree, they pierced Him with a lance, finally they buried Him."[199] It is remarkable that Augustine could write all this, given the fact that the Gospels are very clear that it was Romans, not Jews, who tortured and executed Jesus. Under Roman law, Jews had no power to crucify. Still, the false charge of deicide (killing God) arises again and again throughout Christian history, and it has been invoked to justify innumerable outrages.

Thus when the friar calls Auschwitz a new Golgotha, he is not merely eclipsing the Jewish victims by using Christian imagery. More than this, he is eclipsing them in a way that evokes two thousand years of supposed Jewish culpability. By comparing Auschwitz to the place where Jews supposedly killed Jesus, he obliterates Jewish suffering even as he implies that Jews are guilty and deserve whatever punishment they might receive. If the film had been honest about the content of the *Maly Dziennik*, if it had voiced regret about that content or at least attempted to contextualize it historically, perhaps the use of Christian rhetoric to explain the meaning of Auschwitz would not seem so offensive. As it is, however, one cannot help but leave the film feeling sickened.

The Martyrdom of Edith Stein

On the occasion of the canonization of Edith Stein, national director of the Anti-Defamation League (ADL) Abraham H. Foxman, and Rabbi Leon Klenicki, the ADL's director of Interfaith Affairs, co-authored this statement in the *Jerusalem Post*:

> We as Jews feel that we have lost Edith Stein twice. The first time was at her conversion to Catholicism. The second time is with her canonization, by which some groups appropriate her as a Christian martyr even though her death relates to the Jewish focus of the Holocaust.
>
> Seen in this manner, Edith Stein becomes a Jewish text for a Christian pretext, an excuse whereby the church can claim the same

victimization which its own anti-Jewish practices foisted on innocent
Jewish lives.[200]

It is a strong statement, and it deserves serious consideration. Edith Stein
was a philosopher and teacher who had been raised as a Jew but who had
become an atheist at the age of fourteen. In adulthood she became a
Catholic; in 1933, at the age of forty-two, she entered a Carmelite convent
in Germany, taking the name Sister Teresa Benedicta of the Cross. As
hostilities against Jews in Germany rose, Edith and her sister Rosa, who
had also converted, fled to a convent in Holland. It was there that the two
of them were arrested by the Nazis. Both perished at Auschwitz.

If Stein was murdered because she was a Jew, how did it happen that
she was canonized as a Catholic martyr? Shortly before the arrest of the
two Stein sisters, the archbishop of Utrecht had issued a letter protesting
Nazi actions in Holland. In response to this statement, all Jewish Catholics
in Holland, including the Steins, were rounded up and deported, and most
were subsequently murdered. Thus, in the eyes of the Vatican, Stein was
killed specifically because she was a member of the Roman Catholic
Church. In other words, she was a martyr for the faith.

It is this claim that angered Foxman (a Holocaust survivor himself),
Klenicki, and many others. In their eyes, canonizing Stein was a way of
"Christianizing" the Holocaust and at the same time obscuring the
Church's long history of antisemitism. Lifting her up as a saint seemed an
affront to the millions who went to their deaths holding firm to their
Jewish faith. It also seemed to send a disturbing message to contemporary
Jews: only if you convert will your lives be meaningful in the eyes of the
Church.

This is not at all what the pope had intended when he added Stein's
name to the list of the holy. As a Pole who had witnessed Nazi brutality
firsthand during the war, John Paul II hoped that by drawing attention to
Stein's fate he could honor all of those who had suffered during the
Holocaust: "From now on, as we celebrate the memory of this new saint
from year to year, we must also remember the *Shoah*, that cruel plan to
exterminate a people, a plan to which millions of our Jewish brothers and
sisters fell victim."[201] The fact that the canonization only exacerbated
tensions seemed to come as something of a surprise to him. One point in
particular most angered those who objected to the Church's decision. No
one questioned Stein's intellectual brilliance or her moral character. No
one doubted that in the short time between her arrest and her murder, she

had exhibited extraordinary peace of mind as well as compassion for her fellow prisoners, particularly for children. No one doubted that she had faced death courageously. What was disturbing, however, was the meaning that she herself attributed to her death.

Stein was born in 1891 on the Day of Atonement (also called Yom Kippur), the day the Jewish calendar sets aside for confessing sins, performing acts of repentance, and asking for forgiveness. Though the date of Yom Kippur changes from year to year and thus did not often coincide with her birthday, the holy day was nonetheless her favorite. In conformity with Jewish tradition, she and her entire family observed the ancient ritual of penitential fasting, and in her autobiography she notes that "none of us dispensed ourselves from this fast even when we no longer shared our mother's faith nor continued observing any of the ritual prescriptions when away from home."[202]

Following her adoption of Catholicism, Stein's primary symbol of atonement became the crucifix of Jesus—hence her chosen name, Teresa of the Cross. Through the cross, she believed, the world had been reconciled to God. Hoping to make that reconciliation visible in her own life, she composed the following testament in 1939: "I ask the Lord to accept my life and death to his honor and glorification, for all the intentions of the Sacred Hearts of Jesus and Mary and the church, especially for the preservation, sanctification and perfection of our Holy Order, particularly the Carmels of Cologne and Echt, *for the expiation of the unbelief of the Jewish people* and so that the Lord may be welcomed by his own people and his kingdom come in majesty."[203] The word translated here as "expiation" is *Sühne*, which means "atonement."[204] In other words, Stein offered her life in the hope that her fellow Jews would give up their error and accept the message of Jesus as the truth. It was this fact that angered those who protested her canonization. They saw the Church's action as a blatant reinforcement of what theologian Franklin Littell has called the "myth of supersession," or the belief of many Christians that Judaism has been superseded by Christianity and that the ancient Jewish covenant with God has therefore been nullified.[205]

The hurt and anger caused by Edith's canonization is clearly represented in the film *Edith Stein: Stations of an Extraordinary Life*. Produced in Germany in 1982, *Edith Stein* is a curious mixture of genres. It opens with scenes of an actress preparing for her role as the famous convert. Looking at slides and photographs of Edith and her family, studying the handsome features of the woman whom she is to represent, the actress asks questions, trying to immerse herself into the role. The effect of this opening is to remind viewers that what they will be watching is not the events of history. It is, rather, one telling of those events, a telling that relies on the interpretive skill of actors, writers, directors, producers, and technicians. Even the costuming must be rehearsed, as the actress playing Edith is taught how to put on the habit of a Carmelite nun and how to fold her hands inside of it.

Aside from this "behind the scenes" segment, the film also relies on documentary footage from World War I (during which Stein worked as a Red Cross nurse), from Kristallnacht (the "Night of Broken Glass" in 1938, when Jewish stores, businesses, and synagogues were attacked), and from World War II. The narrative thread of the work is provided by reenactments of events in Edith's life and by commentary taken from her writings, voiced by the actress playing her part. Interspersed are interviews with people who knew Stein and with experts who offer background and context.

One of these interviews is particularly striking, not only for its content but also for its placement. It comes very near the end of the film, providing literally the last word, though horrific images of barbed wire and emaciated corpses follow. The interview is with Jewish thinker Shalom ben-Chorin. Reflecting on Stein's offer of herself in atonement for the Jewish people, ben-Chorin asks, "What is there to atone for here? She remains entirely biased in the traditional Christian sense that [Jesus'] blood washes over us and our children, a point only scarcely testified to in [the Gospel of] Matthew which proclaims that the crucifixion of Jesus represents a lasting guilt that must be atoned for." The passage that ben-Chorin refers to is Matthew 27:25, which most scholars agree is of dubious historical value. Despite its questionable origins, however, the story that Matthew recounts of Jews clamoring for the crucifixion of Jesus, crying "His blood be on us and on our children!" is stubbornly fixed in the imaginations of many Christians. By including this interview, *Edith Stein* not only acknowledges the controversy that the saint's canonization engendered, but also clearly explains the source of the antagonism.

Behind many Christians' attitudes towards Judaism is the notion that the God worshiped by Jews is harsh and angry while the God of Jesus is kind and loving. This notion not only does not accurately describe Jewish and Christian images of God, but it is in addition a Christian heresy. In the second century, a Christian thinker named Marcion declared that there was not just one God. Rather, there were two: the evil god of the Hebrew

Bible (what Christians often call the Old Testament) and the good Father of Jesus who is revealed in the New Testament. Marcion went so far as to declare that Christians should disavow the Hebrew Bible. His ideas were declared anathema by orthodox Christianity, but this fact has not prevented many contemporary Christians from embracing them.

Indeed, it seems that the makers of *Edith Stein* have embraced them as well. In one of the scenes that is supposed to reenact events in the saint's life, Edith (at this point an avowed atheist) is in a bar with her university friends arguing about religion. In her discussion she dismisses both Christian notions of God and what she refers to as "the idea of the Jews of a punishing and vengeful God." Later, when she explains to her mother why she has become a Catholic, she says, "Mother, the God that I speak of is not the Jewish God of retribution who pays man back for his sins for seven generations and more, who makes Jews tremble for fear of death. The God that I mean is love, forgiving, and life-affirming love."

This cinematic Edith apparently subscribes to the Marcionite view of two deities. In fact, however, her statements are utterly out of sync with the real Edith's own writings. Stein was quite conscious of the Jewishness of Jesus and felt privileged to share his Jewish heritage. She envied the religious piety of her mother, a devout Jew, and she continued to accompany her family to synagogue services even after she had become a Catholic. She saw Jesus as the fulfillment of Judaism rather than as its renunciation, and she often called attention to the Jewish roots of many Christian beliefs, prayers, and practices. While she did hope that Jews would come to accept Jesus as she had, and while she felt that Christian belief in the resurrection was superior to Jews' beliefs about life after death, she did not draw a distinction between "the God of the Jews" and the God to whom she drew close through Catholicism. Though the film is wise enough to include an explanation of why Jews were upset about the canonization, it also exacerbates that very antagonism.

Perhaps the reason that *Edith Stein* struggles to understand why a Jewish atheist would convert to Catholicism, and that it therefore places words in her mouth that Stein herself would never have uttered, is that the saint's spiritual journey remains something of an enigma to her biographers. We can say with confidence that her conversion was not rooted in a rejection of the "punishing and vengeful God" of Jews. Yet exactly what steps led her to adopt a religion so foreign to her upbringing and so little understood by her family remain unclear. The 1995 film *The Seventh Chamber of Edith Stein* focuses on precisely this issue: the interior life of the saint. The "seventh chamber" of the title is a reference to the spiritual masterpiece written by sixteenth-century Carmelite Saint Teresa of Avila entitled *The Interior Castle*. In this book, Teresa describes seven stages or "chambers" that a soul goes through on its journey towards God. *The Interior Castle* had a tremendous effect on Stein and was in fact primarily responsible for her conversion. She read it one night while visiting the home of a friend, staying up all night to finish it. At the end, she closed the book and remarked, "This is the truth."

 In a highly stylized scene in *The Seventh Chamber*, Edith teaches Teresa of Avila's ideas to a younger nun who is trying to decide whether or not to leave the convent. She describes each of the first six stages and how the soul gradually leaves behind its worldly cares and enters more deeply into the life of God. When the girl asks what is to be found in the seventh chamber, Edith replies, "I don't know it yet. It's still ahead of me." Immediately, a train whistle sounds and we see a dark tunnel leading to a stark white room. The seventh chamber, we realize, will be the site of Stein's death.

This is not the only scene in which *The Seventh Chamber* adopts a dream-like, surrealistic tone. When during her tenure as a university professor she overhears two of her colleagues favorably discussing the Nazi party, Stein rushes down a flight of stairs, trips, and tumbles to the bottom. Lying on the floor in a cruciform position, her head oozing blood, she is suddenly transported to a dark and crowded ballroom where masked dancers twirl to music played by skeletons. The sequence is disjointed and confusing as Edith sees events from her past and from her future mixed together with the dancers' steps.

In the final scene of the movie, Edith has just been "selected" for the gas chambers. We see her move off towards her fate, and then she appears in the stark white room we glimpsed earlier. This is the seventh chamber, the place where Edith will be murdered. It is also, according to *The Interior Castle*, "God's dwelling place." It is the place where the soul is united to God, where, according to Teresa of Avila, "He alone and the soul rejoice together in the deepest silence."[206] As the film ends, we see Edith in the white room, naked and huddled in a fetal position, being held by her (long-dead) mother.

It is difficult to know what to make of this final scene. In her *Interior Castle*, Teresa of Avila writes that in the seventh chamber of the interior castle, a soul "has no more fear of death than it would of a gentle rapture."[207] Indeed, in an earlier segment of the movie, when Stein and some of her fellow nuns are keeping watch at the deathbed of an elderly sister, one of the younger women asks Edith, "Doesn't death scare you?" The saint resolutely shakes her head. Yet the film hesitates when it comes to Edith's own death. On the one hand, Stein is compassionate and courageous, confronting a Nazi officer on behalf of a motherless girl for whom she has been caring: "The little one must live," she tells him. On the other hand, when she herself is condemned to death, the film shows us her utterly appropriate fear. The last words Stein speaks are, "I'm frightened, Mother."

Two interpretations come to mind. The first is simply that the makers of the film are unable to believe that anyone could face such a horrific death without fear; at the final moment, anyone would succumb to terror. This interpretation is supported by a conversation Stein has with a Nazi officer shortly before she arrives at Auschwitz. The officer, whose name is Heller and who had been a colleague of Stein's at the university, accuses her of pride: of deliberately seeking martyrdom so as to become a saint. In response, Edith asks, "Do you believe I never asked myself if my choice to share my adoration of Christ was really a sincere choice? Or if I'd renounced the world out of pride rather than admit my doubts? Out of deep fear of probing deep into my heart? I really don't know. I'm not able to answer."

Her speech leaves open the possibility that the "sainthood" of Edith Stein is no truer than her life was—that it is simply the result of self-deception, self-flattery, distortion, and falsehood. This interpretation is never entirely ruled out by the film. And yet, it does not fit well with the next exchange between Heller and Edith. The officer, who has clearly been in love with Stein for quite some time, asks her, "Why didn't you search for a safe place?" Edith answers, "You're wrong, I did search. And I found one!" She gazes at the train car in which she is being transported and nods slowly to herself. She does not seem to be a woman running away from herself, a woman with a fear of probing deeply into her own heart.

A second interpretation of her death scene is more intriguing. In the *Interior Castle*, Teresa of Avila describes the love that God has for humanity. Using highly feminine imagery, she writes, "For from those divine breasts where it seems God is always sustaining the soul there flow streams of milk bringing comfort to all the people of the castle."[208] In the end, Edith is held to the breasts of her own mother, the mother who gave birth to her and who wept when she became a Catholic, but who never renounced her wayward daughter. Her Jewish mother rocked her at her birth, and, the film suggests, it is God, the God of the Jewish Jesus, who rocks her gently in the "seventh chamber" of her death.

The Pope and the Holocaust

In 1933, five years before the events of Kristallnacht awakened the world to the intentions of the Nazis, Edith Stein wrote a letter to Pope Pius XI asking him to issue an encyclical in defense of the Jews. In response, she received a letter offering her and her family a papal blessing. The encyclical she desired was never issued, though in 1937 the pope published a document entitled "*Mit brennender Sorge*" ("With Deep Anxiety") which asserted, "Whoever exalts race, or the people, or the State, or a particular form of State, or the depositories of power…above their standard value and divinizes them to an idolatrous level, distorts and perverts an order of the world planned and created by God; he is far from the true faith in God and from the concept of life which that faith upholds."[209] Though the tone is condemnatory, neither the Nazis nor the Jews are mentioned by name. Moreover, when in the same encyclical the pope affirmed the value of the Old Testament for Christians, it was primarily because those books of the Bible "record the story of the chosen people, bearers of the Revelation and the Promise, repeatedly straying from God and turning to the world."[210]

This is hardly the kind of document that Stein might have hoped for. Whether the Christmas Eve broadcast that Pius XI's successor, Pope Pius XII, issued in 1942 was much better is a matter of some debate. In that speech the pope urged all people to take a vow to serve human society: "Humanity owes this vow to those hundreds of thousands who, without any fault of their own, sometimes only by reason of their nationality or race, are marked down for death or gradual extinction."[211] The pope's defenders see his statement as a clear indictment of the genocide that was already beginning to claim millions of Jews. His detractors see it as too little too late.

The story of Eugenio Pacelli, who became Pope Pius XII and whose cause for sainthood was introduced in 1964, is fraught with controversy. Hailed as a beacon of peace on the one hand, and decried for failing to speak out more strongly against Hitler on the other, Pius XII has come under increasing scrutiny in the past several years. One of the earliest literary indictments of his war-time actions was Rolf Hochhuth's *The Deputy*. This play, which appeared in 1964, charged that the pope had sacrificed morality for political gain. Much the same point is made by

Carlo Ponti's film *Massacre in Rome*, based on the novel *Death in Rome* by Robert Katz. Both the novel and the film depict events that actually took place in 1944, when a German SS brigade in Rome was attacked by Italian partisans. In retaliation for the attack which killed 32 soldiers, the Germans rounded up 320 Italians for execution.

Massacre in Rome (1973) stars Richard Burton as German Lieutenant Colonel Herbert Kappler and Marcello Mastroianni as Father Pietro Antonelli, an Italian priest who learns of the Germans' planned reprisals and who seeks to stop them. When Antonelli's pleading with Colonel Kappler brings no results, the priest asks the head of his religious order to intercede with the pope on behalf of the condemned Italian prisoners, many of whom are guilty of nothing other than being Jews. The Father General agrees, and he sends Antonelli off to wait for him while he speaks with the pontiff. We watch as the priest waits and prays and paces back and forth, and we follow his gaze to a painting on the wall—the image of Eugenio Pacelli, Pope Pius XII.

When the Father General returns, he does not have good news to report. The pope, it seems, is reluctant to antagonize the Germans because he sees them as the last bulwark against Communism. He has offered to publish a statement after the slaughter decrying the use of violence against innocent civilians, but in the meantime, he will not intervene on the prisoners' behalf. Hearing the news, Father Antonelli walks away in disgust.[212]

Another film set in Rome during the last years of World War II offers a similar assessment of the pope's actions. *The Scarlet and the Black* (1986) is based on the novel *The Scarlet Pimpernel of the Vatican* by J. P. Gallagher and on the real life of Irish Monsignor Hugh O'Flaherty. Working in the Vatican during World War II, O'Flaherty helped over 4000 imprisoned Allied soldiers to safety and is credited with protecting numerous Jews by having Catholic baptismal certificates made out in their names. The movie focuses on O'Flaherty's story, but it includes several scenes featuring Pius XII as well.

The film opens in 1943. The Italian army has recently disintegrated, and thousands of escaped Allied prisoners of war are flocking to the Vatican in hopes of finding food and shelter there. Meanwhile, the German army has occupied Rome and is trying to intercept the POWs. Gregory Peck plays the tall, handsome Monsignor O'Flaherty who, with the help of numerous friends, hides the refugees in safe houses throughout Rome. Christopher Plummer plays Colonel Kappler, who does his best to put an end to O'Flaherty's operations. Kappler could simply arrest the monsignor in his quarters, but he is forbidden by his superiors from entering Vatican City; the papal domain is neutral territory, and entering it without permission would bring about a diplomatic crisis that the Nazis would like to avoid. As a wan, bespectacled Pius XII (Sir John Gielgud) looks on, German soldiers paint a white line on the pavement marking where the pope's authority ends and Nazi rule begins.

From the start, what concerns the pontiff is that the Vatican remain unbiased in the war that is raging across Europe. When he discovers that O'Flaherty is sheltering refugees, he tells him, "Each of my priests must do as his conscience tells him. I only ask that whatever action is taken, it does not affect Vatican neutrality." As the cinematic pope sees it, if the Vatican were thought to be on the side of the Allies, the world could make no protest if Germany invaded it.

Political neutrality is not all that concerns the pope, however. When O'Flaherty shows no signs of stopping his work to save prisoners of war, the pope summons him to an audience in the basement of Saint Peter's. There he shows him the "irreplaceable treasures" of the Church: manuscripts and paintings, rare icons and jeweled chalices, all carefully packed away lest they be destroyed by the bombs that are ravaging the city. Moving among the stacked crates, the pope explains his position: "Conquerors may come and go, but the eternal Church must remain. My greatest single duty is to preserve the continuity of the centuries: the heritage and existence of the holy Church. I have been condemned by many for not speaking out against Nazism, for making a concordat with Hitler which guaranteed the life of the Church in Germany." Turning to O'Flaherty, he asks, "Was I wrong?" When O'Flaherty replies, diplomatically, "It may not have seemed so at the time, Holy Father," the pope remarks simply, "Well, perhaps I could have done more."

It is this "more" that is at issue. In actuality, in 1935, then-Cardinal Pacelli did speak out against those who were "possessed by the superstition of race and blood cult," calling them "miserable plagiarists who dress up old errors in new tinsel."[213] In 1939, following the invasion of Poland, he wrote, "We find premeditated aggression against a small work-loving, peaceful people on the pretext of a threat which never existed nor was possible. We find atrocities and illicit use of means of destruction against old men, women and children. We also find contempt for freedom and for human life, from which originate acts which cry to God for vengeance."[214] His defenders point to these speeches as evidence of the pope's courageous work for peace, and they note that even though no names are mentioned, everyone knew who the target of his remarks was.[215] Detractors reply that the pontiff had no qualms about naming names when it came to the Spanish civil war, as he referred to "the principles taught by the Church and proclaimed with such nobility by the Generalissimo" and sent a telegram to Franco offering congratulations upon the occasion of Spain's "Catholic victory."[216] Why then was he hesitant to accuse the Nazis outright of the atrocities they were committing?

The concordat of 1933 mentioned by Pius XII in his speech to Monsignor O'Flaherty is also a matter of much debate. The agreement, signed by Pacelli himself (before becoming pope, he was the Vatican's Secretary of State), was the fruit of long negotiations between the Church and Germany. It gave the Church permission to maintain and regulate Catholic life in that country, and it offered state recognition and support of Catholic schools. It also required the Vatican and the German Church to refrain from meddling in "political" affairs. Thus the Church could legally make no protest when Nazis began deporting Jews to concentration camps and gas chambers.

Why would the Church sign such a document? Cardinal Pacelli in 1933 wrote that the concordat was a triumph for the Church since it guaranteed that a newly-compiled body of ecclesial regulations could be enforced in Germany without interference. He stressed that "the Code of Canon Law is the foundation and the essential legal presupposition of the concordat."[217] On the other hand, he maintained later that he had signed the document under duress, trying to protect the Church from persecution. Defenders of the pope accept this explanation, maintaining that if Pius XII had not signed the agreement, individual churches would have been closed and the Church itself would have lost all moral influence in Germany. Detractors point out that Catholics made up more than a third of Germany's population and that a concerted effort to resist Hitler could have crippled the dictator. They cite an incident from 1941 as evidence. In that year, when Hitler was at the height of his powers, Catholic bishop Clemens von Galen preached against the murder of thousands of Germans who had been deemed mentally infirm. Crowds of ordinary Catholics showed up to protest against the "euthanasia" program, holding demonstrations at the local cathedral. Shortly thereafter, the program was curtailed.[218]

The *Scarlet and The Black* sides with those who regret Pius XII's relative inaction against the Nazis. When the cinematic pope tells O'Flaherty,

"The essence of statesmanship is compromise," the Irish monsignor asks, "Is it ever right to see innocent people in mortal danger and turn your back on them?" The pope responds by saying that everyone must do as his conscience dictates, but he urges O'Flaherty, "Think of what I have said. God guide your decision." Clearly he hopes that O'Flaherty will abandon his work for refugees. The Monsignor's conscience, however, dictates otherwise.

One scene in the *Scarlet and the Black* should be noted not so much for what it includes as for what it leaves out. Early in the movie, Nazi Colonel Kappler meets with representatives of Rome's Jewish community to assure them that he intends them no harm. However, in order to guarantee his continued good will, the Jews must come up with one hundred pounds of gold in the next thirty-six hours. News of the exorbitant ransom comes to the ears of Monsignor O'Flaherty who immediately responds by donating the gold cross that hangs around his neck. He pledges to approach his friends for help, and in a series of brief shots immediately following, we see people from all walks of life offering up their jewelry, including parishioners in a Catholic Church.

What *The Scarlet and the Black* does not mention is that the pope himself was approached through various emissaries for assistance with the collection. The pontiff responded by offering not a contribution but rather a loan. No time limit was set for its repayment and no interest was to be charged, but the Vatican made clear that the money was to be returned at some point. In the end, the loan was not needed; the full amount had been collected and paid to the Germans. Rome's Jews were deported anyway.[219]

At the end of the movie, when the Allies have liberated Rome, *The Scarlet and the Black* offers its strongest indictment of Pius XII. The pope seeks O'Flaherty out and tells him, "I wanted you to know that in my heart, I honor you." He continues, "The real treasures of the Church, what makes it imperishable, is that every once in a while, someone comes to it, my son, like you." The Irishman's face remains impassive as he receives this praise from the supreme pontiff. We next see contrasting images: on the one hand, Pius XII on his balcony giving papal blessings to cheering throngs; on the other, O'Flaherty, praying alone before an altar. Which man, the film asks wordlessly, was truly the servant of God?

No such questions trouble the documentary *The Story of the Pope*, a tribute to the papacy and to the 262nd successor to Peter, Pius XII. Begun in 1942 at the instigation of the pontiff himself, this film, narrated by Fulton J. Sheen, portrays the pope as an "angelic shepherd" who works tirelessly for peace while caring for his "sheep" around the world. Throughout the movie, the loneliness of the pope is stressed. We see him hurrying from appointment to appointment, constantly surrounded by guards and constantly constrained by Vatican protocol from living a normal human life. Sheen tells us, "He told this narrator that all the pains and agonies of the world, if concentrated in a single heart, could not equal what he suffered in being named the chief shepherd of the Church." Tall, with an erect posture and a thin, reedy voice, the pope offers his ring to be kissed by dignitaries and heads of state, factory workers and girls in white First Communion dresses, cardinals, nuns, and tourists. Only for a few moments a day can he walk peacefully in solitude, pacing through an olive grove while saying his prayers. Besides detailing the life of Eugenio Pacelli, the movie also provides glimpses into the life of the Vatican itself, from its janitors to its guards and artists. It conveys a kind of timelessness that mirrors the conviction of the pope in *The Scarlet and the Black* that though conquerors may come and go, the Eternal Church will remain. Outside the Vatican war may be raging, but inside its walls only calm and peace can be found. Indeed, the narrator feels it necessary to correct the "misconception" that the pope is simply an ascetic and contemplative who lives "only in shades and shadows of the cross." On the contrary, we are assured, the pope "has his finger on the pulse of contemporary civilization."

The Story of the Pope especially highlights Pius XII's work for victims of war. We see "the Church's vast organization" mobilized to track down missing persons and POWs, as well as huge cabinets filled with files maintained so that information gleaned in one part of the world can be shared with another. "The Holy Father," we are told, "is particularly proud that he located and befriended thousands upon thousands of Jews who had become victims of a totalitarian cruelty."

It is true that the Vatican aided thousands of Jews, in many cases by offering Vatican passports and offering help with emigration. After the war, numerous Jewish groups offered thanks to the pope and praised the Church's efforts on their behalf, and their testimony must be taken seriously. On the other hand, as historian Susan Zuccotti points out, much of this gratitude was misplaced: "Men and women of the Church in Italy certainly deserved to be recognized and thanked, but the pope had very little to do with their activities.... Nuns, monks, and priests—some, perhaps, embarrassed by the pope's silence on one of the most important moral issues of the century—were quite willing, even eager, to share credit for their own dedication and heroism with the Holy Father."[220]

Moreover, one can't help wondering what might have happened if "the Church's vast organization" had been utilized to resist Hitler more strongly. By the close of 1942, the Vatican knew that Jews were being murdered in gas chambers, and they had reports that the number of dead was already in the millions. Regular accounts of Jews being deported to Auschwitz were sent to the Holy See, as were details about the horrors being perpetrated in Poland.[221] It is thus true that the pope "had his finger on the pulse of contemporary civilization"; tragically, though, that fact seems to have made little difference.

In sum, *The Story of the Pope* glosses over the Church's role in the war and in the Holocaust. One cannot help but see as ironic the film's final words:

> In a day when the world is suffering from the nemesis of mediocrity and the dearth of great leadership, when people tend to lose their moral responsibility, it is indeed consoling to know that someone in the midst of chaos is keeping the blueprints of a moral order, and that a great voice still rings out proclaiming that peace is grounded not on power but on justice and on love.... Never in history has there been so many shorn and bleeding lambs. Rarely before has God in his providence given to their sorrow and their broken hearts one who merited more the glorious title "Pastor Angelicus": Angelic Shepherd.

The Holocaust at Home: *Au Revoir, Les Enfants*

In the movie *Au Revoir, Les Enfants* ("Goodbye, Children"), the war seems very far away. True, the boys in the French boarding school suffer cold and hunger. They sell jam on the black market and huddle in the basement during air raids. But most of their days are taken up with lessons and playground squabbles, and they care more about getting a date with the piano teacher than about politics or international affairs. Julien Quentin, the young protagonist of the film, has to ask his older brother what a "Yid" is, and when told that the word refers to Jews, he asks, "What are they guilty of?" "Being smarter than us," says his brother, "and crucifying Jesus." "The Romans did that!" exclaims Julien, who leaves the conversation as confused as he was before.

If Julien is uncertain about how to treat Jews, however, the priest who runs the school is not. One day Father Jean brings three new students into the boys' midst. He introduces one as Jean Bonnet, and as he leaves him to the care of the dormitory prefect, he tenderly kisses the top of the new boy's head. Jean Bonnet, we discover, is really Jean Kippelstein, a Jewish refugee whose father has been arrested and whose other relatives are missing. The priest is hiding him and the other two boys in the hope that they can blend in among the students and thus elude the Gestapo.

Father Jean appears in only a few scenes of the movie. In one, he advises Julien not to become a priest because the job is too rigorous. In another, he preaches to the parents of the schoolboys, nearly all of whom are well-off, warning, "Worldly wealth corrupts souls and withers hearts. I understand the anger of the poor when the rich feast so arrogantly." His voice is steady and clear as he prays for people who are suffering, hungry, and persecuted.

It is equally steady when he is arrested by the Gestapo for harboring Jews. As he and the three Jewish students are led out of the gates of the school, Father Jean calls out the phrase "*Au revoir, les enfants.*" He does not say, "*Adieu,*" the French word for a parting that is final. Instead he uses *au revoir*, or "I'll be seeing you." It is a hopeful gesture on his part, and the boys summon their courage to respond in kind, crying out, "*Au revoir, mon père!*" ("See you, Father!") Their hope is misplaced, however. As the film comes to a close, an adult voice tells us that the three boys died in Auschwitz, and that the priest died in Mauthausen. "I will remember every second of that January morning until the day I die," says the narrator as the camera closes in on young Julien's face. A tear streams down the boy's cheek.

The narrator is Louis Malle, who wrote the script for, directed, and produced *Au Revoir, Les Enfants* (1987). As a boy, Malle attended a boarding school near Fountainebleu run by Carmelite priests. There he became friends with a boy who, as he was to discover, was a Jew. "Through the eyes of Julien Quentin," Malle writes, "I have tried to evoke this first friendship—brutally destroyed—and my discovery of the real world—its violence, its prejudices."[222] The inspiration for the film came not only from his friendship with a Jewish child, but also from the quiet heroism of the headmaster of the school Malle attended, Lucien Bunel, whose religious name was Père Jacques. Père Jacques was posthumously awarded the Medal of the Just by the government of Israel in 1985, and in 1990, his cause for canonization was formally opened.

There are some discrepancies between the priest who appears in *Au Revoir, Les Enfants* and the real Père Jacques, and examining some of these will give us insight into both Malle's vision as a filmmaker and into the relation between sanctity and cinema. Malle himself makes no apologies for the historical inaccuracies of his film. He comments, "Memory is not frozen, it's very much alive, it moves, it changes."[223] He did not set out to produce a documentary but rather to evoke a time and place and series of events that affected him deeply as a child. The movie is told from the perspective of a twelve-year-old boy; there is not one scene in which Julien Quentin does not appear, and if we know things that he does not, it is only because we have the advantage of over fifty years of history from which to interpret the events that changed his life.

As historian Francis Murphy points out, some of the differences between Father Jean and Père Jacques are quite significant.[224] In one scene of the film, the Jewish child Jean Bonnet goes up to receive the Eucharist during Mass. Why he does so is not explained. Malle observes, "It's not quite clear in the film if it's partly provocation or partly Bonnet trying to be as much of a conformist as possible, wanting to do what everyone does."[225] In any case, as Father Jean moves along the Communion rail distributing the Host, he stops short at the sight of the boy. Momentarily frozen, he then moves past the Jewish child and places the wafer on the tongue of the child next to Jean, who happens to be Julien. Viewers might react to this scene with outrage: how could the priest endanger the Jewish boy this way, setting him apart from his classmates? As the scene unfolds, however, it is clear that Father Jean is simply taken aback when he sees Bonnet. He acts not out of malice but rather out of reflex.

That is, Catholic teaching holds that the bread received in Communion is not "merely" a symbol of Jesus. It is actually, albeit in a mysterious and metaphysical way, the body of Christ itself. The bread consecrated by a priest is thus reserved only for those who believe in what is called the "real presence" of Jesus. When Father Jean does not offer the Host to Bonnet, he is acting out of his long years of training as a priest. Seeing a non-Catholic attempting to receive the Catholic sacrament, he instinctively turns away.

However we feel about Father Jean's treatment of Bonnet, it is important to recognize that the scene has no basis in history. Père Jacques had anticipated the problems that having Jewish students in a Catholic school might pose, and he arranged for the three new boys to stay in a classroom during religious services. This was not to prevent "unbelievers" from receiving the Body of Christ, but rather out of respect for the Jewish heritage of the students. He forbade any attempt to convert the boys to Christianity.

A second scene is equally troubling and also is not based in fact. Towards the end of the movie, Father Jean confronts a young man named Joseph who works in the school's kitchen. Joseph has been stealing provisions and selling them on the black market, something that many of the boys (including Julien) know because they have been both suppliers for and beneficiaries of the young man's trade. Father Jean tells the boys involved that he ought to expel them all for their illegal activity, but that out of consideration for their parents, he will not. Joseph, on the other hand, he fires. Out of bitterness, Joseph denounces the priest to the Gestapo, bringing disaster on the school. Here Father Jean appears to coddle the rich while meting out stern justice to the kitchen servant. In actuality, however, it was a former student who betrayed the school under torture by the Gestapo.[226] Joseph and his dismissal are creations of Malle's imagination.

Historian Murphy suggests that these incidents are included because they suit Malle's philosophical perspective. The movie, he believes, seeks to convey the universal corruption of humankind: of the Nazis who ruthlessly hunt down children, of the French who collaborate with their German invaders, and even of Julien, who inadvertently gives Bonnet's identity away when the Gestapo come looking for Jean Kippelstein. Given this agenda, it is necessary that even Father Jean be portrayed as less than morally perfect. He must be flawed as all people are flawed; he must be corrupt as all are corrupt.

Thus we see how a filmmaker's most basic presuppositions can affect his or her presentation of saintly virtue. To be sure, *Au Revoir, Les Enfants* did not intend to produce a historically accurate picture of Père Jacques. We see the priest only as the young Malle might have, from a distance and unclearly. Moreover, at the time the movie was produced, Père Jacques's cause for sainthood had not yet been introduced, and the director would have had no reason to take a hagiographical approach to him. Still, it is good to keep in mind how cinema can reshape history, and why. By showing the flaws of each character, Malle places the Nazis on a continuum of human failing. The Gestapo are not monsters from another realm but are human beings. Any of us, the movie seems to suggest, could become like them.

Christian Saviors in Holocaust Cinema

All of this brings us to one final issue: whether or not it is appropriate for movies to feature Catholic saints who lived during a time when Jews were being murdered in the very heart of Christian Europe. Surely many Christians did act with tremendous compassion and courage during the Holocaust, and surely their stories deserve to be told. Yet, the risk is that these stories will overshadow both Jews' own efforts to save themselves (such as occurred in the Warsaw Ghetto uprising) and Christianity's generally dismal record in its treatment of Jews.

Historian Judith Doneson observes that popular cinema depicts Jews as a people who are eternally condemned for their rejection of Christ, but whose continued existence is necessary "to test the qualities of mercy and goodness incumbent upon good Christians." Regarding cinematic relations between Christians and Jews, she writes, "The relationship exists on two levels: one depicts the Christian/gentile in his attempts to rescue the weak Jew; the other reflects a sexual attitude whereby the male Christian saves a female Jew because he loves her."[227]

For example, regarding the first level, it is Monsignor O'Flaherty in *The Scarlet and the Black* who helps the Roman Jewish community pay the gold ransom the Nazis have demanded of them. We see the priest promise confidently that his many friends will come to the Jews' assistance, and we see him contribute his own gold cross to the collection. However, there is no comparable scene in which a rabbi or other Jewish leader shows such determination or resourcefulness. The Jews are portrayed as fearful on the one hand and as gullible on the other, believing that Kappler will actually honor his promise of safety.

In *Edith Stein: Stations of an Extraordinary Life*, Edith plays the double role of both strong Christian and weak Jew. In one scene, she recites the text of her final testimony, the document that angered so many because of its conversionary tone. She prays, "I ask the Lord to take my life and death...for the atonement of the unbelief of the Jewish people...." Here Edith is the savior-Christian, offering her life for her misguided brothers and sisters.

However, Doneson's second level of Christian/Jewish interaction is illustrated in the film as well. In her relationship with the Nazi Heller, Stein assumes the role of the weak and sexualized Jew, love-object of the masculine German officer. Heller's character is an invention of the script; the man did not exist in real life. He is, as the literature accompanying the video suggests, "a symbolic person—a thread—which moves through the story representing the apparent acceptance or compliance of the German people with Nazism, the adoption of the new social order including anti-Semitism." As an invention, however, he does more than symbolize the German people. His desire for Edith and her refusal of his "love" tap into the very dynamic that Doneson warns of. It sexualizes Stein in a way that does not correspond to history and that reinforces the stereotype of the weak and therefore erotically compelling Jew.

Another trend which we must be wary of is the tendency of film to express what Ilan Avisar calls a Christian ideology: "the fostering of Christian concepts and values which use the Holocaust trauma as a convenient setting to express Christian attitudes, and thereby distorts or blurs the enormity and uniqueness of the Jewish genocide."[228] Avisar writes with reference to films such as *The Diary of Anne Frank*, *The Mortal Storm*, and *The Pawnbroker*, but the same can be said of *The Story of the Pope* and *Maximilian*. Both of these movies compare the suffering of the Holocaust to the suffering of Jesus, and both promise that the suffering will end in the salvific healing of Christ.

For example, *The Story of the Pope* ends with the declaration that the "shorn and bleeding lambs" (an implicit comparison between those who have suffered during the war and both Jesus the Paschal lamb and the lost sheep in the parable of the Good Shepherd) have been provided by God with an angelic shepherd, the pope. This pope is not merely a man, however; he is the representative of God on earth, a stand-in for the risen Christ. Both the opening and closing scenes of the film focus on a statue of a young man, presumably Jesus, carrying a lamb across his shoulders. The movie conveys the triumphalist conclusion that the suffering of this world is as nothing when compared with the promises of the Son of God.

Likewise, *Maximilian* concludes with images of Kolbe praying in his starvation block, alone among corpses. When his torturers come to give him the lethal injection, the priest willingly holds out his arm and then slumps to the floor murmuring, "Love the Immaculata." As he dies, an image of the Virgin Mary fills the screen, and a voice intones words from the New Testament's Book of Revelation. The text is read each year on 15 August, the Feast of the Assumption of Mary, the day Catholics celebrate the taking of Jesus' mother to heaven. (Kolbe died on 14 August and was cremated the following day.) Here is a portion of the reading with which the film concludes: "And a great sign appeared in heaven—a woman clothed with the sun. Now the salvation and the power and the kingdom of our God and the authority of his Christ have come. Rejoice, then, O heavens, and you that dwell within."

Given Kolbe's devotion to the Virgin, and given the curious fact that he died on the eve of one of the most important Marian holidays, it is appropriate that *Maximilian* should end with hope that salvation will come to him, as Catholics believe it did to Mary. The point is not that the movie should end in unyielding despair. The point is rather that as a whole, Christian films about the Holocaust, in their eagerness to portray suffering as redemptive, skip too quickly from death to resurrection. Linking the horror of the *Shoah* with the cross of Jesus, they assume from the outset that the story will have a happy, or at least salvific, ending.

Thus even films that criticize Christianity's inaction during the Holocaust are unable to resist playing off of Christian themes and images. *Massacre in Rome* is a devastating indictment of Pope Pius XII, and yet it ends with a particularly Christian image: a Catholic priest, an innocent man, a spotless victim, freely choosing to join the line of doomed prisoners as each kneels to receive a bullet to the head. Likewise, though *The Scarlet and the Black* is critical of the pope, it concludes by showing us an example of a true Christian man, Monsignor O'Flaherty, kneeling in prayer before a crucifix. Text at the end of the film informs us that after the war, O'Flaherty frequently visited the Nazi Colonel Kappler in his prison cell, and that some years later he officiated at Kappler's baptism.

It is important to remember people such as O'Flaherty and the countless other men and women who showed real moral courage during the dark years of the *Shoah*. We need to take their lives into our own hearts and constantly measure ourselves against them. Yet, we also need to remember that if their actions had been the norm, there would have been no Holocaust. Cinema can lull us into a kind of complacency, believing that what we see on the screen somehow erases the horrors that preceded it. We need to resist concluding too quickly that we know what suffering means and that we know that in the end, it will be insignificant in the light of God. Holocaust scholar Lawrence Langer warns us to be wary of how we remember the *Shoah*: "When we speak of the survivor instead of the victim and of martyrdom instead of murder, regard being gassed as a pattern for dying with dignity, or evoke the redemptive rather than the grievous power of memory, we draw on an arsenal of words that urges us to build verbal fences between the atrocities of the camps and ghettos and what we are mentally willing—or able—to face."[229]

Finally, we need to listen closely to those who actually endured the trains and the camps, giving their voices priority over any cinematic presentation. In this light, Holocaust survivor Wiesel offers the following caution: "Think before you substitute your memory for theirs. Wait until the last survivor, the last witness, has joined the long procession of silent ghosts whose judgment one day will resound and shake the earth and its Creator. Wait...."[230] Perhaps when Christians come to terms with the hatred of Jews that plagues Western civilization; when churches' involvement in the Holocaust is acknowledged and repented of; when theologies refuse any temptation towards triumphalism; perhaps then will be the time for more cinematic saints from Auschwitz. Until then, it would be wise to heed Wiesel's advice: Wait.

9

Hail Mary

Introduction

When Hala Pzoniak in *Polish Wedding* (1998) is chosen to crown the statue of the Virgin Mary in her Detroit parish's annual procession, no one but her family knows that the unwed teenager is pregnant. Her secret is revealed only as she is about to place the traditional ring of flowers on Mary's head. The parish priest, gradually becoming aware of the startling news that is rippling through the crowd, can barely contain his fury. Charging towards the statue of the Virgin, he attempts to drag Hala away in disgrace. The girl's mother rushes to her rescue, however, and as she and her daughter pass through the rows of parishioners, the faithful fall to their knees in awe, blessing themselves reverently. The pregnant girl has become a living icon of the Virgin.

The Virgin Mary enjoys a popularity that crosses national, religious, racial, and gender lines. She has a prominent place in Christian theology, liturgy, and art, but she is also, as it turns out, a movie star. This chapter begins by outlining the history of Mary's journey from obscure Jewish woman to Mother of God and Queen of Heaven. It explains Catholic beliefs concerning Mary, including teachings about the Immaculate Conception, the Annunciation, the Virgin Birth, the perpetual virginity of Mary, and the Assumption.

It also examines how these teachings have found expression in the cinema. Conventional portrayals of Mary found in such movies as *King of*

Kings and the more recent *Mary, Mother of Jesus* give viewers the impression that what they are watching is an accurate portrayal of the "real" Mary—the Mary of history, the one who lived and breathed and mourned her executed son. Even Jean-Luc Godard's controversial *Hail Mary* (*Je vous salue, Marie*, 1985), set in modern times (Mary is a basketball-playing high-school student and Joseph a cab driver), adopts a literalist mentality when it comes to Mary's virginity and pregnancy. The assumption of these films seems to be that what is recorded in the New Testament is to be understood as historically accurate. In reality, however, the Mary of history is all but lost to us. We know next to nothing about who she was or what she was like.

Perhaps this is the reason that any number of films choose not to concern themselves at all with the Mary of history, opting instead to explore the Mary of culture, tradition, and dogma. For example, the 1943 classic *The Song of Bernadette*, which was nominated for eleven Oscars, tells the story of a peasant girl from Lourdes, France who claimed to see visions of a beautiful lady who called herself the "Immaculate Conception." The woman of the visions was identified by Catholic faithful as Mary, and the site where the apparitions occurred became an internationally-known destination for pilgrims seeking miraculous healing. While the film tells us little about the Mary who walked the streets of Nazareth, it does capture the piety of nineteenth-century rural France, and its enormous popularity upon release shows how fervently a war-weary nation was longing for the reassurances of a heavenly mother.

Taking account of the enormous number of documentaries and feature films in which Mary plays a role would require several volumes; one chapter cannot hope to do them all justice. The bulk of this segment of the book, therefore, will focus on only one particular aspect of Marian cinema: its portrayals of sexuality and womanhood. Mary has become a controversial figure in the debate over women's roles in society and in the Church. On the one hand, many see the virgin as the epitome of holiness, as an example of femininity at its best. Explains Pope John Paul II, "*The Church sees in Mary the highest expression of the 'feminine genius'* and she finds in her a source of constant inspiration. Mary called herself the 'handmaid of the Lord' (Luke 1:38). Through obedience to the Word of God she accepted her lofty yet not easy vocation as wife and mother in the family of Nazareth. Putting herself at God's service, she also put herself at the service of others: a *service of love*."[231]

On the other hand, some feminists criticize the use of Mary as a model. For example, radical theologian Mary Daly maintains that holding Mary up as the ideal woman turns all women into slaves. She notes that Catholic tradition praises Mary for her obedience in agreeing to bear God's son, but in Daly's eyes, this obedience is simply submission. She observes, "Physical rape is not necessary when the mind/will/spirit has already been invaded."[232] In her estimation, Mary was God's victim rather than God's favored daughter, and using Mary as a model for all women turns those women into targets of oppression.

Thus a marked ambiguity characterizes theological debate about the importance of Mary, and it shapes cinematic portrayals of her as well.

The Mary of History

During the Enlightenment, when European intellectuals began to trust human reason more than religious faith, a new trend in biblical scholarship took root. It was an attempt to differentiate between what history could tell us about Jesus—about the man who walked and taught and laughed and was crucified—and the faith-claims that his followers made about him after his death. As part of this development, Gospel accounts were carefully sifted to differentiate *ipsissima verba* (words thought to have been actually spoken by Jesus) from words and ideas supplied by the evangelists when they wrote their gospels forty or more years after the crucifixion. Literary and historical-critical methods were devised by which scholars began to distinguish various layers of oral and written tradition, and a consensus emerged that much of what appears in the Gospels stems from the world-views of the first Christians rather than directly from Jesus. The gospel writers, in other words, were not objective recorders of history. They were instead passionate followers of Jesus who shaped their accounts of what he had said and done based on their own and their communities' new-found faith.

Of course, no distinction between the Jesus of history and the Christ[233] of faith can be absolute. Some scholars might wish to assert that it is literally historically accurate to say that Jesus was the Son of God: that he was divine in an absolute and objective sense independent of what people did or did not believe. Others might suggest that the effect Jesus had on people—the fact that he engendered messianic hope in them—is part of who he was historically and cannot be separated out from his life-story. In other words, these scholars would say, people had faith in Jesus as the messiah precisely because of who he was historically. In any case, though, it is quite clear that many of the traditions and dogmas associated with Jesus stem not from his own time but from decades or even centuries later. For example, the notion that Jesus was both fully human and fully divine was not established as orthodox Christian belief until the Council of Chalcedon in 451 CE, roughly four hundred years after Jesus's death. It was not a belief that would have been familiar to even his closest followers during his own lifetime.

If it is difficult to extricate from the New Testament a clear picture of who the Jesus of history was apart from the faith-claims made about him, it is even more difficult to say with confidence what Jesus's mother might have been like. After all, Mary is mentioned relatively little in the gospels, and many of the stories about her and words attributed to her are of questionable historical origin. This has not stopped innumerable movie-makers from portraying Mary's life on the big screen, however. Where history has failed, tradition and imagination have been more than happy to step in.

For instance, the opening credits of *Mary, Mother of Jesus* (1999) assert, "While dramatic license has been taken, we believe this film reflects the spirit and historical significance of the biblical story of Mary and Jesus." The statement is somewhat misleading. Presumably, "the historical significance of the biblical story of Mary" lies in the effects that story has had on religion and culture over the past two thousand years, not in the historical accuracy of the story itself. However, the film is not about the two millennia since the Gospels were written; it is rather about Mary. What the statement seems to be trying to say, then, is that while some events in the film are fictional, the rest have their basis in history. This assertion, however, is precisely what is open to question.

Our best sources for information about Mary are the four gospels in the New Testament, and these provide a sketchy picture of her at best. In the Gospel of Mark, for example, Mary is barely mentioned. (Mark's gospel is believed by most scholars to have been written well before the other three and was one of the sources used by both Matthew and Luke.) Moreover, the mention that she does receive is hardly laudatory. She first appears while Jesus is preaching: "A crowd was sitting around [Jesus]; and they said to him, 'Your mother and your brothers and sisters are outside, asking for you.' And he replied, 'Who are my mother and my brothers?' And looking at those who sat around him, he said, 'Here are my mother and my brothers! Whoever does the will of God is my brother and sister and mother' "(3:32–35). This incident is placed directly after a passage in which Jesus' family has tried to restrain him because they believe that he is not in his right mind (Mark 3:21).[234] The contrast set up by Mark conveys the message that while Jesus' blood relatives do not understand him, his followers can be counted as his true family. This is hardly a favorable presentation of the woman who gave Jesus birth.

Mark's contrast between the family of Jesus, on the one hand, and those who followed him, on the other, is continued later in his text. According to Mark, when Jesus was preaching in his hometown he managed to astound his hearers with his wisdom: "[The hearers] said, 'Where did this man get all this? ...Is not this the carpenter, the son of Mary and brother of James and Joses and Judas and Simon, and are not his sisters here with us?' And they took offense at him. Then Jesus said to them, 'Prophets are not without honor, except in their hometown, and among their own kin, and in their own house'" (6:2–4). These words of Jesus differentiate between those who are willing to honor his message and those who are not, with his family (his own kin, his own house) falling into the latter category.

If Mark's gospel were the only one to appear in the New Testament, it is hard to imagine that Mary could ever have become the object of worldwide adoration that she is today. Mark essentially presents her as a shadowy figure who is dismissed by her son for not recognizing his true identity. To see why Mary became such a beloved figure in Christianity, we must turn instead to the gospels of Matthew and Luke. These two biblical books portray Mary as a woman blessed by God and destined to change the world.

In Matthew, Mary enters the scene as a virgin living in Bethlehem who conceives a child by the Holy Spirit, is visited by wise men from the East and flees to Egypt with her newborn son and husband (who has been told in a dream that Mary became pregnant through the power of God) to avoid the wrath of King Herod's soldiers. In Luke, on the other hand, the virgin Mary is living in Nazareth when she is told by an angel that she will conceive a child.[235] She and her husband travel to Bethlehem, are visited by shepherds (no wise men are mentioned), go to Jerusalem to present their child in the temple, and return home to Nazareth without any sojourn into Egypt. The accounts offered by Matthew and Luke of Jesus's birth and Mary's role in it are virtually incommensurable and are regarded by most scholars as having little historical value.[236] Nonetheless, as we will see, they have profoundly shaped Christian beliefs about the mother of Jesus.

Two incidents in the fourth gospel of the New Testament, the Gospel of John, also add to popular imagination regarding Mary. The first takes place at a wedding where the celebration's hosts have run out of wine. Mary, a guest at the affair, comments on this fact to her son, who responds, "Woman, what have you to do with me? My hour has not yet come."[237] Persisting in her worry about the lack of wine at the party, Mary tells the servants present to do whatever Jesus asks of them. Jesus then instructs the servants to fill some jars with water, and the water is miraculously transformed into wine (John 2:1–10).

Many scholars, while appreciating the theological significance of this story, doubt that it has any basis in history. Catholic biblical expert John P. Meier notes that "if we are asked whether there are sufficient indications that at Cana of Galilee the historical Jesus actually performed some astounding deed involving water and/or wine, a deed that the disciples with him considered a miracle, the answer must be negative." He explains that "the story is a creation of the Evangelist himself, using a number of traditional themes."[238]

The second incident from John's gospel that affects popular images of Mary takes place during Jesus's crucifixion. Hanging on the cross and looking at one of his disciples, Jesus says to his mother, "Woman, here is your son." Then, turning to the disciple, he says, "Here is your mother." From that hour, according to the gospel, the disciple took Mary into his own home (John 19:26–27). Scholars do allow that the mother of Jesus may have been present at the crucifixion. However, we should observe that even if the passage is historically accurate, it tells us little about Mary herself; we do not know what she may have been thinking or feeling or if she was at the cross as a disciple or simply as a grieving mother. Nonetheless, the image of Jesus's mother standing bravely by during her son's execution remains a stirring theme in art, literature, and, of course, film.

The Mary of Faith

Catholic artist Corita Kent is said to have once remarked, "The nice thing about Mary is that her son turned out so well."[239] According to the recent film *Mary, Mother of Jesus* (produced by Robert and Eunice Kennedy Shriver), the reason Jesus turned out so well is precisely because he had such a wise and compassionate mother. Mary, in this film, is the source of many of Jesus's teachings, including the parable of the Good Samaritan.

Her influence on her son is confirmed by her husband as he lies dying surrounded by his family. Gasping for breath and struggling to speak, Joseph confides to Mary, "Everything he is, you made him."

Mary, Mother of Jesus, which as we saw seeks to convey the "historical significance of the biblical story of Mary," is a composite of incidents taken from various canonical gospels. It includes the Annunciation and the shepherds from Luke, but it also takes Joseph's dream, the wise men and the flight into Egypt from Matthew. Speeches from John are sprinkled throughout, and the resurrection scene is also heavily influenced by John's account.

Most interesting is the way the film presents the controversial episode in which Jesus's mother and brothers are looking for him. Mark, recall, indicates that the relatives were trying to apprehend Jesus because they thought him demented. Matthew and Luke don't mention that motivation but do acknowledge that it was both Jesus' mother and his brothers who were trying to reach him. In *Mary, Mother of Jesus*, however, not only is there no suggestion that the family thinks that Jesus is out of his mind, but the brothers of Jesus are completely omitted.

Perhaps we should not be surprised that the film would leave out mention of the brothers (in Greek, *adelphoi*) of Jesus. After all, if Jesus had brothers, they presumably were conceived by Mary in the normal fashion, and thus Mary would have at some time ceased being a virgin. To say this, however, would contradict a Catholic teaching of long standing: that Mary not only conceived Jesus as a virgin but remains a virgin perpetually.

The virginal conception of Jesus is clearly attested to in the Gospel of Matthew, though neither Mark nor John makes any reference to it and the Gospel of Luke is ambiguous on this point. It is possible that Mary's virginity was a Matthean innovation—in other words, that he was the first to proclaim it. It is also possible, however, that Matthew was merely drawing on a tradition already circulating among followers of Jesus. In any case, it did not take long before Christian tradition began to assert not only that Jesus had been conceived virginally but also that his birth did not violate the bodily integrity of Mary. The apocryphal[240] Infancy Gospel of James, written most likely in the late second century, reports that when the time came for Mary to give birth, a great light appeared in the cave where she was staying, and when the light withdrew, the baby Jesus appeared. The midwife attending the birth exclaimed, "I have a new sight to tell you; a virgin has brought forth, a thing which her nature does not allow." Another woman, refusing to believe the news, declares, "As the

Lord lives, unless I put (forward) my finger and test her condition, I will not believe that a virgin has brought forth." However, when she prepares to test Mary's virginity, her hand withers as if consumed by fire. "I have tempted the living God!" she exclaims.[241]

This early tradition was later codified in Church proclamations. For example, Leo the Great declared in the year 449 CE that Mary brought Jesus forth "without the loss of virginity, even as she conceived Him without its loss."[242] This tradition developed despite the passage in Luke's gospel that describes Jesus's parents presenting him in the Temple in accordance with the law that says, "Every male that *opens the womb* shall be called holy to the Lord" (2:23).[243]

As Christian tradition evolved, Mary came to be declared not only to have conceived and given birth in a virginal way, but to have remained a virgin all her life. The perpetual virginity of Mary is not alluded to at all in the gospels. Indeed, Matthew's text, which is the only one to assert unambiguously that Mary conceived virginally, says that Joseph "had no marital relations with her *until* she had borne a son" (1:25),[244] which would seem to indicate that following Jesus's birth the couple assumed normal sexual relations. Nevertheless, the perpetual virginity of Mary gained acceptance as early as the fifth century and continues to be part of regular Catholic teaching. Explains the *New Catholic Encyclopedia*, "The significance of Mary's virginity after the birth of Jesus consists in the reverence due to Mary as the sanctuary of God's presence on earth through her role in the Incarnation and also through her role as the new Eve, totally dedicated to the service of God as the handmaid of the Lord, closely associated with her divine Son in the work of Redemption."[245] The implication of the passage seems to be that had Mary been a sexually active woman, whether or not she had borne other children, she would have been somehow less dedicated to the service of God and therefore less worthy of reverence.

This negative assessment of sexuality helps explain one of the most persistent errors that Catholics and non-Catholics alike make when talking about Mary: confusing the Immaculate Conception with the Virgin Birth. That is, when many people hear the phrase "Immaculate Conception," they believe that it refers to the idea that Mary conceived Jesus without having had sex. The unspoken but very real implication is that having sex makes one non-immaculate, or, in a word, dirty. As essayist Marina Warner observes, "Accepting the Virgin as the ideal of purity implicitly demands rejecting the ordinary female condition as impure."[246]

In fact, however, the dogma of the Immaculate Conception refers to the conception of Mary, not to that of her son. The dogma states that though Mary was created in the normal fashion by her parents, at the moment of her conception God intervened on her behalf to remove the stain of original sin from her soul. She was spared the effects of the first sin committed by Adam and Eve in the Garden of Eden and was thus a pure vessel in which the Son of God could begin his life on earth.

The fact that people continue to confuse the Immaculate Conception with the intercourse-free conception of Jesus points to the deep and powerful influence that Mary's virginity has had on both Christian and popular imagination. Women in our culture are often divided into two categories; they are either maidens or they are sluts, with no grey area in between. If a woman acts on her sexual desires, she is cast as a fallen daughter of Eve. Comments Warner, "There is no place in the conceptual architecture of Christian society for a single woman who is neither a virgin nor a whore."[247]

Neither, it can be argued, does Christian society look kindly on even married women's sexual activity. Warner explains, "Accepting virginity as an ideal entails contempt for sex and motherhood, with the result that far from remaining a privileged state undertaken by a few women of vocation, virginity and sexual chastity become a general condition of sinlessness applicable to both the married and the unmarried."[248] Even a sexual thought can cause a woman to be banished from the realm of the pure, as Richard Benjamin's *Mermaids* (1990) illustrates. In *Mermaids*, Winona Ryder plays a young girl obsessed with stories about Catholic virgins and martyrs. After she kisses the boy of her dreams for the first time, she is overcome by guilt. She resolves, "I will starve myself until I purge every single thought about Joe Peretti from my soul." Panicked and mortified by her momentary concession to her sexual urges, she becomes convinced that she is pregnant. The fact that she has never had intercourse does not comfort her at all: "Mary didn't even *kiss* Joseph, and look what happened to her!"

Holding Mary's virgin motherhood up as an ideal puts women in an untenable position, and it is precisely this point that the movie *Polish Wedding* wishes to make. The movie, written and directed by Theresa Connelly, opens with a series of alternating images: of the Virgin Mary, on the one hand, and of courtesans and love-goddesses on the other. The film tells the story of a Polish-American family living in Detroit. Bolek Pzoniak (Gabriel Byrne) is the titular head of the Pzoniak clan, but it is his wife

Jadzia (Lena Olin) who wields the most emotional power in the family. Though her job is to clean bathrooms in a nearby manufacturing plant, she carries herself like royalty: "I'm a queen," she explains to her friend. "I have five children. I'm a queen!" Jadzia is carrying on a none-too-discreet affair with a wealthy executive, and her baker-husband has all but resigned himself to his status as a cuckold. When their teenaged daughter Hala becomes pregnant, however, Bolek and Jadzia are forced to examine their views of love and sexuality more deeply.

Hala is an unwed high school dropout who sneaks out of her parents' house at night to run barefoot through the streets and alleys of her moonlit neighborhood. The father of her unborn baby is a young police officer with whom she has had sex only one time—in a field near the local church. Her pregnancy complicates her life for several reasons but most of all because it threatens her ability to participate in the upcoming Church procession. Hala, as it happens, has been chosen to place a crown of flowers on the church's statue of the Virgin Mary, an honor given annually to one of the girls from the parish. In conferring the honor, the local priest explains, "To lead the Virgin's procession is a high and solemn privilege reserved for one who embodies all that we prize in womanly virtue: innocence, chastity and purity." Hala's pregnancy would seem to indicate that she is not the best representative of these virtues.

Or is she? Why, the movie asks, does sexual activity make one less innocent or less pure? Why is chastity privileged above the very activity that makes life possible: making love? At one point in the film, Bolek, frustrated with his wife's unfaithfulness, asks her, "Don't you believe in anything more important than yourself? Your religion? God?" Jadzia, pointing to her baby grandson whom she is holding in her arms, replies, "Nothing on earth is more sacred to me than this. Making life and love. That's my religion." Though eventually Jadzia abandons her extra-marital affair and returns to her husband's bed, she never surrenders her conviction that it is her sexual and generative powers that matter most.

This conviction is solidified in the movie's final scene, in which Hala marches in the procession to honor the Virgin. As she approaches Mary's statue to crown it with flowers, she becomes aware of a growing murmur from the crowd. Boys begin to taunt her, ridiculing her for pretending to be a virgin. Standing in front of the statue, she prays to Mary for help, asking what she should do. Suddenly, she places the ring of blossoms on her own head, yelling to the crowd, "Put this in your pipe and smoke it!" The parish priest, realizing that he has been duped, threatens to strike Hala with an upraised hand, but the girl's mother comes to her rescue. Then Jadzia, wearing a tight-fitting red dress, walks the pregnant Hala, dressed in white, through the crowd. No longer taunting, the crowd has become reverent. Kneeling in awe and blessing themselves with the sign of the cross, they allow Hala and her mother to process through their midst with dignity and honor. The movie's point becomes clear. Life is sacred, the film asserts, and women should be honored for their sexuality instead of condemned because of it.

Virgin and Goddess

It is appropriate that *Polish Wedding* chooses the crowning of Mary as the festival at which Hala's pregnancy is discovered and then celebrated. Traditionally, Mary is crowned in the month of May. A Marian Hymn entitled "Bring Flowers to the Rarest" includes this chorus: "O Mary! we crown thee with blossoms today/Queen of the Angels, Queen of the May." Another, entitled "'Tis the Month of Our Mother" exults, "All hail to dear Mary/The guardian of our way/To the fairest of Queens/Be the fairest of seasons, sweet May." As it happens, the month of May is named for the Roman goddess Maia, who ruled the forces of growth. In ancient Ireland and throughout the Celtic world, the first day of May marked the beginning of the summer season. May-Day (also called Beltaine) was celebrated in honor of Bel, fire god and life-giver. Youths would observe the festival by spending the night in the woods, dancing around a maypole, and choosing a May Queen, often accompanied by a May King (also known as Jack-in-the-Green) dressed in green clothing to symbolize growth and fertility. When Christians crown Mary with blossoms, they are hearkening back to this very ancient ritual that celebrated fecundity.

The fact is that many of the traditions associated with Mary are prefigured, if not directly influenced, by pre-Christian art and ritual. For example, statues of the Egyptian Goddess Isis from the sixth century BCE show the divine mother seated on a throne and offering her breast to her infant son Horus, a pose that Mary often assumes in medieval Christian art.[249] Isis later came to be worshiped throughout the Hellenistic world, where she was called "Mother of All Things" and "Queen of Heaven," titles later given to Mary.[250]

Likewise, the virgin goddess Diana/Artemis was honored throughout the ancient world until worship of her was repressed by the Emperor Theodosius in 380 CE. Some scholars argue that it is no mere coincidence that it was in Ephesus, site of an ancient temple dedicated to Diana, that Mary was first proclaimed to be the *Theotokos* or the Mother of God. One scholar explains that after worship of Diana had been forbidden, "the people, deprived of their goddess, readily turned to Mary instead."[251] Recognizing that devotion to Mary mimics devotion to pre-Christian goddesses, the Catholic Church carefully distinguishes its veneration of Mary from worship of a goddess. Mary, according to Catholic teaching, is not divine. As the Mother of God she is entitled to praise and honor, but she does not partake of the godliness of her son Jesus. The faithful, however, are not always so fastidious in making such distinctions.

Pray for Us Sinners

One of the most beloved prayers in Catholic tradition is called the "Hail Mary." Often recited as part of a ritual known as praying the rosary, the Hail Mary ends with these words: "Holy Mary, Mother of God, pray for us sinners now and at the hour of our death." There is no better intercessor in heaven, many Catholics believe, than the Virgin Mary. When all else fails, sinners can turn to her with the confidence that there they will find a sympathetic ear. In her capacity as mother, she is seen as being much more approachable than is her sometimes-forbidding son. Priest-novelist Andrew Greeley tells this joke to explain Catholics' devotion to the Virgin: One day Jesus was walking around heaven and noticed that several people had been admitted who really did not belong there. Irritated, he went to Saint Peter (according to tradition, the gate-keeper of heaven) and complained, "You really ought to be doing a better job. We need more quality control around here!" To this, Peter replied, "Don't blame me. I turn them away, but they go to the back door and your mother lets them in!"

Mary's sympathy for sinners extends even to those with whom she would seem to have the least in common: those who commit sins of the flesh. The rather odd fact is that though Mary has frequently been invoked to suppress women's sexuality, she is also often portrayed as a friend to lovers, even illicit ones. As an example of Mary's lenient attitude towards lovers, consider the following. According to one medieval legend, the abbess of a certain monastery "fell into the sin of wantonness" with her page and became pregnant. The nuns in the abbess's convent reported their superior to the local bishop, and the abbess, afraid of what the bishop would do, turned to Mary for help. Mary spirited the abbess's baby away so that when the bishop arrived to investigate, he found nothing out of the ordinary and admonished the nuns for making false accusations.[252]

Another story concerns a young virgin named Beatrice who was led into sin by an amorous cleric. Unable to withstand the temptations of the flesh, the girl left her convent and joined her lover, but the man proved unfaithful and soon abandoned her. Alone and ashamed, Beatrice turned to prostitution and lived as a harlot. Fifteen years later, she returned to her former home and asked the gatekeeper, "Do you know one Beatrice, formerly the custodian of this convent?" The gatekeeper replied, "Yes, she is a very worthy lady, holy and without reproach from her childhood, who has lived in this convent to this day." The Virgin Mary, as it turns out, had taken the young girl's place so that no one would notice her absence. From that day on, Beatrice resumed her place in the convent, and as long as she lived she gave thanks to the Virgin.[253]

This story finds its cinematic counterpart in a 1959 film entitled *The Miracle*, based on Karl Vollmöller's play of the same name. Set in Spain during the Napoleonic wars, *The Miracle* stars Carroll Baker as Teresa, a postulant[254] in a convent, and Roger Moore as the English captain who captures her heart. Unlike in the medieval legend, however, in *The Miracle* Mary apparently has a vindictive side. Though she takes the place of Teresa while the postulant pursues her love affairs, she demands quite a high price for her services.

The story begins in a convent in Spain, where young Teresa is scrubbing floors as penance for the crime of having read "godless literature": *Romeo and Juliet*. When she pauses in her work to go watch a local festival, she remembers to ask leave first from the statue of the Virgin Mary that presides over the chapel. Mary, we learn, is the only mother Teresa has ever known. The girl was left at the convent when she was only a baby by a Gypsy woman, and she has never known her true family. Having grown up among the good sisters, Teresa intends to take her vows someday soon and become a bride of Christ. She intends this, that is, until the English Captain Michael Stuart rides into town.

Stuart falls in love with the beautiful Teresa and asks her to marry him. She refuses him, but it is clear that her heart is torn. Praying in the chapel, she cries to Mary, "How can you leave me to make such a choice by myself?" As a storm begins to rage outside, Teresa throws off her postulant's robes and sets off into the night in search of Michael. It is then that the miracle of the movie's title takes place. As the empty chapel darkens and thunder and lightning crash outside, the statue of Mary comes alive and dons the clothing that Teresa has just cast off. When the Mother Superior of the convent comes looking for her missing postulant, she finds Mary (disguised as Teresa) kneeling in the chapel, her face glowing with holiness.

Meanwhile, Teresa rushes into the nearby town in search of her captain, only to discover that the village has been engulfed in flames. Napoleon's soldiers have raided the village and are killing indiscriminately. After a narrow escape, Teresa finds herself in the company of some Gypsies who take her in and treat her as one of her own. It is from them that Teresa learns that her beloved is dead—pierced by a French bayonet. In despair, she shouts defiantly, "Christianity is a faith which betrays its believers. I'm no Christian!" and she agrees to marry one of the Gypsy men. Misfortune strikes again, however, as both her husband-to-be and his brother are slain.

At this point, Teresa decides (quite reasonably) that she is a danger to men, and she resolves to love no more. This does not stop men from falling in love with her, however. Pursuing a career as a singer, Teresa attracts the notice of a famous matador who desires her hand in marriage. She refuses him but agrees to attend one of his fights, only to watch as he is gored to death by a bull. Her bad fortune has struck again.

Soon, however, Teresa's luck begins to change. Now famous as a singer, she travels to Paris where, as it happens, she runs into Captain Michael Stuart. Quite alive and still in love with Teresa, he once again asks her to marry him. The two begin to plan for the future, but war intervenes. Michael is summoned to fight Napoleon once again, and as she waits anxiously for his return, Teresa prays for his safety. It is at this point that she comes to a heartbreaking realization: the only way to keep Michael safe is to leave him and to return to her convent. This she does, leaving behind a note begging the soldier not to follow her.

Four years have passed by the time that Teresa returns to the village where she was raised. The town is now desolate. Meeting an old woman at a dried-up well, Teresa learns that for the past four years there has been no rain. The crops have withered, the cattle have all sickened and died, and a baby wails from hunger because its mother has no milk to offer. Noting that these misfortunes began at just the same time that the statue of Mary in the convent chapel disappeared from its pedestal, the old woman muses, "Some say our virgin left us in anger because our people of the valley had fallen away from God."

The real reason for the drought, though, is Teresa's sinful departure from the convent. Lying face down on the chapel floor, Teresa prays simply, "Forgive me." At that moment the statue of Mary miraculously returns to its pedestal and rain begins to fall, watering the thirsty ground. When the nuns of the convent arrive at the chapel to give thanks to God, they find Teresa (no longer in postulant's robes but now in the garments of a full-fledged nun) kneeling before the altar under the impassive gaze of the miraculous statue.

Perhaps it should come as no surprise that Mary in this movie is associated with rain and with the fertility of crops. As we have seen, many Marian traditions have roots in ancient religious rituals and myths. In this case, Mary's abandonment of the village and the subsequent withering of all living things call to mind the story of Demeter and Persephone in Graeco-Roman mythology. According to that story, the virgin Persephone was stolen by her uncle Hades and taken to the underworld. When her mother, Demeter, heard of the crime, she searched the world over for her lost child. The ancient poet Homer describes the cosmic effects of Demeter's grief: "And she made this the most terrible year on this earth that feeds so many, and the most cruel. The earth did not take seed that year... And the cattle many times pulled their bent ploughs in vain over the land, and many times the white barley fell uselessly upon the earth. And in fact she would have wiped out the whole race of talking men with a painful famine...if Zeus hadn't noticed it, and thought about it in his heart."[255] Only when Demeter was reunited with her daughter did the earth begins to flower again; only when Teresa returns to her "mother" Mary do the rains begin to fall in her village.

The Second Eve

As protectress of the earth, Mary reprises the role of Eve, the first woman created by God. Eve's name means "life-bearer"; she is referred to in the Bible as "mother of all living" (Gen 3:20). Together with her husband Adam (whose name comes from the Hebrew word for "earth"), Eve was placed in the Garden of Eden to enjoy its fruits. As everyone knows, however, a serpent in the garden convinced Eve and Adam to eat from the one tree that God had forbidden them to touch: the tree of the knowledge of good and evil. Because of their trespass, the pair was sent out from their paradise. God also punished them further, vowing to Eve, "I will greatly increase your pangs in childbearing; in pain you shall bring forth children,

yet your desire shall be for your husband, and he shall rule over you."
Moreover, God placed an angel with a flaming sword to guard the tree of
life so as to ensure that Eve and her husband would one day have to die
(Gen 3:16, 24).

Eve is remembered as the cause of sorrow and death in the world.
Mary, on the other hand, came to be thought of in Christian theology as a
new Eve, one who brings joy and life into creation. Saint Paul, in his
comparison between Jesus and Adam, set the stage for the development of
this tradition. In his Letter to the Romans, Paul wrote, "For just as by the
one man's disobedience the many were made sinners, so by the one man's
obedience the many will be made righteous" (5:19). Adam and Eve
brought sin. Jesus, through his mother Mary, brought redemption. This
connection between Mary and Eve is often depicted in art. Innumerable
statues of the Virgin present her standing serenely atop a once-fearsome
but now-defeated serpent. Eve may have succumbed to the reptile's wiles,
but Mary has triumphed over its sting.

In recognition of her role as the new (and improved) "mother of all the
living," Christian tradition has held that Mary was spared the punishments that Eve received. She had no pain in bearing her son, many
Christians believe, and as God's chosen vessel she was not tempted by
sexual desire. Moreover, she did not simply die and return to dust, as God
had threatened would be the fate of Eve. Instead, at least according to
Catholic teaching, Mary now lives in heaven. How did this happen?
According to the proclamation issued by Pope Pius XII in 1950 (one of the
few times that the privilege of infallibility has been utilized by a pope),
"[T]he Immaculate Mother of God, the ever Virgin Mary, having
completed the course of her earthly life, was assumed body and soul into
heavenly glory."[256] This teaching is known as the dogma of the
Assumption. While the pope's proclamation leaves open the question of
whether or not Mary died before she was assumed, it is adamant that she
now resides with God: "It is forbidden to any man to change this, our
declaration, pronouncement, and definition or, by rash attempt, to oppose
and counter it. If any man should presume to make such an attempt, let
him know that he will incur the wrath of Almighty God and of the Blessed
Apostles Peter and Paul."[257]

Hail Mary

The contrast between Eve and Mary is the sub-text of Jean-Luc Godard's
controversial *Hail Mary*, which was condemned upon its release by Pope

John Paul II and was panned by most critics. Roger Ebert of the *Chicago Sun-Times*, reflecting on the furor that the film caused, commented that "the people on the picket line will be protesting a film most of them have not seen and will not see. The irony is this: With their special devotion to Mary, they are perhaps the only people in town who might find this film genuinely interesting."[258]

In *Hail Mary*, Anne Gautier plays Eva, a young student of science and philosophy who listens attentively while her boyfriend/professor lectures about the origins of life in the universe. The professor is convinced that, contrary to what many scientists think, "The astonishing truth is that life was willed. A prior intelligence programmed life. It preserved life." We did not emerge from an amino-acid soup, says the professor; rather, our ancestors, in the form of primitive bacteria, came from space: "We wonder what an extraterrestrial looks like. Go to a mirror and look at yourself."

The professor is married but is having an affair with Eva, whom he insists on calling Eve. There can be no doubt about the significance of Eva's name; when she and her lover go away together for a vacation, it is to the "Paradise Villa" that they head. There Eva/Eve toys with an apple until finally she picks it up and slowly, delicately, bites into it. The affair between the two ends badly. The professor heads home to his wife and child, and Eva is left in despair, sobbing, "The world's too sad."

By contrast, the relationship between Mary, the basketball-playing teenager, and Joseph, her taxi-driving boyfriend, starts badly but ends with marriage and the subsequent birth of a son. Mary is a virgin. She declares to Joseph, "I sleep with no one. I touch no one," and she wards off his sexual advances. It is only after she is confronted at her father's gas station by a small girl and her seedy-looking Uncle Gabriel that she discovers that she is pregnant. When she tries to explain to Joseph that she has never slept with anyone, she meets with understandable skepticism.

Eventually Gabriel convinces Joseph that Mary is telling the truth, and the two young people come to a kind of agreement about what kind of physical relationship they will share. The movie includes a long scene in which Joseph learns from Mary how to tell her that he loves her. At first he does it wrongly, reaching out to touch her belly while declaring his love. Eventually, however, he learns that he must withdraw his hand rather than reaching it out to her; to say "I love you," he must pull away from her body rather than approaching it. Mary tells Joseph, "The hand of God is upon me, and you can't interfere."

There is an element of insincerity in the film's insistence that the way to love is to withdraw from the flesh. When the movie was released, outraged Christians complained about the amount in the nudity in the film (which is considerable) and about one scene in which Mary visits her family doctor and undergoes a gynecological exam. Much of this material, however, is actually germane to the plot. After all, it seems natural that a young woman who finds herself pregnant would spend considerable amounts of time contemplating her body, and one hopes that any mother-to-be would seek out the advice of a physician.

Moreover, as critic Ebert observed in his open letter to the Catholic cardinal of Chicago, Mary's visit to her doctor "serves as a reminder that this woman was not only the mother of Christ, but also, in every respect, a human being with apprehensions and fears. A central fact of Catholicism is that God became man, but when we sentimentalize the figure of Mary into a bloodless, asexual abstraction, we diminish the meaning of that fact."[259] At the heart of the term "Incarnation" is the Latin word *carnis*, or "flesh." To deny the value of the body is to deny the central proclamation of Christianity: that God became flesh.

Ironically, however, it is precisely this that *Hail Mary* seems bent on doing. The story that the professor in the movie tells his students, the story of our beginnings in outer space, implies that earth is not really our home. The professor tells his admiring students to listen to an inner voice to discover their true origins: "That Voice deep in our consciences whispers, if we listen: you're born of something, somewhere else, in Heaven. Seek and you will find more than you dream of."

His words mirror those of the ancient Gnostics who despised this earth and their own flesh and who sought a way back to the spiritual realm whence they came. The Gnostic story called "The Hymn of the Pearl," in which a princely soul must leave heaven and travel to Egypt (symbol of darkness and error), putting on the "filthy and impure garment" of the body makes precisely this point. The prince's parents write him a letter urging him not to forget his true nature: "From your father, the King of Kings, and your mother, the Mistress of the East, and from your brother, our next in rank, to you, our son, in Egypt, greetings: Awake and rise from your sleep and hear the words of our letter! Remember that you are a son of Kings and see the slavery of your life."[260] This hymn, written perhaps in the second century CE, reminds its readers that they too do not belong to this material realm and that their destiny lies outside of the flesh. In Godard's film, Mary herself diminishes the importance of the body. When she asks her doctor, "Does the soul have a body?" he answers, "The body has a soul." Replies Mary, "I thought it was the opposite." Later, she declares, "Let the soul be body. Then no one can say that the body is soul, since the soul shall be body." The central element of personhood is, for Godard's version of Mary, the soul. The soul may temporarily become body, but it remains soul nonetheless, the constant marker of identity.

Since *Hail Mary* enshrines this sort of Gnostic sensibility, it is curious that it opts to include some intensely focused shots of Mary's nude body that apparently have nothing whatsoever to do with the plot. Much of the film's nudity is, as noted above, quite in keeping with the story and seems utterly appropriate. Close-ups of Mary's pubic region, however, close-ups that last for several seconds and that detach that part of her body from the rest of her, serve no apparent purpose. If the body is really unimportant, if our soul is the reminder of and the vehicle towards our true destiny, one can't help but wonder why Mary's pelvis should be such an object of intense interest.

Il Miraculo

A far more intriguing interpretation of the Eve/Mary dichotomy can be found in Roberto Rossellini's no less controversial film *Il Miraculo* (*The Miracle*, 1948).[261] When it was released, the movie was denounced by New York's Cardinal Francis Spellman and the Catholic Legion of Decency as being sacrilegious; however, its director has described it as being "an absolutely Catholic work."[262] The film tells the story of Nanni, a demented, homeless peasant woman who meets a stranger one day in the hills outside her town. Convinced that the man is Saint Joseph, Nanni babbles to him foolishly, thanking him for graces he has given her in the past and begging him to take her with him to heaven. She desperately wants to be with God, despite the fact that the local villagers have told her that "Loonies don't go to heaven." For his part, the stranger (played by Federico Fellini, who wrote the story on which *Il Miraculo* is based) says nothing, simply offering Nanni more and more sips from the bottle of wine that he carries with him.

Eventually, Nanni becomes drunk and falls back on the grass of the hillside, murmuring to herself, "Oh, what paradise. What paradise!" She is Eve in a Garden of her own making, though the rugged Italian hills seem anything but edenic. Nonetheless, Nanni is enchanted by her encounter with the stranger. Lying on the grass, pulling some of it up and chewing on it as if she were one of the goats that she has been caring for, Nanni is at one with the earth. Her body is that of a peasant, fleshy and ill-clad in a cast-off dress she has been given by the local nuns. Growing more and more intoxicated by the wine, she begins pulling at her clothes, complaining about how hot and sweaty she is. She then falls asleep, and when she awakens she is alone save for a few goats that nuzzle her to remind her that it is time to return to the village. She does not realize that her afternoon on the hillside has changed her life entirely.

Nanni's identification with Eve is confirmed in a scene that takes place soon after in the local church. There, as the pious kneel and pray, Nanni spies a basket full of apples and manages to steal one. The beggar Cosimino, who once was her suitor, sees her take the apple and begs for a bite, but she refuses him. This refusal is important, as it differentiates her story from Eve's. In the biblical story of Genesis, we are told that Eve ate the fruit of the forbidden tree, "and she also gave some to her husband, who was with her, and he ate. Then the eyes of both were opened, and they knew that they were naked; and they sewed fig leaves together and made loincloths for themselves" (3:6–7). This passage is often interpreted in Christian tradition as the awakening of the pair to their own sexuality. The fact that Nanni does not share the apple with her suitor Cosimino indicates that she has not yet undergone such an awakening. Though she has eaten of the fruit, she is still innocent of its implications. Her eyes have not yet been opened.

Indeed, even after Nanni discovers that she is pregnant, she does not believe that she has ever engaged in sexual activity. The village women scoff at her, sneering, "She pretended she was a saint!" Nanni, however, denies that she has had sex with anyone: "It's the Lord's grace," she tells them. She is now both Eve and Mary: both earth mother and virgin mother. She tells one of the nuns who dishes out soup to the poor that she has no need to go to Confession because she is already favored by God. The villagers, however, find her claim laughable. Their teasing takes on an ugly tone when one day they catch Nanni in the street and begin to mock her. Placing a blanket around her shoulders and putting a pot on her head, they parade her through the narrow alleyways, taunting and laughing. At one point Nanni stumbles to her knees, and, lifting her eyes to heaven, she prays, "Lord, forgive them." Eve, Mary, Jesus—all of Christian salvation history is embodied in this poor demented creature.

It is precisely this paradox that director Rossellini hoped to convey in making *Il Miracolo*. He explains, "Here we have a mad woman afflicted by some sort of religious fixation. However, besides her fixation, she also has a real deep faith.... Some of the things she believes in, I admit, may seem blasphemous, but her faith is so huge that it rewards her."[263] The contrast between Nanni's faith and the villagers' hypocrisy is emphasized when Nanni, who was chased from the town by the villagers' cruelty, returns one day only to see the townspeople walking in a procession and singing a hymn of praise to the Virgin Mary. The irony is clear: as long as faith makes no real claims on them, the villagers can afford to be devout. If the Virgin were actually to appear in their streets one day, however, they would drive her out just as they drove out poor Nanni.

Rossellini does not forget that according to the Gospel of Luke, the Virgin Mary was in fact sadly neglected even as she was about to give birth to Jesus. According to Luke's infancy narrative, Mary, who was traveling with her husband Joseph, bore her son not in the comfort of an inn but rather in a stable. Nanni also can find no consolation when her labor begins. She climbs the hillside and approaches the village church for help, but its gates are locked, a further reminder from Rossellini that Nanni's faith surpasses even the faith of those who profess to serve God. In despair, Nanni hears the bleating of a goat and follows it up to the church's stable. There she gives birth, exclaiming, "God, my God. My God. My child... My creature. My blood. All mine." As the baby whimpers, she opens her blouse to feed it, and thus ends *Il Miraculo*.

In Rossellini's film, the two paradigms that Christianity offers to women, earth mother and virgin, combine in startling ways. One interpreter of *Il Miraculo* paraphrases Saint Paul's letter to the Romans to describe the central theme of the film: "All nature groans the pains of childbirth until is revealed in man and the whole cosmos the glory of the children of God."[264] In Nanni we see both nature and glory, both flesh and its redemption. Nanni is a repellent character, foolish and dirty, and yet she has a dignity that will not be denied. She refuses to succumb when the nun doling out soup tells her that she must confess her sins; she knows that she has not sinned, and she will not repent for something that she has not done. Moreover, her concern for her unborn baby is tender and protective. Running from the abuse of the townspeople, she assures it, "My blessed child. Don't worry. I'll defend you." She knows what is right and what is wrong, and she is willing to defend her humanity against everyone who tries to deny it. She is by far a more compelling Mary figure than the ethereal virgin of *Hail Mary*.

In sum, we can see in film both a veneration of Mary's status as pure virgin and a resentment against the unrealistic standard that this imposes on all women. Mary is deeply loved as a kindly nurturer but also feared as a demanding mother who is satisfied with nothing less than utter self-renunciation. She is both earth mother and pure vessel. As a model for women, she functions in film as both a faithful follower of God and a powerful goddess in her own right.

One more point: the fact that in Rossellini's *Il Miraculo* Nanni is, as the villagers claim, "loony," should not surprise us. Many of the figures that history now calls saints were mocked and ridiculed in their own day. Even Jesus, as we have seen, was thought by some to be out of his mind. There is often a very fine line between sanctity and insanity, and more than one saint has strayed over that line from time to time. The relationship between holiness and psychosis will be the next topic to address as we near the end of this tour through cinematic saintliness.

10   Saint or Psychotic?

Introduction

When Pierre Janet published his book *The Mental State of Hystericals* in 1901, he listed the following among the symptoms of hysteria: hyperaesthesia, in which certain parts of the body are constantly painful and cannot be subjected to the slightest contact; paralyses and contractures, which result in difficulty of motion, speech, and swallowing; and mental confusion, in which the patient experiences intellectual disturbances and an absence of attention. He also noted that two of his patients, independently of each other, complained of pains so severe that they felt as if an animal were gnawing at their insides.[265]

Consider now the following excerpt from the autobiography of Saint Teresa of Avila:

> With the severest afflictions, I spent three months…sometimes it seemed that sharp teeth were biting into me…. I was so shrivelled and wasted away…that my nerves began to shrink causing such unbearable pains that I found no rest either by day or by night….
>
> …only the Lord can know the unbearable torments I suffered within myself: my tongue, bitten to pieces; my throat unable to let even water pass down…everything seeming to be disjointed; the greatest confusion in my head; all shrivelled and drawn together in a ball. The result of the torments…was that I was…unable to move as though I were dead; only one finger on my right hand it seems I was able to move. Since there was

no way of touching me, because I was so bruised that I couldn't endure it, they moved me about in a sheet, one of the nuns at one end and another at the other. This lasted until Easter. My only relief was that if they did not touch me, the pains often stopped…. The paralysis, although it gradually got better, lasted almost three years.[266]

Was Teresa of Avila a hysteric? Did she suffer from mental illness? If she did, should we no longer think of her as a genuine "mystic"? Should we no longer to think of her as a saint?

What this chapter hopes to do is to explore the complex and often murky territory that lies at the juncture between mental illness and spiritual greatness. It is a simple fact that saintly behavior often appears to us as eccentric at best. Other words that might come to mind are "freakish" or "demented" or "deranged." Nor is it the case that what appears to us as strange would in all cases have seemed perfectly normal in the saint's own context. Saint Clare of Assisi, for example, fasted so severely that she was ordered by both her bishop and by her friend, Saint Francis, to begin eating again. Even in an age that prized asceticism, Clare's behavior was beyond the pale. Likewise, the self-mortifications of Saint Catherine of Siena were so extreme that many of her contemporaries thought her a fanatic.

Hysteria and Mysticism

Hollywood has shown a keen interest in exploring the line between madness and sanctity. Significantly, virtually all of the films centering on this theme have had women as their main characters. It is not entirely clear why this is so, but perhaps one reason is that historically, many mental illnesses, and hysteria in particular, have been thought to afflict women far more often than men. The word "hysteria" actually comes from a Greek word for the uterus (as in the term "hysterectomy"). In ancient Greece, hysteria was thought to be a disease of the womb. Plato's *Timaeus* speculated that when a woman's uterus was barren, it would become distressed and begin to stray around the body; in its wandering, according to the philosopher, the uterus moved upward into the chest cavity and caused difficulty in breathing and swallowing. This difficulty, he continued, drove women "to extremity, causing all varieties of disease."[267]

The identification of hysteria with uterine dysfunction did not end with the Greeks. Roman medical authorities recommended regular sexual intercourse as the best treatment for the malady. Conversely, physicians in the eighteenth century attributed hysteria not to a lonely womb but rather to sexual *over*indulgence. A woman who was diagnosed as hysterical was thought to be at the same time to be morally suspect.

In the twentieth century, Sigmund Freud also attributed hysteria to sexual dysfunction, though he did so in a novel way. Whereas earlier ages had assumed that women's physical problems were responsible for their psychological symptoms, Freud theorized that the reverse was true: that repressed mental and emotional traumas expressed themselves physically in the bodies of hysterics. The most famous patient diagnosed as hysterical by Freud was a young woman whom he called Dora. Throughout her adolescence, Dora had suffered various symptoms including headaches, attacks of nervous coughing, and complete loss of voice. Freud's convoluted analysis of Dora's case concluded that Dora was repressing her love for the husband of her father's mistress. When this man (a friend of the family) had approached Dora when she was only fourteen and had grabbed and kissed her, Dora had run away in fear and revulsion. In response to this reaction, Freud remarks, "Instead of the genital sensation which would certainly have been felt by a healthy girl in such circumstances, Dora was overcome...by disgust." He adds, "I should without question consider a person hysterical in whom an occasion for sexual excitement elicited feelings that were preponderantly or exclusively unpleasurable."[268]

Freud's interpretation of Dora's behavior might seem incredible to us. After all, what Dora undergoes can be interpreted as the sexual abuse of a minor. Nonetheless, it has long been the case that women who do not act as their societies expect them to have been labeled as hysterical or as mentally ill or sometimes simply as "crazy." At other times, such women have been diagnosed as possessed by the devil or, worse, as having willingly espoused themselves to Satan. As we will see, numerous saints have at times been thought of as madwomen or witches or both. Precisely because the saints so often tread beyond the boundaries of polite society, they are sometimes viewed with suspicion and fear.

Movies have made much of the ambiguity of saintly women's lives. Notably, however, nearly all of the films that deal with this theme hold out at least the possibility, if not the certainty, that the women in question are truly holy. Perhaps because of Hollywood's fear of offending the faithful, or perhaps because of filmmakers' desire for complexity in their characters, movies that question saints' sanity often end up suggesting that the saint is more clear-headed than the rest of the world is.

The point of these speculations is that we need not make too fine a distinction between mental illness and "real" mystical experience. As we saw in chapter four, what makes a person a mystic is not that he or she encounters God in a way that is inaccessible to the rest of humanity. Rather, mysticism consists in having psychologically distinct experiences that manifest clearly and intensely a grace that is available to all of us. Thus the criterion by which apparently mystical experiences can be judged is not whether the person who has them is sane but rather whether the experiences genuinely reflect the grace of God.

How have Christians understood this grace? The New Testament author Paul contends that the fruits of the Holy Spirit are love, joy, peace, patience, kindness, generosity, faithfulness, gentleness, and self-control (Gal 5:22–23). Thus, psychologically-unusual experiences that lead to an increase in virtue and good works might be understood as genuinely "mystical" whether or not the person who has them is also afflicted with mental illness. Saint Teresa of Avila urged the sisters in her convent, "This is the reason for prayer, my daughters, the purpose of this spiritual marriage: the birth always of good works, good works." If a spiritual experience, no matter how intense, does not lead to an increase of charity, then according to Christian tradition it is not to be trusted. On the other hand, experiences that open people up to the gifts of the Spirit can, in Christian tradition, be thought to come from God, no matter the psychological state of the one who has them.

Either/Or: Science Versus Religion

Thus in a diagnosis of holy women's lives there is really no reason for us to have to choose between saintliness and psychosis. Unfortunately, a number of movies fail to grasp this point and turn the question of sanctity-versus-insanity into a battle between religion and science. The premise of these films is that one must choose either faith or reason: that saintly characters are either genuinely holy or simply mad, with no options in between. In *The Song of Bernadette*, for instance, religion pits itself against the arrogance of secular science. *Agnes of God*, conversely, deems those who believe in God either tragically naive or deliberately self-deceptive. What neither of these films seems to understand is that one might be both blessed and psychologically disturbed, both holy and insane.

The truth is that science and faith need not be seen as contraries but rather can be understood as complementary modes of human self-exploration and expression. Science and religion conflict only to the extent that math and poetry do, or physics and music, or biology and painting. By framing their stories in terms of atheistic scientists battling pious church-goers, the films in question do justice to neither reason nor faith. Instead, they provide caricatures of both and leave us with a deeper understanding of neither.

The Song of Bernadette

The Song of Bernadette is based on the true story of Marie Bernarde Soubirous, a nineteenth-century French peasant girl. At the age of four-teen, Bernadette began seeing visions of a beautiful lady whom she referred to as "Immaculate Conception" and who was later identified by the faithful as the Virgin Mary. Bernadette died at the age of thirty-five and was canonized in 1933. The grotto in Lourdes where the visions are believed to have occurred has become a site of international pilgrimage.

The grotto's fame is due largely to the waters that flow there and that are thought to contain healing powers. In *The Song of Bernadette*, the beau-tiful lady of Bernadette's visions tells the girl to dig in the dirt of the grotto and to wash herself in the spring that she will find there. When Bernadette does this she finds only mud, but obediently she smears her face and arms with it. At this point the crowd around her, who have come more out of curiosity than piety, begin to laugh at the girl. One of the local func-tionaries cries out, "Citizens! At last you've seen with your own eyes what we officials have known all along: that this story of the Blessed Virgin was born in a sick and warped mind!" The town's officials, rather than being pleased to have an apparent saint in their midst, attempt to discredited Bernadette. In their opinion, her claims of divine intervention are dangerous and will lead to religious fanaticism, reversing humankind's progress towards enlightened reason. They can only feel dismay when, shortly after Bernadette has been led away from the pool of mud by her mother, a spring of clear water begins to bubble up from the site, and a blind man who washes in it claims to have been cured. From their point of view, this "miracle" will only fuel the people's superstitious beliefs.

In their ongoing efforts to have Bernadette's reputation undermined, the local officials summon the town doctor so that he can examine the girl and pronounce her to be insane. For his part, the doctor is willing to consider that Bernadette is suffering from cerebral anemia, catalepsy, or hysteria. Upon closer inspection, however, he discovers that the girl's pulse and reflexes are normal and that she is obviously not feeble-minded. He concludes that he can find no scientific explanation for her visions. Hearing this conclusion, the imperial prosecutor (Vincent Price), who is eager to have Bernadette's claims proven false, asks impatiently, "Science excludes fraud. It excludes mental disease and a miraculous occurrence. I venture then to ask science, what is left?" To this the doctor responds thoughtfully, "Yes. What is left?"

What is left, of course, is the possibility that science is simply wrong and that Bernadette's visions really do come from God. Jennifer Jones, the actress who plays the young saint, appears in the film with a kind of ethereal beauty. According to cinematographer Arthur Miller, who won an Oscar for his work in the film, Jones's saintly countenance is no accident. Miller illuminated the actress with reflected rather than direct light, and he used a spotlight behind her head in order to create a halo effect. In addition, he under-lit the other actors in any scene in which Jones appeared.[269] The result is a visual depiction of holiness; viewers cannot help but sense Bernadette's goodness and piety.

When the local officials in Bernadette's town are unable to discredit the girl's visions, they bring in a professor of psychiatry and neurology to examine her. The psychiatrist is confident that the Virgin Mary's alleged appearances can be explained by a mental defect in Bernadette: "Such delusions are a usual symptom of paranoia," he says loftily. He and the imperial prosecutor begin an examination of the girl, asking her to close her eyes and stand on one foot and do multiplication problems in her head. Their investigation is interrupted, however, by the parish priest. He, though skeptical at first, has come to believe that what Bernadette saw was genuine. The priest arranges for the girl to live in a convent that will allow her a life of quiet prayer. Not everyone in the convent is pleased with this, however. One nun tells the girl that she ought to be thankful that she did not live in former times, when "creatures who boasted of equivocal visions and produced springs as if by magic were burned at the stake."

Eventually, however, even this nun becomes convinced of the saint's holiness, largely because of Bernadette's patience in suffering. The imperial prosecutor also comes to regret his earlier skepticism. In the end, he falls to his knees at the grotto where the faithful are holding a candlelight vigil, and he too prays to the Virgin. As for Bernadette, she undergoes a long investigation at the hands of the Church. Though she dies before any definitive conclusion is reached as to the merit of her visions, audiences know that Bernadette is the genuine article. As the girl lies on her deathbed, the beautiful lady appears to her once more, and, as the film comes to a close, bells begin to ring. We come to believe the truth of what the priest in the movie has said: "To those who believe in God, no explanation is necessary. To those who do not, no explanation will suffice." Religion has trumped the pretensions of science, and for those with eyes to see, faith has been vindicated at last.

Agnes of God

If *The Song of Bernadette* celebrates the victory of faith over science, *Agnes of God* heads in the opposite direction. The movie stars Meg Tilly as naive young Sister Agnes and Jane Fonda as the tough psychiatrist Martha Livingston who is investigating the murder of Agnes's newborn child. Anne Bancroft plays Mother Miriam Ruth, the superior of the convent who distrusts psychiatry in general and Dr. Livingston in particular.

The premise of the movie is that Sister Agnes has given birth to a baby in a Montreal convent one dark night, and the infant is later found strangled and stuffed into a trash can. How the girl became pregnant, and who killed her baby, are the mysteries to be solved. Agnes herself is an unreliable witness. When the psychiatrist asks her how babies are born, Agnes answers, "Well, I think they come from—an angel lights on their mother's chest and whispers into her ear. That makes good babies start to grow. And bad babies come from when a fallen angel squeezes in down there, and they grow, grow, till they come out down there. I don't know where good babies come out." She claims no memory of having given birth or even of seeing the baby that the doctor and the police keep asking her about.

Much of the movie centers on the battle between religion and science. Mother Miriam challenges Dr. Livingston to explain how it happened that Agnes at one point developed the stigmata, imitations of the wounds Jesus received when he was nailed to the cross. "Do you think hysteria could do that?" she demands. Replies the doctor coolly, "It's been doing it for centuries." Later, Livingston accuses the nun of deliberately keeping Agnes from learning about the world around her: "Poverty, chastity, and ignorance is what you live by!" The battle lines are clearly drawn. From the doctor's perspective, science is the bearer of enlightenment and progress, and religion is a superstition that twists consciences and darkens minds. In the mother superior's eyes, psychiatry is a cold and hyper-rational machine that arrogantly refuses to recognize the higher truth of religion.

To its credit, the film does not rigidly maintain this dichotomy. The psychiatrist is shown to have spiritual struggles of her own, and Mother Miriam emerges as a compassionate and level-headed woman with worldly sensibilities and a strong intelligence. Yet, ultimately, the movie cannot reconcile or even illuminate the separation that it sets up between reductionistic rationality and gullible faith. Arguing about who might be the father of Agnes's baby, the mother superior suggests that there may be no father at all—that the child may be the product of a virginal conception: "A miracle is an event without an explanation!" she declares. This possibility is judged "insane" by the doctor, who contends that Agnes was raped or seduced or perhaps seduced a man herself. She thinks that religious belief can shed no light on Agnes's life: "Everything that Agnes has done is explainable through modern psychiatry." Mother Miriam cannot believe what she is hearing. She asks, "That's what you believe she is? The sum of her psychological parts?" In reply, the doctor shouts, "That's what I have to believe!"

Part of what is at issue between the characters of Martha Livingston and Mother Miriam is whether or not Agnes is a saint: whether or not she is, as the Mother says, "attached to God. Left in his hands at birth." The doctor dismisses this possibility out of hand. "Show me a miracle!" she demands, though when Agnes's bleeding palms and apparently inexplicable pregnancy are pointed out, Livingston scoffs that both have purely natural explanations. The film thus leaves no middle ground between faith and reason. One can accept either the findings of science or the promises of religion, but not both.

The last few scenes of *Agnes* only serve to reinforce this conclusion. At her court hearing, Agnes reveals that she was impregnated by a lover, presumably an angel, who "opened his wings" and lay on top of her. All the while, she says, the lover sang to her this song: "Charlie's neat, Charlie's sweet, Charlie's a dandy." Reflecting on Agnes's story, the doctor comments at the very end of the film that she doesn't know if the song had been sung by a field hand trying to seduce the young nun, or if it was a lullaby Agnes remembered from her childhood, and if then the father of the baby was "hope, and love, and desire, and a belief in miracles."

Given all that the doctor has adamantly and defiantly argued throughout the entire script, this comment comes as an unsatisfactory resolution to the serious issues that the film has attempted to raise. The dynamics of *Agnes of God* make the nun's holiness dependent on the origin of her child. Either she was seduced by a laborer, in which case she is merely to be pitied, or she was impregnated by "a belief in miracles," in which case she is beloved of God. The trial shows that the baby's father was not in fact an angel. After all, what kind of angel would sing the kind of ditty that Agnes repeats during the trial? If Agnes was not impregnated by divine will, then the movie must conclude that the girl is psychotic. Just before the credits begin to roll, the doctor says of Agnes wistfully, "I want to believe that she was blessed." This half-hearted wish to the contrary, *Agnes of God* ends up siding with the claims of science over those of religion.

Both/And: Holiness and Mental Illness

Both *The Song of Bernadette* and *Agnes of God* rely on a dichotomy between science and religion. One vindicates faith while the other opts for the path of reason. Several other films, however, see the relation between holiness and mental illness as being more complex. *Breaking the Waves*, for example, features a character with a history of psychiatric disturbances who is nonetheless truly holy. Likewise, in *Household Saints* we see a young woman confined to a mental hospital who is vindicated by the film as having been a saint. Finally, *The Messenger*, which tells the story of Saint Joan of Arc, leaves both the question of Joan's sanity and the question of her sanctity open. By introducing a character called simply "The Conscience," the movie allows us into the interior of Joan's psyche, and viewers are asked to judge for themselves about the character of what they find there.

Breaking the Waves
Lars Von Trier's exquisite film *Breaking the Waves* (1996) centers on a character named Bess (played by Emily Watson), a simple-minded young woman living on the Scottish seacoast. Impulsive, prone to emotional outbursts, and sexually inexperienced, Bess falls in love with Jan, a rugged worker who makes his living on the oil rigs of the North Sea. Bess marries Jan despite the misgivings of the elders of her church, a grim lot who distrust Jan as an "outsider" to their ways. When Jan asks the church minister why there are no bells in the steeple, the minister answers icily that they do not need bells in order to worship God. Bess confesses that she loves church bells, though, and she giggles that she and Jan should put some in the church.

Throughout the film, we are able to eavesdrop on the prayers that Bess offers up to God. Moreover, we get to hear God's replies as well. That is, when Bess kneels and prays aloud in her desolate church, she acts as both pray-er and answerer, pleading with God in her own voice and then closing her eyes, dropping her tone an octave and responding as if she were God himself. Viewers can't decide if Bess is just playing a childish game of make-believe or if she is truly demented and believes that God is speaking to her. The fact that she has a history of mental illness, having been treated by a psychiatrist after the death of her brother, inclines us towards the latter opinion.

The turning point of *Breaking the Waves* comes when Jan is seriously injured in an accident on an oil rig. Bess feels responsible for this tragedy; missing him during his long stints on the rigs, she had prayed that Jan would come home to her, and now he has indeed come home, though as a paraplegic. (When Bess confides her feeling of responsibility to Jan's doctor, he says gently, "Wow. What powers you possess. Do you really believe that you possess such powers?") Despite her feelings of guilt, however, she is overjoyed to have Jan by her side again.

Jan is not quite so pleased to be home. Despairing because he is unable to make love with his wife, he encourages her to seek out as many sexual experiences as she can and to come back and tell him about them. Bess at first refuses. Gradually, however, she becomes convinced that if she does what Jan asks, she will restore him to health. Thus Bess begins her slow descent into a suffering that will either destroy her or save Jan, or perhaps both. She begins by trying to seduce Jan's doctor, a kind man who feels protective of her and who turns her down as gently as he can. She then moves on to strangers, fondling a man on a bus and picking up men in a bar. Eventually, she convinces a local boatman to take her to one of the ships anchored offshore. There she is subjected to brutal sex and is nearly murdered. All of this she does with the conviction that in some mystical way, her suffering will lead to Jan's being cured.

At this point, the townspeople decide that Bess has gone too far. The Church casts her out, and even her own mother refuses to open the door when Bess shows up sobbing and pleading to be let inside. The kindly doctor intervenes on her behalf, begging Jan, whose condition is deteriorating rapidly and who is expected to die soon, to sign papers committing Bess to a psychiatric hospital. The doctor tells him, "She's suffering from delusions regarding your condition." Jan agrees to sign, and the next time Bess shows up to visit her husband's sickbed, she is carted off by police.

She manages to escape from her captors, however, and she determines to go once again to the ship where she had been attacked. We can only imagine what happens to her there, but soon after this she is rushed back to the hospital, broken and bleeding. After a brief conversation with her mother, who could not in the end bear to shun her only daughter, Bess dies.

After the death, an investigation takes place to determine if the doctor was negligent in caring for Bess. The doctor tells the magistrate that since Bess's death, he has changed his opinion of what condition she was suffering from. He says, "Instead of my writing neurotic or psychotic there, I might just use a word like—'good.'" The magistrate peers at him in disbelief: "The deceased was suffering from being *good*?" The doctor acknowledges that his judgment sounds absurd, and he allows his previous assessment of her as suffering from mental illness to stand. Nonetheless, we are given reason to believe that what the doctor says is true. As we see soon after, Jan has in fact recovered from what was supposed to be his deathbed. He can now get about with crutches, and we know that one day he will walk without them.

Indeed, Jan is well enough to trick the minister of the church that cast Bess out. Refusing to allow the church people to bury her, he fills her coffin with sand instead. He and his friends then take Bess's body on their ship, and, after an emotional scene, they commit her to the sea. It is then that the doctor's assessment of Bess as "good" is vindicated. The next morning, though there are no other ships in the area and there is nothing natural that could be the cause, Jan and his friends hear a magical sound: the ringing of bells, the bells that Bess loved so dearly.

Bess was good. Bess was psychologically unstable. Bess had a clarity of spirit that made those around her love her and that in the end was rewarded by the heavens.

Household Saints

In Nancy Savoca's, *Household Saints* (based on the novel by Francine Prose), the questions of sanctity and sanity are given similarly complex treatment. In *Household Saints*, the saint in question is Teresa Santangelo, a mousy young woman who dresses in drab brown clothes and who wants more than anything to become a Carmelite nun. Teresa is the only daughter of Catherine and Joseph Santangelo, hard-working Italian-Americans who run a sausage shop and who have for the most part abandoned their Catholic upbringing. When Joseph's mother Carmela dies,

Catherine packs away all of the old woman's holy pictures and crucifixes, hoping never to look at them again.

Things don't work out quite the way Catherine had planned, however. One might say that the responsibility for this lies with the couple themselves; when their daughter was born in 1952, they named her Teresa Carmela, a name that evokes not only the child's extremely religious grandmother, but the Carmelite spiritual tradition and two great Carmelite saints as well (Thérèse of Lisieux and Teresa of Avila). Little Teresa Santangelo was fated from the start.

When she is seven or eight, Teresa's obsession with religion begins to take root. The year is 1960, and rumors are growing that the pope will soon reveal the famous "secret of Fatima"—the words supposedly delivered by the Virgin Mary to three shepherd children in Portugal in 1917. When Teresa overhears another child talking about the upcoming revelation, she takes it upon herself to ensure that the pope's words will promise hope rather than disaster. Sitting in her bedroom in her Catholic school uniform, she prays, "Dear God, please let the news from Our Lady's letter be good." She vows to sit without moving for five minutes to add weight to her request.

When days pass and the pope makes no statement regarding the apparition at Fatima, Teresa becomes despondent. "I know I did something wrong," she sobs. Looking in despair around her bedroom, she gets up from her bed and waters the plant that she had been neglecting. She rips up a math exercise that she had not completed with absolute neatness, and she re-does it with painstaking accuracy. Teresa is on her way to becoming perfect for God.

Her desire for perfection is reinforced when in high school she wins an essay competition (the topic: "Why Communism is anti-Christ") and receives as her prize a copy of *The Story of a Soul*. This little book is the autobiography of Saint Thérèse of Lisieux, the nineteenth-century saint also called "The Little Flower." In her memoirs, Saint Thérèse described what has come to be known as the "Little Way." One need not perform extraordinary feats to be pleasing to God, said Thérèse; one need only perform small tasks with love. Teresa Santangelo takes this advice to heart and redoubles her efforts to be worthy of Jesus's attention.

It is when her parents refuse to let her become a nun that Teresa stops eating. She tells her mother that she simply isn't hungry, but underlying her lack of appetite is a challenge. She tells her father, "When you let me join the Carmelites, that's when I'll eat," to which he replies, "Then you starve!" Eventually Teresa gives in to her hunger and wolfs down some of the family's sausage. She interprets her capitulation as a sign of spiritual weakness. She asks Jesus, "Why have you abandoned me?" and tells him that she wants nothing more than to be a saint for him. "So that is my sin—to want too much. And this is my punishment—to be nothing." She believes that satisfying her bodily needs has condemned her to a life of ordinary human sinfulness.

The lengths to which Teresa will go in her desire to please Jesus become clear when she meets up with a law student named Leonard who is studying at Saint John's University. Leonard is seemingly oblivious to Teresa's naïvete and believes that her religious preoccupations are simply the normal piety of any Catholic girl. He clumsily lures Teresa into his bedroom and then tells her to take off her clothes. She does this without hesitation, observing of herself, "I feel that I am following someone else's orders. It must be God." When the sexual act is over and Teresa has stained the sheets with blood, she states flatly, "I'm going to hell." She begins to question her own devotion to God, asking plaintively, "What if this is all the Devil's work? Or worse, what if it's only real life, plain and simple?"

Unsettled by the possibility that she is merely imagining God's approval of her obedience to him, she embarks on an even more severe regimen of tasks. She scrubs crumbs out of the toaster with a toothbrush, and she lies on her floor at night with arms stretched out in a cruciform position. Her efforts are finally rewarded. One day when she is ironing Leonard's red checked shirt, Jesus appears to her wearing nothing but the shroud he was buried in. He thanks her for taking such good care of one of his lambs, and she offers to wash and iron his robe for him. Suddenly the whole room is filled with red checked shirts, and Teresa and Jesus share a hearty laugh together.

At this point, both Leonard and Teresa's parents realize that something has gone seriously wrong. Teresa dresses herself in a bridal veil and vows not to leave her room lest she miss Jesus's next visit. She refuses to eat until she can share her food with him, and she will not sleep unless she can dream of him: "Oh my sweet Jesus, when will we see each other again?" Consulting a mental hospital, Teresa's parents learn that their daughter is suffering from "acute hallucinatory psychoses brought on by a particularly difficult and prolonged adolescent psychosexual adjustment, no doubt aggravated by a somewhat obsessional religious nature." Teresa is admitted to the hospital, where she continues to pursue the Little Way of Saint Thérèse, scrubbing floors and ironing sheets.

It is clear that Teresa has real psychological handicaps. What is not made clear to viewers is if Teresa is simply mentally ill or if she is really receiving apparitions as well. When Jesus visits her, we see the room filled with red shirts as clearly as she does. When after this incident her parents arrive to take her home, however, we see with them that what Teresa believed to be miraculous signs of Jesus's love are simply ordinary pastel-colored shirts hanging in a closet. When Teresa claims to be playing cards with God the Father, Jesus, and Saint Thérèse ("The Little Flower isn't much of a pinochle player," she says), we feel inclined to believe her, and yet, when she confides that God the Father is fond of the same sins as her earthly father is, cheating at cards and tipping the meat scales with his thumb, we begin to think that Teresa's visions are nothing more than infantile projections.

Nor is the question settled at the end of the film. When Teresa dies unexpectedly, her father becomes convinced that the girl was a saint. Flowers bloom where the day before there were only weeds, and Teresa's body gives off the scent of roses. Her mother, however, is unconvinced: "She was crazy, Joseph. She went crazy ironing shirts in her boyfriend's apartment. There have been no miracles here!"

Her mother's skepticism notwithstanding, the story of Teresa Santangelo takes on the appearance of hagiography. At her funeral, the faithful leave notes asking for favors, and, according to the narrator of the film, every one of those favors was granted. Moreover, the family's sausage was said to begin working miracles, curing everything from heart disease to cancer. To those who would scoff at the story, the narrator sums up the meaning of Teresa's life: "She saw God in her work. How many of us can say that?"

Indeed, though Teresa seems quite clearly to be emotionally unbalanced, underlying her activities is a genuine love of God and a sincere desire to serve. It would be wrong to trivialize her spiritual intensities as mere craziness, as her mother does. For all of her misguided notions, Teresa follows a path that has been trod by innumerable spiritual worthies: seeking God in the details of everyday life. It is a path that most of us would find far too demanding.

The Messenger

By one count, there have been as many as thirty films made about Saint Joan of Arc.[270] We seem never to tire of this fifteenth-century peasant who, at the behest of what she understood as heavenly voices, led an army to victory and brought Charles VII to the French throne. Both hailed as a prophet and vilified as a harlot and heretic in her own day, she has since come to symbolize any number of causes: individualism, feminism, French patriotism, faithful Catholicism, and anti-clericalism, among them.[271] In film, depictions of Joan range from Maria Falconetti's passionate and tortured portrayal of the saint in Carl Theodor Dreyer's *La Passion de Jeanne d'Arc* (1928) to the wholesome and hearty performance of Leelee Sobieski in Christian Duguay's mini-series *Joan of Arc* (1999).

One of the most interesting approaches to Joan, however, can be found in Luc Besson's *The Messenger*, starring Milla Jovovich (1999). This interpretation of the saint's life is distinctive precisely because it takes seriously the possibility that Joan's voices may have been the product of her own desires for revenge and for fame rather than signs from God. While the movie does not directly raise the question of mental illness, Jovovich's performance at times calls to mind the mannerisms of someone suffering from schizophrenia. By the end of the film, we are not sure if we have been watching someone in need of psychiatric treatment, someone destined by God to restore the fortunes of France, or both.

It is nothing new to suggest that Joan may have been suffering from some mental disturbance. In 1922, the Australian physician Charles MacLaurin described Joan's voices as a delusional compensation for the girl's failure to develop sexually. According to sources close to the saint, Joan never menstruated, and this, according to MacLaurin, was the root of her trouble: "The mighty forces which should have manifested themselves in normal menstruation manifested themselves in her furious religious zeal and her Voices." The physician continues, "It is not for one moment to be thought that Jeanne ever had the slightest idea of what was the matter with her; ...the only thing that she did not know was that her delusions were entirely subjective—that her Voices had no existence outside her own mind."[272]

The Messenger does not speculate about the menstrual life of the saint. However, it does provide in one scene a motive for Joan's thirst for battle. This scene, which has no basis in the historical record, takes place in Domrémy, Joan's place of birth. Joan is a young girl, perhaps eleven or twelve, and English soldiers invade the village. In a panic, Joan rushes home and is greeted by her sister, who quickly hides her in a closet. The sister, however, does not have time to hide herself, and when three of the soldiers burst in, one of them impales her with his sword. He then rapes the poor girl's corpse as Joan huddles inside the cupboard, watching.

A flashback of this event occurs during Joan's first battle. Convinced that her voices have commanded her to crown Charles VII the king of France, Joan has gone to the exiled Charles and somehow convinced him to let her lead an army against the English and their Burgundian collaborators. Charles, sensing political gain, has agreed to her proposition and outfitted her with armor and horse. Her first military venture takes place at the city of Lyons, which has been under siege. During this battle Joan is pierced by an arrow, and in a delirium born of pain she sees the face of the loathsome English rapist with his sword, and she hears her sister's screams. Awakening with a start, she manages to rise from her bed and rejoin the fight just in time to hear that victory has been declared.

The victory has come at a tremendous price, however. Joan surveys the battlefield and sees mangled bodies everywhere. Decapitated heads and limbs lie about on the ground, and crows pick among the bodies. Shocked and wild-eyed, Joan keeps repeating to herself, "This is not possible. This is not possible." Looking at her own hands covered in blood, she shouts, "I must confess! I must confess!" and summons a priest to hear her sins. Over and over again, in a frenzy, she assures her soldiers that everything will be fine, everything will be just fine—obsessively she comforts them even as her eyes show the panic of a trapped and wounded animal.

The victory at Lyons allows Charles to travel to Rheims to be crowned, but Joan is not satisfied that she has completed her mission. She continues to fight the English even though Charles shows less and less inclination to support her. Eventually she is taken captive and is charged before an ecclesiastical court with the crime of heresy. The English wish to see her denounced as a witch so that her reputation as a heroine will be destroyed.

During her trial, the same kind of compulsive muttering that she exhibited after her first battle marks Joan's speech. She holds her hands in front of her mouth like a frightened child, and she flicks her head about as if suffering from a tic. When asked if she has ever killed someone in battle she says, "No. Maybe. But only to defend myself!" She has none of the composure that marks so many other Hollywood versions of her life. Instead, she is frantic and unsure of herself.

The most interesting feature of *The Messenger* is its introduction of a character called "The Conscience," played by Dustin Hoffman. The

Conscience shows up in Joan's prison cell and torments her by digging relentlessly into the motives that have guided her campaign against the English. Joan defends herself by pointing to all of the signs from God that she has received: the voices that spoke to her, the wind and clouds that accompanied her visions, and, most importantly, the weapon that she found as a girl and subsequently carried into battle. She declares belligerently to The Conscience, "The sword lying in the field. That—that was a sign." The Conscience answers calmly, "No, that was a sword in a field. You didn't see what was, Joan. You saw what you wanted to see." The Conscience then calls into her question her assertion that she has never killed anyone, or, if she has, that it was only in self-defense. She stands by her claim: "I never took pleasure in hurting anyone!" The Conscience asks, "Really?" At this point Joan falls to her knees in despair.

During her trial, Joan is given the opportunity to save herself if she will only acknowledge that she is a heretic. If she signs a recantation she will be condemned to prison, but at least her life will be spared. Threatened by the flames of the executioner's pyre, the girl reluctantly makes her mark on the page that the bishop holds before her. At that moment The Conscience appears before her: "You know what you just signed? You just signed away His existence. For you, He's a lie. An illusion. In the end it was you who abandoned Him." Joan is left in despair. Abandoned by King Charles and by France, and having turned away from her God, she has nothing left but her chains and her grief.

In her prison cell, The Conscience makes one last appearance: "You want to confess? I'm listening." Here Joan comes to grips with the truths that have haunted her and which she has refused to see. She makes her confession: "I saw so many signs. Ones I wanted to see. I fought out of revenge and despair. I was all the things that people believe they are allowed to be when they're fighting for a—a cause. I was proud, and stubborn. Selfish. Yes. Cruel." Compassionately, The Conscience lays his hand on her head and absolves her. At this point, Joan is ready to face her death. She renounces her earlier recantation and is led to the site of her execution. The movie's last scene is of Joan, eyes wide in terror and pain, as the flames catch the hem of her shift and engulf her. Through the flames we see a cross held aloft, sign of Joan's faith.

Saintly Insanity

In his translation of the biblical Book of Job, Stephen Mitchell remarks, "Any idea about God, when pursued to its extreme, becomes insanity."[273] Perhaps the saints simply make the mistake of believing too much—having too much faith in the God whom they love, or trusting too much that in the end, God will redeem them. The saints are connoisseurs of extravagance. They compose their lives on the vast canvasses of heaven, and so it is no wonder that those lives stretch beyond the boundaries of the puny frames that this earth provides.

Any film that hopes to capture saintly lives must thus keep its own limits in mind. The best cinematic depictions of holiness will find ways to point audiences beyond what they see and into the depths of the human heart. Those depths are not always beautiful. Sometimes in fact they are hideous. But our only hope of portraying holiness on screen is to proceed with courage, believing, like Bess and Teresa and poor Joan of Arc, that what we see is only the beginning of what there is to know.

Additional Titles of Interest

The following is a *partial* list of additional documentaries, docudramas and feature films about saints and saintly figures.

Martyrs

Documentaries

Fourteen Flowers of Pardon: St. Maria Goretti (60 mins.)
Irish Martyrs (47 mins.)
Passion of the Saints, vol. 1: *Blood of Martyrs* (1996, 50 mins.) Learning Channel
Pillars of Faith: Martyrs to Christianity (1999, 48 mins.)

Docudramas and Feature Films

Becket (1964) Stars Richard Burton
Joan of Arc (1948) Directed by Victor Fleming, Stars Ingrid Bergman
Joan of Arc (1954) Directed by Roberto Rossellini, Stars Ingrid Bergman
Joan of Arc: France's Call for Arms (1996) Stars Catherine Sage
Joan of Arc: The Virgin Warrior (2000) Stars Mira Sorvino
Saint Joan (1957) Directed by Otto Preminger, Stars Jean Seberg
Trial of Joan of Arc (1962) Directed by Robert Bresson, Stars Florence Carrez

Ascetics and Mystics

Documentaries

The Letters of St. Thérèse (420 mins.) Thirteen parts, Eternal Word Television Network (EWTN)

Miracle of St. Thérèse (1959, 115 mins.) French with English dubbing

Passion of the Saints, vol. 2: *Hermits: Monks and Madmen* (1996, 50 mins.) Learning Channel

Passion of the Saints, vol. 3: *Mystics and Miracles* (1996, 100 mins.) Learning Channel

Pioneers of the Spirit: Hildegard of Bingen (24 mins.)

Pioneers of the Spirit: Julian of Norwich (1997, 24 mins.)

Pioneers of the Spirit: Teresa of Avila (1997, 24 mins.)

St. Thérèse of the Child Jesus (1997, 90 mins.)

Seeds of the Desert: The Legacy of Charles de Foucauld (38 mins.)

Teresa of Avila: Personality and Prayer (390 mins.) Thirteen parts, narrated by Thomas Dubay

Thérèse: Living on Love (55 mins.)

Docudramas and Feature Films

Clare of Assisi (1993) One-woman drama, Stars Karen Lee Hodgson

Faustina (1995) Life of Blessed Faustina Kowalska

Teresa de Jesus, Spanish with English subtitles. EWTN

Apostles and Missionaries

Documentaries

Legends of Ireland: Saint Patrick/Brendan the Navigator (1998, 52 mins.)

Mary Magdalen: An Intimate Portrait (43 mins.)

Pillars of Faith: New Testament Witnesses (1998, 48 mins.)

The Story of the Twelve Apostles (100 mins.) History Channel

Docudramas and Feature Films

Paul the Emissary Stars English actor Garry Cooper

Peter and Paul (1981) TV Miniseries, Stars Anthony Hopkins, Robert Foxworth

St. John in Exile (1986) Stars Dean Jones

St. Patrick: The Irish Legend (2000) TV Miniseries, Stars Patrick Bergin

 Miracle Workers

Documentaries

Padre Pio: 50 Years of Thorns and Roses (60 mins.)
Padre Pio: A Great Man of Our Century (55 mins.)
Padre Pio: Man of God (55 mins.)
Padre Pio: The Priest Who Bore the Wounds of Christ (390 mins.) Thirteen parts from EWTN

Docudramas and Feature Films

Touch (1997) Based on an Elmore Leonard novel

 Saints to the Poor

Documentaries

Blessed Mother Katharine Drexel (60 mins.)
Citizen-Saint—The Life and Miracle of Frances Cabrini (73 mins.)
Francis and Clare of Assisi (1999, 30 mins.)
Intimate Portrait: Mother Teresa (1999, 60 mins.)
Mother Teresa: A Life of Devotion (1987, 50 mins.) A&E Biography series
Mother Teresa: In the Name of God's Poor (1997, 93 mins.) Hallmark Production
Saints in the Making: Katharine Drexel (29 mins.) Narrated by Benedict Groeschel
Saints in the Making: Pierre Toussaint (28 mins.) Narrated by Benedict Groeschel

Docudramas and Feature Films

Don Bosco (1935) In Italian with Spanish dubbing
Don Bosco (1988) Stars Ben Gazzara
Francis of Assisi (1961) Directed by Michael Curtiz, Stars Bradford Dillman
The Small Miracle (1951) Boy takes donkey to Assisi in hopes of a cure

Saints of the Holocaust

Documentaries

Maximilian Kolbe (21 mins.)
Ocean of Mercy (60 mins.) Features Faustina Kowalska, Maximilian Kolbe

Docudramas and Feature Films

The Assisi Underground (1985) Priest aids Jews in Italy

 # Mary and Joseph

Documentaries

Bernadette (45 mins.)
Betania: Land of Grace (58 mins.) Marian apparitions and healings in Venezuela
The Blinking Madonna (1995, 57 mins.) Statue of Mary in Boston appears to blink
The Cloak of Juan Diego (28 mins.)
The Holy Snakes of the Virgin Mary (47 mins.) In Greece, snakes appear for Mary's feast
Intimate Portrait: The Virgin Mary (60 mins.)
Joseph: The Man Closest to Christ (60 mins.)
Miracles: Lourdes, Fatima, Guadalupe and Knock (60 mins.)
Our Lady in Scripture and Tradition (390 mins.) Thirteen parts, EWTN
Our Lady of Guadalupe (70 mins.)
Woman Clothed With The Sun (270 mins.) Marian apparitions

Docudramas and Feature Films

Apparitions at Fatima (90 mins.)
Bernadette (1987) Stars Sydney Penny
Blessed Art Thou (2000) Monk miraculously becomes pregnant woman
Mary of Nazareth (1996) Directed by Jean Delannoy
The Miracle of Our Lady of Fatima (1952) Stars Gilbert Roland

 Teachers and Preachers

Documentaries

Company: Inigo and His Jesuits (52 mins.)
A Downright Account—Cardinal Newman (60 mins.)
A Gift of God: Josemaria Escriva (57 mins.)
Pioneers of the Spirit: Augustine of Hippo (1997, 24 mins.)
Pioneers of the Spirit: Ignatius Loyola (24 mins.)
St. Augustine: His Life and Spirituality (90 mins.) Three parts, narrated by Benedict Groeschel
St. John Neumann (28 mins.)

Docudramas and Feature Films

Loyola, The Soldier Saint (1952)
Mary (1994) Australian film about Mary MacKillop
A Time for Miracles (1980) Stars Kate Mulgrew as Elizabeth Seton

 Other

Island Soldiers: The History of the Celtic Saints (1997, 180 mins.)
Pillars of Faith: Celtic Saints (1998, 48 mins.)
Return Of The Saints, (1996, 50 mins.) Cardinal Hume gives tour of England's saints
Saints' Gallery (158 mins.) Four parts, Saints in art
Saints with Sister Wendy (1998, 60 mins.) Famous nun looks at artwork featuring saints

Notes

[1] See www.suntimes.com/ebert/ebert_reviews/1999/11/111202.html.

[2] *Time*, 29 December 1975, cover.

[3] William James, *The Varieties of Religious Experience* (New York: New American Library, 1958) 216. The characteristics of which James speaks can be found on pp. 216–18.

[4] Augustine, *Confessions*, trans. R. S. Pine-Coffin (New York: Penguin Books, 1961) 175.

[5] Ibid., 169, 181. This translation of Romans appears in the *Confessions*. Unless noted otherwise, all biblical citations are from the New Revised Standard Version (NRSV) of the Bible.

[6] John Henry Newman, *Cardinal Newman's Meditations and Devotions* (New York: Longmans, Green and Co., 1893) 301–302.

[7] James, *The Varieties of Religious Experience*, 217.

[8] Ibid.

[9] John of the Cross, *The Ascent of Mount Carmel*, trans. and ed. E. Allison Peers (New York: Triumph Books, 1991) 57.

[10] This is an English-dubbed version of a German film. The English translation of the original German title is "The Death of the White Marabut."

[11] Catherine of Genoa, *Purgation and Purgatory: The Spiritual Dialogue*, trans. Serge Hughes, Classics of Western Spirituality series (New York: Paulist Press, 1979) 131.

[12] For a fascinating journey into the process of canonization, see Kenneth L. Woodward, *Making Saints: How the Catholic Church Determines Who Becomes a Saint, Who Doesn't, and Why* (New York: Simon and Schuster, 1990).

[13] Woodward, *Making Saints*, 147.

[14] Catherine C. Mooney, *Philippine Duchesne: A Woman with the Poor* (New York: Paulist Press, 1990) 9.

[15] Ibid., 13.

[16] Ibid., 15.

[17] Thomas Aquinas, *Summa Theologica*, 3 vols., Part I, q. 92, art. 1, ad 1., trans. Fathers of the English Dominican Province (New York: Benziger, 1947) 1:466.

[18] Augustine, *The Trinity* XII.3.10, trans. Edmund Hill, ed. John E. Rotelle (Brooklyn: New City Press, 1991) 328.

[19] Mooney, *Philippine Duchesne*, 23.

[20] *The New Saint Joseph Baltimore Catechism*, second ed. (New York: Catholic Book Publishing Co., 1962–1969) 154.

[21] Karl Rahner, "Christianity and the Non-Christian Religions," in *Later Writings*, volume 5 of *Theological Investigations*, trans. Karl-H. Kruger (New York: Crossroad, 1966) 123.

[22] James, *The Varieties of Religious Experience*, 298.

[23] Rudolf Otto, *The Idea of the Holy*, trans. John W. Harvey (New York: Oxford University Press, 1923) 12.

[24] Ibid., 16.

[25] This translation is provided by Stephen Mitchell, *The Book of Job* (New York: HarperCollins, 1979) 6.

[26] Ibid., 73.

[27] Ibid., 79.

[28] Ibid., 33.

[29] Otto, *The Idea of the Holy*, 79.

[30] Mitchell, *The Book of Job*, 88.

[31] Michael Bird, "Film as Hierophany," in John R. May and Michael Bird, eds., *Religion in Film* (Knoxville: University of Tennessee Press, 1982) 4. Many of the insights in this chapter were inspired by this very fine essay by Bird.

[32] Rudolf Arnheim, *Film as Art* (California: University of California Press, 1957) 11.

[33] Ibid., 57.

[34] Siegfried Kracauer, *Theory of Film: The Redemption of Physical Reality* (Princeton: Princeton University Press, 1960) 39, 306.

[35] Paul Tillich, *Systematic Theology*, 3 vols. (Chicago: University of Chicago Press, 1951) 1:237.

[36] Ibid., 239.

[37] Paul Tillich, *Dynamics of Faith* (New York: Harper and Row, 1957) 9.

[38] Ibid., 97.

[39] Sara R. Horowitz, "But Is It Good for the Jews?: Spielberg's Schindler and the Aesthetics of Atrocity," in *Spielberg's Holocaust*, ed. Yosefa Loshitzky (Bloomington: Indiana University Press, 1997) 119.

[40] Otto, *The Idea of the Holy*, 68–70.

[41] Cited by Peter Brown, *The Cult of the Saints* (Chicago: University of Chicago Press, 1981) 82.

[42] Alban Butler, *Lives of the Saints*, 4 vols., ed. Herbert J. Thurston and Donald Attwater (Maryland: Christian Classics, 1990) 1:138.

[43] Peter Brown, *The Cult of the Saints*, 82.

[44] Ellwood E. Kieser, *The Spiritual Journey of a Showbusiness Priest* (New York: Paulist Press, 1996) 322.

[45] Clinton J. Doskey, "Readers Respond: Delille Piece Fictional," *Clarion Herald*, 2 March 2000. See clarionherald.org/20000302/artltr.htm.

[46] "The Acts of Andrew," in *The Other Bible*, ed. Willis Barnstone (San Francisco: Harper and Row, 1984) 462.

[47] Quoted in Peter Brown, *The Cult of the Saints*, 7.

[48] This abbreviation means "Before the Common Era." It is equivalent to BC which means "Before Christ." Most scholars prefer to use BCE and CE (Common Era) to designate time rather than BC and AD (*Anno Domini*, or "Year of the Lord"). They do this in recognition of the fact that not everyone sees the birth of Jesus as the central event of history.

[49] Plato, "Apology," in *Five Dialogues*, trans. G. M. A. Grube (Indianapolis: Hackett, 1981) 44.

[50] Plato, "Phaedo," in *Five Dialogues*, 100, 121.

[51] Ibid., 152.

[52] Ibid., 119.

[53] Christopher Reeve, *Still Me* (New York: Ballantine Books, 1999).

[54] For example, in the book of Genesis, God forms the earth-creature (*ha'adam*) from the dust of the ground, but only after God blows life into its nostrils does it become a *nephesh*—a living being (2:7).

[55] On this point, see John A. T. Robinson, *The Body: A Study in Pauline Theology* (London: SCM Press, 1966).

[56] Athanasius, *Saint Antony of the Desert* (Rockford IL: TAN Books and Publishers, 1995) 56.

[57] "The Second Treatise of the Great Seth," in *The Other Bible*, 117, 119. Emphasis added.

[58] "Open Letter to Universal Pictures from The American Society for the Defense of Tradition, Family and Property," printed in the *New York Times*, 12 August 1988, A7.

[59] Andrew Greeley, "Blasphemy or Artistry?" *New York Times*, 14 August 1988, A1.

[60] There have been numerous recent books published about the life and death of the historical Jesus. One of the most respected is John P. Meier's three-volume work entitled *A Marginal Jew: Rethinking the Historical Jesus*, which was published as part of the Anchor Bible Reference Library. See especially volume 1, *The Roots of the Problem and the Person* (New York: Doubleday, 1991).

[61] "The Martyrdom of Polycarp," in *Early Christian Writings*, trans. Maxwell Staniforth (New York: Penguin Books, 1968) 160–61.

[62] Ibid., 157–61.

[63] Les Keyser and Barbara Keyser, *Hollywood and the Catholic Church* (Chicago: Loyola University Press, 1984) 27.

[64] James M. Skinner, *The Cross and the Cinema* (Connecticut: Praeger, 1993) 37.

[65] Jacobus de Voragine, *The Golden Legend*, 2 vols., trans. William Granger Ryan (Princeton: Princeton University Press, 1993) 1:103.

[66] Ibid., 1:154–56.

[67] Alban Butler, *Lives of the Saints*, 1:256. Emphasis added.

[68] Kathleen Norris, "Maria Goretti—Cipher or Saint?" in *Martyrs*, ed. Susan Bergman (San Francisco: Harper San Francisco, 1996) 308.

[69] Ibid.

[70] The Greco-Roman god of light.

[71] Derek Jarman, *At Your Own Risk* (New York: Overlook Press, 1992) 83.

[72] Woodward, *Making Saints,* 130.

[73] Ibid, 123.

[74] www.suntimes.com/ebert/ebert_reviews/1989/10/377301.html.

[75] For a detailed account of Popiełuszko's murder, see John Moody and Roger Boyes, *The Priest and the Policeman* (New York: Summit Books, 1987). The book draws on the authors' expertise as correspondents for *Time* magazine and the *Times of London*.

[76] Susan Bergman, "Twentieth-Century Martyrs: a Meditation," in *Martyrs*, 9.

[77] This word derives from the Greek word *hagios*, which means "holy." The word "hagiography" refers to literature that tells of the lives and deaths of the saints.

[78] Redemptus Maria Valabek, citing documents from the committee assigned to Bakanja's case, in the Carmelite periodical *Carmel in the World*. Valabek's article was translated by the New York Times, and excerpts of it appeared in that newspaper on 29 January 1995, 47.

[79] Gustavo Gutiérrez, *A Theology of Liberation*, trans. and ed. Caridad Inda and John Eagleson (Maryknoll, New York: Orbis Books, 1973) 13.

[80] See Penny Lernoux, *Cry of the People* (New York: Penguin Books, 1982) 79.

[81] Gutiérrez, *A Theology of Liberation*, 265.

[82] For a discussion of medieval sainthood and asceticism, see André Vauchez, *Sainthood in the Later Middle Ages*, trans. Jean Birrell (New York: Cambridge University Press, 1997).

[83] Emile Cioran, *Tears and Saints*, trans. Ilinca Zarifopol-Johnston (Chicago: University of Chicago Press, 1995) 60.

[84] For this taxonomy of pain, I am indebted to the work of Ariel Glucklich. See especially his book *Sacred Pain: Hurting the Body for the Sake of the Soul* (New York: Oxford University Press, 2001).

[85] Henry Suso, *The Life of the Servant*, in *Henry Suso*, trans. and ed. Frank Tobin, Classics of Western Spirituality series (New York: Paulist Press, 1989) 87–93.

[86] Ibid., 87.

[87] Armando Favazza, *Bodies Under Siege: Self-Mutilation and Body Modification in Culture and Psychiatry* (Baltimore: Johns Hopkins University Press, 1987, 1996) 285, 46.

[88] Ibid., 49.

[89] Ibid., 275.

[90] Rudolph Bell, *Holy Anorexia* (Chicago: University of Chicago Press, 1985) 20.

[91] Ibid., 53.

[92] John of the Cross, *The Ascent of Mount Carmel*, 58.

[93] Ludwig Bieler, ed., *The Irish Penitentials* (Dublin: Dublin Institute for Advanced Studies, 1975) 131.

[94] Caroline Walker Bynum, *Holy Feast and Holy Fast* (Berkeley: University of California Press, 1987) 246.

[95] Angela of Foligno, *Memorial*, in *Complete Works*, trans. Paul Lachance, Classics of Western Spirituality series (New York: Paulist Press, 1993) 163.

[96] Nicholas H. Barker, "The Revival of Religious Self-Flagellation in Lowland Christian Philippines, www2.hawaii.edu/ ~ millado/flagellationfolder/flagella-tion6.html.

[97] Ibid.

[98] Angela of Foligno, *The Book of Blessed Angela of Foligno* in *Complete Works*, 141–42.

[99] Ibid., 141.

[100] Karl Rahner, "Mystical Experience and Mystical Theology," in *Jesus, Man, and the Church*, vol. 17 of *Theological Investigations*, trans. Margaret Kohl (New York: Crossroad, 1981) 97.

[101] Teresa of Avila, *The Book of Her Life* in *Saint Teresa of Avila: Collected Works,* 3 vols., trans. Kieran Kavanaugh and Otilio Rodriguez (Washington, DC: ICS Publications, 1987) 1:251.

[102] Ibid.

[103] David Livingstone, *Dr. Livingstone's Cambridge Lectures*, ed. William Monk (London: Deighton, Bell & Co., 1860), cited by Norman E. Thomas, ed., *Classic Texts in Mission and World Christianity* (Maryknoll, New York: Orbis Books, 1995) 68.

[104] Norman Perrin and Dennis C. Duling, *The New Testament: An Introduction* (San Diego: Harcourt Brace Jovanovich, 1982) 266.

[105] David J. Bosch, *Transforming Mission: Paradigm Shifts in Theology of Mission* (Maryknoll NY: Orbis Books, 1991) 81.

[106] Cited by Bosch, *Transforming Mission*, 218.

[107] This story appears in Alban Butler, *Lives of the Saints*, 2:478–79.

[108] For another film featuring an animal-saint, see Robert Bresson's *Au Hasard, Balthazar*, in which the title character is a donkey.

[109] The word "friar" comes from the Latin word for brother. Unlike monks, who generally remain in one monastery all their lives, friars move from place to place, owning no property.

[110] The terms "exclusivist," "inclusivist," and "pluralist" are defined by Paul Knitter in an essay entitled "Five Theses on the Uniqueness of Jesus," in *The Uniqueness of Jesus*, eds. Leonard Swidler and Paul Mojzes (Maryknoll NY: Orbis Books, 1997) 3n.2.

[111] Associated Press, *Washington Post,* 19 September 1993, A21.

[112] "Declaration on the Relationship of the Church to Non-Christian Religions," also called "*Nostra Ætate,*" par. 2, in *The Documents of Vatican II*, ed. Walter M. Abbott (New York: America Press, 1966) 662.

[113] Knitter, "Five Theses," 10.

[114] Ibid.

[115] Paul Knitter, "Can Our 'One and Only' Also Be a 'One Among Many?'" in *The Uniqueness of Jesus*, 176.

[116] Junípero Serra, *Writings of Junípero Serra*, 4 vols., ed. Antonine Tibesar, (Washington, DC: Academy of American Franciscan History, 1955) 1:63.

[117] Daniel Berrigan, *The Mission: A Film Journal* (San Francisco: Harper and Row, 1986) 62.

[118] George E. Tinker, *Missionary Conquest: The Gospel and Native American Cultural Genocide* (Minneapolis: Fortress Press, 1993) 42.

[119] Serra, *Writings*, 1:103.

[120] Serra, *Writings*, 1:39, 177.

[121] Sherburne F. Cook, "Historical Demography," in *California*, vol. 8 of *Handbook of North American Indians*, ed. Robert F. Heizer (Washington, DC: Smithsonian Institution, 1978) 92.

[122] Serra, *Writings*, 1:307. Serra used the term *neófitos* to designate Native Americans who had converted to Catholicism. The term *gentiles* referred to native people not yet converted.

[123] Edward D. Castillo, "The Impact of Euro-American Exploration and Settlement," in *California*, 101.

[124] *The Mission* is based on a true story, but none of the Jesuits involved in the events it depicts has been canonized or proposed for canonization. The film is nonetheless included in this book for two reasons. First, the lives of Father Gabriel and his brother Jesuits have much in common with the lives of Jesuit saints Roque Gonzalez de Santa Cruz, Alphonsus Rodriguez, and Juan de Castillo, all of whom were martyred in Paraguay in the seventeenth century. Second, the movie is one of the most important cinematic depictions of Catholic missionizing.

[125] For a description of the Reductions, see Philip Caraman, *The Lost Paradise: The Jesuit Republic in South America* (New York: Seabury, 1976) especially 116–53.

[126] According to the New Testament's Acts of the Apostles, "All who believed were together and had all things in common; they would sell their possessions and goods and distribute the proceeds to all, as any had need." See Acts 2:44–45.

[127] Berrigan, *The Mission*, 12, 21.

[128] See *Hurons, Lower Canada, Algonkins, 1650*, vol. 35 of *Jesuit Relations and Allied Documents*, ed. Reuben Gold Thwaites (Cleveland: The Burrows Brothers Col, 1896-1901) 151, 153, 157. The text can also be found at puffin.creighton.edu/jesuit/relations/relations_35.html.

[129] Peter Fraser, *Images of the Passion: The Sacramental Mode in Film* (Connecticut: Praeger, 1998) 65, 61.

[130] Ibid., 60.

[131] Roger Ebert, *Chicago Sun Times*, 1 November 1991. This review is available at www.suntimes.com/ebert/ebert_reviews/1991/11/678497.html.

[132] Brian Moore, *Black Robe* (New York: Fawcett Crest, 1985) *vii*.

[133] *Leap of Faith* questions the authenticity of Christian healers. A film that explores this subject with a far less suspicious eye is the documentary *Miracle Healers*. The movie has an unintended tragic quality to it, however; one healer who is shown making a lame woman walk is none other than Jim Jones of the ill-fated People's Temple in Guyana.

[134] Paul Molinari, "Saints and Miracles," *The Way* (October, 1978): 291, 293.

[135] R. F. Holland, "The Miraculous," in *Miracles*, ed. Richard Swinburne (New York: MacMillan, 1989) 53–54.

[136] Ibid., 55.

[137] Ibid., 66.

[138] Ibid., 62.

[139] Alban Butler, *Lives of the Saints*, 3:589.

[140] Ibid., 3:177.

[141] Teresa of Avila, *The Book of Her Life* in *Saint Teresa of Avila: Collected Works*, 174.

[142] Holland, "The Miraculous," 65.

[143] "Acts of Peter," in *The Other Bible*, 441.

[144] David Hume, *An Enquiry Concerning Human Understanding* (Chicago: Henry Regnery Co., 1956) 120.

[145] Ibid., 132.

[146] See www.csicop.org/si/online.html.

[147] Joe Nickell, *Looking for a Miracle* (Buffalo: Prometheus Books, 1993) 225.

[148] Ibid., 223–25.

[149] *The Little Flowers of Saint Francis*, trans. Raphael Brown (New York: Image Books, 1958) 192.

[150] Ibid.

[151] Desson Howe, "*Stigmata*: Over-the-Top Omens," in *The Washington Post*, 10 September 1999, N45. This review is available at www.washingtonpost.com/wp-srv/style/movies/reviews/stigmatahowe.htm.

[152] See, for example, "The Gospel of Thomas" in *The Other Bible*, 299–307. See also the following Web site: www.miseri.edu/users/davies/thomas/Trans.htm.

[153] Quoted in Ted Harrison, *Stigmata: A Medieval Mystery in a Modern Age* (New York: St. Martin's Press, 1994) 133.

[154] Robert L. Moody, "Bodily Changes During Abreaction," *The Lancet* (28 December 1946): 934.

[155] Hume, *An Enquiry Concerning Human Understanding*, 118.

[156] Laurie Goodstein, "Child's Close Call Aided Nun's Way to Sainthood," *New York Times*, 11 October 1998, A14.

[157] Molinari, "Saints and Miracles," 299.

[158] See Paul Tillich, *Systematic Theology*, 1:115–17.

[159] Luigi Garlaschelli et al., "Working Bloody Miracles," *Nature* 353 (10 October 1991): 507.

[160] Tillich, *Systematic Theology*, 2:47–55.

[161] Paul Tillich, *The Dynamics of Faith*, 79.

[162] Madeleine L'Engle, *A Circle of Quiet* (Connecticut: Fawcett Crest, 1972) 85–86.

[163] Leonardo Boff, *Saint Francis*, trans. John W. Diercksmeier (New York: Crossroad, 1990) 59–64.

[164] See, for example, Psalm 147:6, "The Lord lifts up the downtrodden (*anavim*); he casts the wicked to the ground."

[165] These quotations are from *Francesco* rather than from the NRSV.

[166] For an account of Vincent de Paul's work with foundling children, see Pierre Coste, *The Life and Works of Saint Vincent de Paul*, 3 vols., trans. Joseph Leonard (Maryland: Newman Press, 1952) 2:255–79. See also his letter to Louise de Marillac, dated January 17, 1640, in Vincent de Paul, *Correspondence, Conferences, Documents*, 8 vols., eds. Jacqueline Kilar and Marie Poole, trans. Marie Poole et al. (New York: New City Press, 1990) 2:8–10.

[167] Boff, *Saint Francis*, 60.

[168] This story can be found in Alban Butler, *Lives of the Saints*, 3:298.

[169] This quote appears in Dorothy Brown and Elizabeth McKeown, *The Poor Belong to Us: Catholic Charities and American Welfare* (Cambridge: Harvard University Press, 1997) 1.

[170] See Kathryn Norberg, "Religious Charity and Cultural Norms in Counter-Reformation France," in *With Us Always: A History of Private Charity and Public Welfare*, eds. Donald Critchlow and Charles Parker (Lanham, MD: Rowman and Littlefield, 1998) 42.

[171] John Chrysostom, in Peter Phan, *Social Thought*, Message of the Fathers of the Church series (Wilmington DE: Michael Glazier, 1984) 138, 157–60.

[172] Ibid., 139.

[173] Coste, *The Life and Works of Saint Vincent de Paul*, 1:87–88.

[174] Alba Della Fazia, *Jean Anouilh* (Boston: Twayne Publishers, 1969) 29.

[175] *Rerum Novarum*, par. 39. See www.vatican.va/holy_father/leo_xiii/encyclicals/documents/hf_l-xiii_enc_15051891_rerum-novarum_en.html.

[176] *Pastoral Constitution on the Church in the Modern World*, also called *Gaudium et Spes*, I.2.26 and I.2.30 in *The Documents of Vatican II*, 225, 229.

[177] www.catholicworker.org/dorothyday/canonization.cfm.

[178] *Shoah* is a Hebrew word meaning "catastrophic destruction." It is often used as another name for the Holocaust.

[179] In Marc Fisher, "The Truth That Can Only Hurt," *Washington Post*, 25 June 1999, C8.

[180] Elie Wiesel, *A Jew Today*, trans. Marion Wiesel (New York: Vintage Books, 1979) 235.

[181] Ibid., 48.

[182] Ibid., 235.

[183] Emil Fackenheim, *God's Presence in History* (New York: Harper & Row, 1970; Harper Torchbook, 1972) 84.

[184] Annette Insdorf, *Indelible Shadows: Film and the Holocaust*, second ed. (New York: Cambridge University Press, 1989) xiii.

[185] Ronald Modras, *The Catholic Church and Antisemitism: Poland, 1933–39* (Switzerland: Harwood Academic Publishers, 1994) 42, 101.

[186] Ibid., 145, 182.

[187] Ibid., 227.

[188] Ibid., 176.

[189] Richard Rubenstein and John Roth, *Approaches to Auschwitz* (Atlanta: John Knox Press, 1987) 152–53.

[190] These figures are taken from the Web site of the Auschwitz Museum in Poland, www.auschwitz-muzeum.oswiecim.pl/html/eng/historia_KL/liczba_narodowosc_ofiar_ok.html. Estimates of the number of victims at Auschwitz vary widely.

[191] Wladyslaw T. Bartoszewski, *The Convent at Auschwitz* (New York: George Braziller, 1990) 10.

[192] Franciszek Piper, "The Number of Victims," in *Anatomy of the Auschwitz Death Camp* (Bloomington: Indiana University Press, 1994) 62.

[193] Rubenstein and Roth, *Approaches to Auschwitz*, 111.

[194] Charles Krantz, "Alain Resnais' *Nuit et Brouillard*: A Historical and Cultural Analysis," in *Literature, the Arts, and the Holocaust*, vol. 3 of *Holocaust Studies Annual*, ed. Sanford Pinsker and Jack Fischel (Greenwood FL: Penkevill Publishing, 1987) 116.

[195] Many millions of others died at the hands of Nazis. Jews, however, were the one group slated for total elimination simply because of who they were.

[196] In Hermann Rauschning, *Hitler Speaks* (London: Thornton Butterworth, 1939) 57.

[197] For a table showing these parallels, see Raul Hilberg, *The Destruction of the European Jews* (New York: Holmes & Meier, 1985) 10–11.

[198] John Chrysostom, "Discourse VI," in *Saint John Chrysostom: Discourses Against Judaizing Christians*, vol. 68 of The Fathers of the Church series, trans. Paul W. Harkins, (Washington, DC: The Catholic University of America Press, 1979) 154.

[199] Augustine, "The Creed," 3:10, in *Saint Augustine: Treatises on Marriage and Other Subjects*, vol. 27 of The Fathers of the Church series, trans. Marie Liguori (New York: Fathers of the Church, Inc., 1955) 301.

[200] www.jpost.com/com/Archive/20.Oct.1998/Opinion/Article-1.html.

[201] Pope John Paul II on the occasion of Edith Stein's canonization. See www.jcrelations.net/stmnts/edith-stein.htm.

[202] Edith Stein, *Life in a Jewish Family 1891–1916: An Autobiography*, vol. 1 of *The Collected Works of Edith Stein*, trans. Josephine Koeppel, ed. L. Gelber and Romaeus Leuven (Washington, DC: ICS Publications, 1986) 72.

[203] Friedrich Georg Friedmann, "Not Like That! On the Beatification of Edith Stein," in *Never Forget: Christian and Jewish Perspectives on Edith Stein*, ed. Waltraud Herbstrith, trans. Susanne Batzdorff (Washington, DC: ICS Publications, 1998) 112. Emphasis added.

[204] A photograph of her handwritten testament appears in Maria Amata Neyer, *Edith Stein: Her Life in Photos and Documents*, trans. Waltraut Stein (Washington, DC: ICS Publications, 1999) 70–71. The pertinent part of the text reads, "…zur Sühne für den Unglaubens des jüdischen Volkes."

[205] Franklin Littell, *The Crucifixion of the Jews* (Macon GA: Mercer University Press, 1986) 30.

[206] Teresa of Avila, *The Interior Castle*, trans. Kieran Kavanaugh and Otilio Rodriguez, The Classics of Western Spirituality series (New York: Paulist Press, 1979) 186.

[207] Ibid., 184.

[208] Ibid., 179.

[209] "*Mit Brennender Sorge*: Encyclical of Pope Pius XI on the Church and the German Reich," par. 8. See www.vatican.va/holy_father/pius_xi/encyclicals/documents/hf_p-xi_enc_14031937_mit-brennender-sorge_en.html.

[210] Ibid., par. 15.

[211] Cited by John Cornwell, *Hitler's Pope* (New York: Viking Press, 1999) 292.

[212] After the release of *Massacre in Rome*, the dead pope's sister and nephew sued author Robert Katz for what they saw as a libelous attack on the Holy Father. They lost the case and appealed, and in the end, the suit was judged inconclusive. See Cornwell, *Hitler's Pope*, 380.

[213] Cited by Margherita Marchione, *Pope Pius XII: Architect for Peace* (New York: Paulist Press, 2000) 26.

[214] Cited by Marchione, 60.

[215] See, for example, Ronald J. Rychlak, *Hitler, the War, and the Pope* (Indiana: Our Sunday Visitor, 2000) 249.

[216] Cited by Cornwell, *Hitler's Pope*, 223.

[217] Cited by Cornwell, 131.

[218] Cornwnell, 198–99.

[219] Ibid., 302.

[220] Susan Zuccotti, *Under His Very Windows: The Vatican and the Holocaust in Italy* (New Haven: Yale University Press, 2000) 301.

[221] Michael Phayer, *The Catholic Church and the Holocaust, 1930–1965* (Bloomington IN: Indiana University Press, 2000) 47–50.

[222] Louis Malle, *Au Revoir, Les Enfants*, trans. Anselm Hollo (New York: Grove Press, 1988) v.

[223] Malle in *Malle on Malle*, ed. Philip French (London: Faber and Faber, 1993) 167.

[224] Francis J. Murphy, "Louis Malle's Portrayal of Père Jacques in *Au Revoir, Les Enfants*," *Proceedings of the Annual Meeting of the Western Society for French History* 24 (1997): 389–97.

[225] Malle in *Malle on Malle*, 173.

[226] Murphy, *Père Jacques: Resplendent in Victory* (Washington, DC: ICS Publications, 1998) 92.

[227] Judith E. Doneson, "The Image Lingers: The Feminization of the Jew in *Schindler's List*," in *Spielberg's Holocaust*, 140.

[228] Ilan Avisar, "Christian Ideology and Jewish Genocide in American Holocaust Movies," in *Literature, the Arts, and the Holocaust*, 22.

[229] Lawrence L. Langer, *Admitting the Holocaust* (New York: Oxford University Press, 1995) 6.

[230] Wiesel, *A Jew Today*, 247. Ellipses in the original.

[231] Pope John Paul II, "Letter to Women (June 29, 1995)," par. 10. Italics in the original. See www.vatican.va/holy_father/john_paul_ii/letters/documents/hf_jp-ii_let_29061995_women_en.html.

[232] Mary Daly, *Gyn/Ecology* (Boston: Beacon Press, 1978) 85.

[233] This word comes from Greek and means "Messiah" or "Anointed One."

[234] The NRSV says that Jesus's family "went out to restrain him, for people were saying, 'He has gone out of his mind.'" However, other translators contend that Mark means to say that it was the family itself thought Jesus to be not in his right mind. On this point, see Raymond Brown et al, eds., *Mary in the New Testament* (Philadelphia: Fortress Press, 1978) 54–59.

[235] This event is known as the Annunciation.

[236] For historical difficulties associated with the infancy narratives, see Raymond Brown et al, *Mary in the New Testament*, 12–14.

[237] This is the Revised Standard Version (RSV) of John 2:4. The NRSV translation is, "Woman, what concern is that to you and me? My hour has not yet come."

[238] John P. Meier, *Mentor, Message, and Miracles*, vol. 2 of *A Marginal Jew: Rethinking the Historical Jesus* (New York: Doubleday, 1994) 950, 949.

[239] Quoted in Kenneth Woodward, "Hail, Mary," *Newsweek*, 25 August 1997, 52.

[240] This word refers to books that circulated in the early Christian world but that were not included in the Bible.

[241] "Infancy Gospel of James" 19:3, 20:1, in Robert Funk, ed., *New Gospel Parallels*, vol. 2, *John and the Other Gospels* (Philadelphia: Fortress Press, 1985) 280.

[242] *New Catholic Encyclopedia*, s.v. "virgin birth."

[243] This is the RSV translation, emphasis added. The NRSV says, "Every firstborn male shall be designated as holy to the Lord."

[244] Emphasis added.

[245] New Catholic Encyclopedia, s.v. "virgin birth."

[246] Marina Warner, *Alone of All Her Sex: The Myth and the Cult of the Virgin Mary* (New York: Vintage Books, 1983) 77.

[247] Ibid., 235.

[248] Ibid., 77.

[249] One such statue can be viewed online at the web site of the British Museum. See www.thebritishmuseum.ac.uk/. Use the "Compass" feature to search for statues of Isis and Horus.

[250] Luther H. Martin, *Hellenistic Religions: An Introduction* (New York: Oxford University Press, 1987) 76.

[251] Anne Baring and Jules Cashford, *The Myth of the Goddess: Evolution of an Image* (London: Viking Arkana, 1991) 550.

[252] Johannes Herolt (called Discipulus), *Miracles of the Blessed Virgin Mary*, Broadway Medieval Library series, trans. C. C. Swinton Bland (London: George Routledge and Sons, 1928) 42–43.

[253] Ibid., 43–44.

[254] A postulant is someone in training to become a nun.

[255] Homer, *The Homeric Hymns*, second ed., revised, trans. Charles Boer (Dallas: Spring Publications, 1970) 117–18.

[256] *Munificentissimus Deus*, par. 44. See www.ewtn.com/library/PAPALDOC/P12MUNIF.HTM.

[257] Ibid., par. 47.

[258] Roger Ebert, *Chicago Sun-Times*, 4 April 1986. The review is available at www.suntimes.com/ebert/ebert_reviews/1986/04/51797.html.

[259] Ibid.

[260] "The Hymn of the Pearl," in *The Other Bible*, 311.

[261] *Il Miraculo* is the second part of a two-part film entitled *L'Amore* (The first part is called *Una Voce Umana*.). *Il Miraculo* is remembered in part because of its role in a landmark legal case. Responding to the uproar caused by the film, the Supreme Court reversed its own 1915 ruling and declared in 1952 that movies are indeed protected by the First Amendment.

262 Roberto Rossellini, *My Method: Writings and Interviews*, ed. Adriano Aprà, trans. Annapaola Cancogni (New York: Marsilio Publishers, 1992) 51.

263 Ibid.

264 See Tag Gallagher, *The Adventures of Roberto Rossellini* (New York: Da Capo Press, 1998) 253. The reference is to Rom 8:22.

265 Pierre Janet, *The Mental State of Hystericals: Significant Contributions to the History of Psychology, 1750-1920, Series C* (Washington, DC: University Publications of America, 1977) 2:325–26, 455.

266 Teresa of Avila, *The Book of Her Life*, 74, 76, 77.

267 Plato, *Timaeus*, trans. Benjamin Jowett (Indianapolis: Liberal Arts Press, 1949) 74.

268 Sigmund Freud, *Dora: An Analysis of a Case of Hysteria* (New York: Collier Books, 1963) 44. Emphasis added.

269 Charles Higham, *Hollywood Cameramen: Sources of Light* (London: Thames and Hudson, 1970) 143, 149.

270 See Nadia Margolis, *Joan of Arc in History, Literature, and Film* (New York: Garland Publishing, 1990) 393–402. Margolis's book was published before *The Messenger* was released, as well as before the 1999 version of Joan's life starring Leelee Sobieski appeared.

271 See Marina Warner, *Joan of Arc: The Image of Female Heroism* (California: University of California Press, 1981) especially 198–275.

272 Charles MacLaurin, *Post Mortem: Essays, Historical and Medical* (New York: George H. Doran Company, 1922) 51, 56.

273 Mitchell, The Book of Job, xiv.

Index

Scripture & Apocrypha

Genesis

2:7	219, n.54
3:6-7	190
3:16	186
3:20	185
3:24	186

Job

1:11	15
7:9-10	29
12:8-9	16
14:11-12	30
31:2-4	15
38:1-3	15
42:6	16

Psalms

147:6	224, n.164

Isaiah

61:1-2	125

Matthew

1:25	178
5:3	127
6:10	81
10:9	128
16:24	128
25:40	133
27:25	153
28:19-20	79

Mark

3:21	175
3:32-35	174
6:2-4	175
10:21	126

Luke

1:38	172
2:23	178
4:18	51
4:21	125
6:20	127
22:42	35
23:34	47

John

2:1-10	176
2:4	227, n.237
3:16	83
14:6	83
15:5-6	83
19:26-27	176

Acts of the Apostles

2:44-45	222, n.126
7:59	48

Romans

5:19	186
7:24	31
8:22	228, n.264
13:14	2

I Corinthians

1:2	11
6:19-20	31
12:27	35
15:22-23	33-4

Galatians

5:19-21	31
5:22-23	196

I Thessalonians

4:16-17	31

Acts of Peter 107

Infancy Gospel of James 177-8

Gospel of Thomas 111-2

Second Treatise of the Great Seth 32

Hymn of the Pearl 188